c|net Do-It-Yourself iPOD PROJECTS

24 cool things you didn't know you could do!

Guy Hart-Davis

McGraw Hill

New York   Chicago   San Francisco
Lisbon   London   Madrid   Mexico City
Milan   New Delhi   San Juan
Seoul   Singapore   Sidney   Toronto

The McGraw·Hill Companies

McGraw-Hill books are available at special quantity discounts to use as premiums and sales promotions, or for use in corporate training programs. For more information, please write to the Director of Special Sales, Professional Publishing, McGraw-Hill, Two Penn Plaza, New York, NY 10121-2298. Or contact your local bookstore.

CNET Do-It-Yourself iPod Projects:
24 Cool Things You Didn't Know You Could Do!

1234567890 QPD QPD 019876

ISBN-13: 978-0-07-226470-8
ISBN-10:   0-07-226470-5

Sponsoring Editor
Roger Stewart

Editorial Supervisor
Jody McKenzie

Project Manager
Vasundhara Sawhney

Acquisitions Coordinator
Carly Stapleton

Technical Editors
James Kim
Lindsey Turrentine

Copy Editor
Sally Engelfried

Proofreader
Raina Trivedi

Indexer
Robert Swanson

Production Supervisor
Jim Kussow

Composition
International Typesetting
and Composition

Illustration
International Typesetting
and Composition

Art Director, Cover
Jeff Weeks

Cover Designer
Jeff Weeks

Cover Illustration
Sarah Howell

This book is dedicated to
Rhonda and Teddy.

About the Author

Guy Hart-Davis is the author of more than 40 computer books on subjects as varied as the iPod and iTunes, Microsoft Office, Windows Vista, Mac OS X, and Visual Basic for Applications. His most recent books include *How to Do Everything with Your iPod & iTunes.*

Contents

Part III   Advanced

Foreword

Few tech toys have had the iPod's impact. It is at once a best-of-breed music player, an *au courant* bauble, a symbol of cultural currency, and an industrial design icon. But that doesn't mean it's perfect: a little do-it-yourself tweaking can make your iPod even better. That's what you'll learn to do in this book's twenty-four hands-on projects.

Inevitably, you will need to replace your iPod's battery, and that project is perhaps the most fundamental how-to in this book. Otherwise, your choices are to live with flaccid battery life; to buy a new player; or to send your iPod back to Cupertino, California, with a check for U.S. $65.95 and endure a week of silence as it goes through an off-site battery replacement. Instead, you can change the battery yourself at home in well under an hour and for a fraction of the cost.

What else will you learn here? Another one of our favorites is a lesson in moving music *from* your iPod *to* a computer. Apple thought you'd never need to know, but as anyone who has experienced a hard drive crash can attest this workaround is essential and provides tremendous peace of mind.

You already know what a difference the iPod has made in your life.

With our DIY projects, you'll move to the cutting edge of the digital media revolution.

Brian Cooley
CNET Editor-at-Large

Acknowledgments

My thanks go to the following people for making this book happen:

- Roger Stewart for getting the project started and keeping it going
- James Kim and Lindsey Turrentine for performing the technical review
- Jody McKenzie and Vasundhara Sawhney for coordinating the project
- Sally Engelfried for editing the text with care and a light touch
- International Typesetting and Composition for laying out the pages
- Raina Trivedi for proofreading the book
- Robert Swanson for creating the index

Introduction

Apple Computer's various models of iPod are beautifully designed portable music and video players—but they also have hidden depths that nine out of ten iPod owners barely suspect. Depending on the model of iPod, you can also record voice notes or high-quality audio on it, read e-mail and books on its screen, use it as extra storage for your digital camera, or even boot your Mac from it. You can even install a different operating system on your iPod to add extra capabilities to it.

Who Is This Book For?

This book is for iPod owners who want to take their iPods and iTunes to the limit and get as much use and enjoyment out of them as possible.

That means you. Read on.

Which iPods Does This Book Cover?

Most of the projects in this book focus on the iPod with video (also called the fifth-generation regular iPod), the iPod nano, and the iPod shuffle. Some of the projects also apply to earlier iPod models, such as the third- and fourth-generation regular iPods and the iPod mini.

Several projects show you how to create and manipulate audio files, using iTunes and other software. These projects apply to any iPod that's still working, from the first generation of regular iPod onward.

Other projects show you how to create text notes and e-mail to put on your iPod. These projects work with any iPod that can display notes on its screen.

What Does This Book Cover?

This book consists of 24 separate projects, divided into three categories: Easy Projects, Challenging Projects, and Advanced Projects. Here are examples of what you'll find:

- **Easy Projects** Turning your iPod into your home hi-fi or your car's stereo source; reading your e-mail on your iPod; using your iPod as a digital voice recorder; putting your vinyl records onto your iPod; and converting your home videos and your DVDs into iPod-friendly formats.

● **Challenging Projects** Using your iPod as a portable hard disk for file transfer and backup; learning techniques to get the most out of iTunes; loading your iPod from two or more computers; and DJing using your iPods, your computer, or both.

● **Advanced Projects** Diagnosing problems that your iPod is suffering—and fixing them; replacing the battery in your iPod; creating a central music library or a music server for your household; booting your Mac from your iPod; or installing a different operating system—iPodLinux or Rockbox—on your iPod to give it different capabilities.

Each project is a self-contained unit, although some projects refer to steps in other projects to avoid repetition. Each project is divided into a number of major steps, with each step providing clear instructions on how to proceed.

You may choose to start with easy projects and move up to more ambitious projects. But the way the book is structured allows you to dive directly into any project that appeals to you.

Each project starts with a list of the iPods to which it applies, details of any extra hardware and software you need, and an idea of the approximate cost, so you know exactly what you're getting into.

Conventions Used in This Book

To make its meaning clear, this book uses various conventions, four of which are worth mentioning here:

● Note, Tip, and Caution paragraphs highlight information you should pay extra attention to

● The pipe character or vertical bar denotes choosing an item from a menu. For example, "choose File | Open" means that you should pull down the File menu and select the Open item. Use the keyboard, mouse, or a combination of the two as you wish.

● The ⌘ symbol represents the Command key on the Mac.

● Most check boxes have two states: *selected* (with a check mark in them) and *cleared* (without a check mark in them). This book tells you to *select* a check box or *clear* a check box rather than "click to place a check mark in the box" or "click to remove the check mark from the box." (Often, the check box will already have the required setting—in which case, you don't need to change it.)

Part I
Easy

Project 1

Play Back iPod Videos on Your TV or Your Friend's Computer

What You'll Need:

- iPod type: iPod with video
- Hardware required: A/V cable or A/V dock
- Cost: $25–$150 U.S.

The iPod with video is a lovely device with a bright, sharp, high-resolution screen—but that screen is only two and a half inches across, big enough for solo watching at home or on the move but not for viewing with company.

To enjoy videos with one or more friends, you'll need to connect your iPod to a TV so that you can play back the videos at a decent size. Alternatively, you can connect your iPod video to your friend's computer and play back videos from the iPod on the computer's screen. This project shows you how to do both.

Step 1: Play Back Videos on Your TV

Computers are well on their way to infiltrating every dwelling, but TVs are way ahead of them and have achieved almost total saturation. So, pretty much wherever you go, you're guaranteed to find a TV into which you can plug your iPod and play back video on a larger screen. You need do nothing more than connect the iPod to the TV, choose the right output settings, and then set the video rolling.

Connect Your iPod to Your TV

To connect your iPod to your TV, all you need is the right kind of cable to carry the video and audio signals. But if you want to play videos from your iPod through your TV frequently, and perhaps play audio through the TV or through your stereo system, you may prefer to get an all-in-one iPod dock.

Connect Your iPod to Your TV with a Cable

The simplest and most direct route is to get a cable that plugs into the iPod and the TV. The cable carries the video signal and audio signal from the iPod to the TV, so when you start playing a video on the iPod, the video appears on the TV screen. You use the iPod's controls to start and stop play (rather than using a wired or wireless remote control) and use the iPod's screen to navigate the menus and set up the video. The iPod's menus don't appear on the TV screen, but as you're holding the iPod, this isn't a problem.

When you want to play videos through your TV only sometimes, a cable is a great solution: it takes only moments to connect, it's compact enough to carry in a pocket, and it's relatively inexpensive (though perhaps not as cheap as it might be).

Your first option is to get Apple's iPod AV Cable (shown below) from the Apple Store ($19.99 U.S.; http://store.apple.com). Slide the 1/8-inch connector into your iPod's headphone port, connect the connectors with the yellow, red, and white markings on the other end of the cable to the corresponding RCA plugs on your TV, and you're in business. If you have an iPod Universal Dock, you can connect the iPod AV Cable to the dock's line-out port rather than the iPod's headphone socket. You can then keep the AV cable plugged in when you remove the iPod from the dock.

note   *The iPod AV Cable (and other equivalent cables) have three bands around the 1/8-inch connector— video, left audio, and right audio. The video band, which is the furthest from the tip of the connector, picks up a video connection in the iPod's headphone socket that a headphone plug simply bypasses.*

Belkin (www.belkin.com) also makes an AV Cable for a 4G/5G iPod. This cable is similar in features and looks to the iPod AV Cable and costs the same ($19.99 U.S.). However, the Belkin cable has the edge on length—at 12 feet, it's twice as long as the iPod AV Cable.

Connect Your iPod to Your TV with a DIY Cable

The iPod AV Cable is stylish and handy, but you may feel it's not worth $20 U.S.; the Belkin cable gives you twice the value per foot but costs the same overall. For a less expensive alternative, visit your local electronics paradise (either online or bricks-and-mortar) and find a standard A/V cable with three RCA plugs at one end (coded red, white, and yellow) and a ⅛-inch A/V plug with three bands at the other end.

To set up your iPod for playback, plug the ⅛-inch connector into your iPod's headphone port, and then plug the yellow, white, and red RCA connectors into the RCA jacks on your TV in this non–color-coded way:

Cable Connector	TV Jack
Red	Yellow
Yellow	White
White	Red

Connect Your iPod to Your TV via a Dock

If you're planning to play videos from your iPod on your TV frequently, you may prefer a connection that keeps the iPod anchored. You can find a variety of video iPod docks at the Apple Store and other online stores, such as GadgetLocker.com (www.thinkdifferentstore.com) and everythingipod.com (www.everythingipod.com). At this writing, these are the leading contenders for your money:

- **iPod AV Connection Kit** The iPod AV Connection Kit ($99 U.S.) is a bundled product that includes the iPod AV Cable (discussed earlier in this project), a Universal Dock, dock adapters for various iPods (but not the iPod with video or iPod nano, each of which comes with its own adapter), an Apple Remote for controlling play remotely, a USB power adapter for charging the iPod, and a USB cable for connecting the dock to the power adapter. This kit enables you to dock your iPod and play back video through the TV using the iPod AV Cable, but it has some drawbacks: the iPod's menus don't appear on the TV screen, so you need to control playback via the iPod's screen—which makes the remote much less useful than if the menus did appear on the TV. You will also end up with dock adapters that you do not need (unless you have a full suite of older iPod models).

- **DLO HomeDock for iPod** The DLO HomeDock ($99.99 U.S.) is a kit that consists of a remote control, a dock module (into which the remote control and the iPod both fit), a six-foot AV cable and an RCA-to-miniplug adapter, and an AC power supply. The HomeDock includes an S-video port that helps you ensure high-quality transmission from the iPod (via the HomeDock) to the TV, but if you buy your video files from the iTunes Music Store, you may not be able to see the difference. The HomeDock doesn't display the iPod's screen (or an equivalent) on the TV.

● **Griffin TuneCenter** The Griffin TuneCenter ($149.99 U.S.; www.griffin-technology.com) is a dock that provides an S-video connection, a composite video connection, and left and right audio channels. On your television, the TuneCenter displays not the iPod's actual screen but a functional equivalent that lets you control the iPod while looking at the TV rather than at the iPod's screen. Apart from displaying video on your TV and playing audio through it, you can display your photos from the iPod. You can also use TuneCenter to play Internet radio stations through your TV or stereo.

● **Valor iLink-L2** The Valor iLink-L2 ($179.99 U.S.; various retailers) is an all-in-one iPod interface for connecting any iPod with a dock connector port to a TV or a stereo system. The iLink-L2 is designed primarily for use in automobiles but also works with regular TVs and stereos that have RCA connectors (in other words, most of them). The iLink-L2 provides an on-screen display that lets you control the playback of videos or music.

tip *Choosing among the different dock options for the iPod with video is a task that, if not quite worthy of Solomon, certainly will cost you some effort. For arguments for and against products, check the user feedback sections of sites such as the Apple Store. You'll find plenty of bias and propaganda, but when you discard these, you'll usually find nuggets of valuable information about each product's strengths and weaknesses.*

Connect your iPod to the dock using the appropriate end of the cable supplied with the dock, and connect the cable's other end to your TV.

Set the iPod to Output the Signal to the TV

To set your iPod to output the signal to the TV, follow these steps:

1. Scroll to the Videos entry on the main menu, and then press the Select button to access the Videos screen (see Figure 1-1).

2. Scroll to the Video Settings entry, and then press the Select button to access the Settings screen (see Figure 1-2).

Figure 1-1

The Videos screen gives you access to your video playlists, video files, and the Video Settings screen.

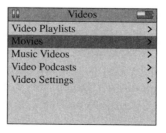

Figure 1-2

On the Settings screen, choose whether to output to a TV and, if so, which format to use.

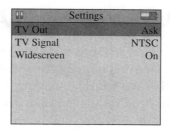

3. Set the TV Out setting to On if you want the iPod always to output the video to TV, or to Ask if you want the iPod to prompt you first. Ask is usually more convenient, as you don't need to switch the setting when you want to play the video on the iPod's screen. The disadvantage to Ask is that you have to deal with the iPod's prompt—TV or Screen?—each time you play a video.

4. Make sure your iPod is set to output the right kind of TV signal for your TV: NTSC or PAL. NTSC is primarily used in North America and Japan, while PAL is used in most European countries.

5. For the Widescreen setting, choose On or Off to suit your TV or your tastes.

6. Press the Menu button to return to the Videos screen.

Start the Video Playing

To play videos on your iPod, follow these steps:

1. If the iPod's not already showing the Videos screen, scroll to the Videos entry on the main menu, and then press the Select button.

2. Scroll to the appropriate category (for example, Movies or TV Shows), and then press the Select button to access it.

3. Scroll to the item you want, and then press the Select button to access it and start it playing.

You can fast forward through the video file by pressing the Fast Forward button and rewind by pressing the Rewind button, but these controls are comfortable only for moving short distances. To move farther, press the Select button to display the scrub bar, and then scroll to scrub forward or backward. When you reach the point you want, press the Select button to hide the scrub bar again.

tip   *When you're playing short videos, you may not want to start each of them playing separately. To make your iPod play them for you, create a video playlist in iTunes, add the videos to it in the order you want, and then synchronize your iPod. You can then set the playlist playing from the Video Playlists entry on the Videos screen.*

Step 2: Play Back Videos on Another Computer

Instead of using a TV as a super-size monitor for your iPod, you can simply play back the videos on your computer using iTunes: double-click the video in your music library, and iTunes starts it playing.

But what you'll often want to do is play back videos from your iPod on someone else's computer. To do so, follow these steps:

1. Make sure iTunes is installed on the computer. If not, download the latest version and install it. For a Windows computer, install the iPod software as well.

2. Choose the window size at which you want to play the video:

   - On Windows, choose Edit | Preferences to display the iTunes dialog box. On the Mac, choose iTunes | Preferences to display the Preferences dialog box.

   - Click the General tab to display its contents.

   - In the Play Videos drop-down list, choose In A Separate Window, In The Main Window, Full Screen, or Full Screen With Visuals. Full Screen or Full Screen With Visuals is usually the best choice (why settle for less?).

   - Click the OK button to close the dialog box.

3. Connect your iPod to the computer. Suppress the synchronization message by holding CTRL-ALT (Windows) or ⌘-OPTION (Mac) from when you connect the iPod until the iPod appears in the Source pane.

4. Click the iPod's entry in the Source pane to display its contents.

5. Double-click the video to start it playing.

Now, where's the popcorn?

Turn Your iPod into Your Home Hi-Fi

What You'll Need:

- iPods Covered: Any iPod
- Hardware Required: Speakers, A/V cable, RF transmitter
- Cost: $15–$350 U.S.

Your iPod is primarily a portable player designed for use with headphones, but there's no reason you can't use it for playing music through speakers in your home. With minimal effort, you can connect your iPod to a pair of powered speakers, a stereo system, or your TV and crank up the volume as high as your ears or your neighbors will tolerate.

Step 1: Play Your iPod Through Speakers

The easiest solution for making your iPod your home hi-fi is to connect the iPod to a pair of powered speakers—speakers that contain an amplifier. You can use either speakers specially designed for iPods or other powered speakers, such as a set that you already have.

Decide What Type of Powered Speakers You Need

Powered speakers come in all sizes and shapes—some of them intricately designed shapes—and capable of delivering widely varying volumes of sound. Use this checklist to decide roughly what kind of speakers you need before you decide whether to get iPod-specific speakers or general-purpose speakers.

- **How many speakers do you need?** Until a few years ago, the trend was for more and more speakers: two speakers for a "desktop" set, two plus a subwoofer for louder listening, and five or seven (plus a subwoofer) for a "home theater" experience. You can still find many sets like this, but there are now many integrated speaker units that give less stereo separation but are much easier to position.

note *In a two-speaker set, such as desktop speakers, the amplifier is usually placed in one of the speakers, driving both. In a speaker set that includes a subwoofer, the amplifier is usually placed in the subwoofer, letting its weight rest on the floor and also allowing the satellite speakers to be compact. 5.1 speaker systems (five satellite speakers and a subwoofer) and 7.1 systems can give great sound but involve a mass of speaker wires.*

- **How much sound do the speakers make?** The best design in the world is useless if the speakers deliver sound too puny for your listening needs.

caution *Manufacturers tend to muddy the question of how loud speakers are by using various measurements of speakers' power-handling capabilities interchangeably. In lay terms, RMS watts (root mean square watts) measure the wattage that the speaker can sustain, while peak output watts measure the loudest wattage that the speaker can produce momentarily. The best way to judge what volume speakers can produce is to listen to them—in a store, at a friend's house, or by proxy when a party is happening next door.*

- **How are the speakers powered?** Some speakers are powered by replaceable batteries; others by rechargeable batteries; and others by AC power. AC power always gives you the loudest sound, but you may want to be able to use the speakers where AC power isn't available sometimes.

- **Are the speakers designed for the kind of music you listen to?** Some speakers are designed for heavy music; others for a range of music; others— a few—for piano-based classical music; and others for games. Choosing the right kind of speakers doesn't guarantee your music will sound good through them, but choosing the wrong kind pretty much guarantees it won't.

Choose Between iPod-specific Speakers and General-purpose Speakers

Choosing between iPod-specific speakers and general-purpose speakers can be difficult. Given that you've got an iPod, you may prefer to buy speakers specifically designed for iPods. For one thing, you can find speakers that match your iPod's design and color. For another, many of the speakers can recharge the iPod as it plays music.

On the other hand, general-purpose speakers tend to be less expensive and give you greater flexibility. (For example, your next audio player might not be an iPod.) Besides, if you've been listening to music from your computer or another portable player, you may already have speakers that you can use. You might as well test those speakers to destruction with your iPod before buying iPod-specific speakers.

Choose iPod-Specific Speakers

Once you've decided you want speakers designed for the iPod, consider these two questions:

- **Do the speakers recharge the iPod?** Some speakers recharge the iPod as it plays. Others just wear down the battery.

- **Do the speakers work with all iPods?** Some speakers are designed only to work with a particular iPod model. Others can recharge various iPods (for example, all iPods with the dock connector) but can accept input from other players via a line-in port. In many cases, the best choice is speakers that use the iPod Universal Dock system, which lets you connect different models of iPods by using suitably shaped plastic inserts.

- **Do the speakers have other special features?** Some speakers include a video-out port (for example, an S-video port) so that you can display photos or videos on your TV. Other speakers let you use your iPod as an alarm clock.

Equipped with the decisions you made in the previous section and in the preceding list, you should now be ready to choose speakers for your iPod.

At this writing, there are far too many models of iPod-specific speakers to discuss here—and by the time you're reading this, there will be many more. You'll probably find plenty of iPod speakers at your local electronics paradise, and you'll find a bewildering variety at online outlets such as the Apple Store (http://store.apple.com), GadgetLocker.com (www.thinkdifferentstore.com), and everythingipod.com (www.everythingipod.com).

To give you some idea of what's available, this section briefly mentions three iPod speakers, ranging from the large to the small.

iPod Hi-Fi

The iPod Hi-Fi from Apple ($349 U.S.) is a large, boom box–like speaker with an iPod dock connector on the top. The iPod Hi-Fi (see Figure 2-1) works with any iPod that has a dock connector but also includes a standard 3.5 mm port that allows you to connect an iPod shuffle, a first- or second-generation iPod, or any other sound source.

Figure 2-1

The iPod Hi-Fi from Apple has generally received good reviews and produces room-filling sound.

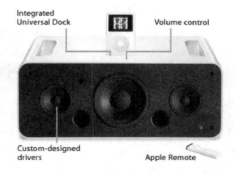

Integrated Universal Dock

Volume control

Custom-designed drivers

Apple Remote

Altec Lansing inMotion Series

Altec Lansing makes a series of speakers called inMotion for different iPod models. The inMotion speakers range in cost from $99.99 to $249.99 (U.S) and are available from various retailers, including the Apple Store (http://store.apple.com). Choose the model that fits your iPod, matches your budget, and delivers the volume you need. Figure 2-2 shows an example of an inMotion speaker.

Figure 2-2

Altec Lansing inMotion is a series of speakers for different iPod models and budgets.

iHome iPod Clock Radio

You can use your iPod's built-in alarm feature (on the Extras | Clock | Alarm Clock menu) to wake you up through a pair of speakers, but the effect may be more dramatic than you want, as there's no way to tell your iPod to start playing quietly.

If you want to wake up to music from your iPod, you may prefer an integrated solution such as the iHome iPod Clock Radio (see Figure 2-3). The iHome ($119.99 U.S.; www.thinkdifferentstore.com) is a clock radio with an iPod Universal Dock on the top, allowing you to connect any iPod with a dock connector. You can also connect any other audio source via a patch cord.

Figure 2-3

The iHome iPod Clock Radio offers a gentler way to wake up than your iPod on its own does.

The iHome starts playing at a low volume and builds up to the volume you've set rather than blasting you out of your bed. The iHome also has a sleep mode that puts your iPod to sleep after you've drifted off.

caution *There's also an iHome model for the original iPod shuffle, the iHome IH18W Portable Travel Alarm Clock. This alarm clock lets you play back music from your iPod shuffle, but it doesn't control the iPod shuffle remotely. (There's a good reason for this limitation: the iPod shuffle doesn't have remote-control capabilities.) So the Sleep function turns off the iHome itself but leaves the iPod shuffle playing unless you turn it off manually; and the alarm uses a buzzer rather than music from the iPod shuffle.*

Sonic Impact i-Pax Portable Speaker System

The Sonic Impact i-Pax Portable Speaker System ($79.99 U.S.; www.amazon.com and other retailers) is a portable speaker system designed solely for the original iPod shuffle. The i-Pax (see Figure 2-4) can run off four AA batteries or an AC adapter.

Figure 2-4

The i-Pax's folding hard case includes a storage slot in which you can park your iPod shuffle (original model) when you're not listening to music on the move.

Step 2: Connect Your iPod to Your Stereo or TV

iPod speakers are a neat solution, and some of them can deliver impressive volume. But if you already have a stereo system, it'll probably make more sense to play your iPod through it than to buy iPod-specific speakers.

And if the TV is the focus of your entertainment system, you may want to harness its speakers to play music.

The easiest way to connect your iPod to your stereo or TV is to use a cable, which should give you good audio quality and no complications. If you find it easier not to have a physical connection, you can use a radio transmitter to send the audio from the iPod to the stereo (see Step 4).

For a typical stereo system that has a receiver, you'll need a cable that has a mini-plug at one end and two RCA plugs at the other end.

note *Some receivers and boom boxes use a single stereo miniplug input rather than two RCA ports. To connect your iPod to such devices, you'll need a stereo miniplug-to-miniplug cable. Make sure the cable is stereo, because mono miniplug-to-miniplug cables are common. A stereo cable has two bands around the miniplug (as on your iPod's headphones), whereas a mono cable has only one band.*

If you have a high-quality receiver and speakers, get a high-quality cable to connect your iPod to them. After the amount you've presumably spent on your iPod and your stereo, it'd be a mistake to degrade the signal between them by sparing a few bucks on the cable.

tip *You can find various home-audio connection kits that contain a variety of cables likely to cover your needs. These kits are usually a safe buy, but unless your needs are peculiar, you'll end up with one or more cables you don't need. So if you do know which cables you need, make sure a kit offers a cost savings before buying it instead of the individual cables.*

Connect your iPod to your receiver as follows:

1. Connect the miniplug to your iPod's headphone port. If you have an iPod dock, connect the miniplug to the dock's line-out port instead, because this gives better sound quality than the headphone port.

2. If you're using the headphone port, turn down the volume on the iPod all the way.

3. Whichever port you're using, turn down the volume on the amplifier as well.

4. Connect the RCA plugs to the left and right ports of one of the inputs on your amplifier or boom box—for example, the AUX input or the Cassette input (if you're not using a cassette deck).

caution *Don't connect your iPod to the Phono input on your amplifier. This is because the Phono input is built with a higher sensitivity to make up for the weak output of a record player. Putting a full-strength signal into the Phono input will probably blow it.*

5. Start the iPod playing. If you're using the headphone port, turn up the volume on the iPod a little.

6. Turn up the volume on the receiver so that you can hear the music.

7. Increase the volume on the two controls in tandem until you reach a satisfactory sound level.

note *Too low a level of output from your iPod may produce noise as your amplifier boosts the signal. Too high a level of output from your iPod may cause distortion.*

Step 3: Use a Remote Control with Your iPod

Getting your iPod to play through speakers, your stereo, or your TV is great—but it's only the first step. Having to get up and go to your iPod to change the song or the volume every few minutes is guaranteed to mar your enjoyment of the music.

In other words, you need a wireless remote control for your iPod. This section discusses the main points to keep in mind when choosing an iPod remote control and then describes a couple of examples of remote controls.

Choosing an iPod Remote Control

When choosing an iPod remote control, first make sure that the remote control works with the type of iPod you have:

- At this writing, you can get some remote controls that work with any dock connector iPod: the iPod with video, the iPod nano, the iPod mini, and the third- and fourth-generation iPods (including the iPod photo). Many remote controls are more limited.

- Remote controls designed for third- and fourth-generation iPods and the iPod mini mostly use the remote control connector next to the headphone connector rather than the dock connector. (Before Apple removed the remote control connector in the iPod nano, using this connector was the smart way to design a remote control.)

- Remote controls designed for first- and second-generation iPods use the remote-control port built into the extra contact ring around the headphone connector.

Once you've assembled a list of remote controls that work with your model of iPod, consider the following criteria as well as their price and looks:

- Does it use infrared (IR) or radio frequency (RF)? RF typically gives better range and works around corners. But IR has the advantage that universal remote controls can learn from some IR remote controls.

- Do you need features for the latest iPods, such as the ability to control your iPod's picture features, or do you simply want to play back music? You may need to read feature lists carefully to make out exactly what a particular remote control can and cannot do. Also read any user reviews you can find, because such reviews are normally honest about shortcomings in the products.

Examples of iPod Remote Controls

This section discusses some of the leading remote controls available at this writing.

Apple Remote with Mac

The Apple Remote with Mac is the slim-line remote control that's included with various consumer-oriented Macs, such as the Mac Mini, the iMac, and the MacBook. You can also buy the Apple Remote separately from the Apple Store (http://store.apple .com) or other retailers for $29 U.S. This remote control is primarily designed for use with the Mac, and by most accounts works well with it. But the Apple Remote also works with iPods—up to a point.

Here are the details:

- The Apple Remote works only with iPods that have the dock connector.

- You can play and pause the music, change the volume, and move to the next or previous song.

- You can't navigate the iPod's menus at all. The Apple Remote has a menu button, but it works only with the Mac, not with the iPod. To navigate the iPod's menus, you need to use the iPod's Click wheel, as usual.

Marware Remote Docking Station

The Marware Remote Docking Station (www.everythingipod.com; $49.99 U.S.) works with all iPods that have dock connectors. The package includes the docking station itself, an IR remote control, a power adapter and a USB cable, and an A/V cable for connecting the iPod to the hi-fi or television.

iPod nano Dock with Remote

The iPod nano Dock with Remote ($29.95 U.S.; www.thinkdifferentstore.com) is a nano-only dock with a 3.5mm stereo port that you can connect to any speakers or receiver via a standard cable. The iPod nano Dock also includes a USB port so that you can connect your iPod nano to your computer or to a power source for charging. The remote control lets you play and pause music, move to the next or previous song, and change the volume.

AirClick

The AirClick from Griffin Technology ($39.99 U.S.; www.griffintechnology.com) is an RF remote control that works with the iPod with video, the fourth-generation iPod (including the iPod photo), and the iPod mini, but not the iPod nano.

The AirClick connects to the iPod via the Dock Connector but doesn't have a pass-through for the dock connector. This means that you can't dock the iPod or play music through the dock connector when the AirClick is connected—so you can't play music on any speakers to which the iPod connects via the dock connector. Connecting the iPod to your speakers or hi-fi via the headphone port, however, works fine.

Step 4: Play Your iPod Through One or More Radios

If you don't need ultimate audio quality, you can play your iPod through your existing stereo system or through any radio almost effortlessly by using a radio transmitter to send the audio from the iPod to the radio on your stereo. See "Use a Radio Transmitter to Play Your iPod Through Your Car Stereo" in Project 8 for a discussion of radio transmitters.

Using a radio transmitter has two main advantages:

- You don't need to connect the iPod directly to the stereo system. Instead, you can keep the iPod to hand so that you can control playback. Alternatively, you can dock the iPod, and then use a remote control to control it.

- You can play the music on several radios at the same time, giving yourself music throughout your dwelling without complex and expensive rewiring.

Audio quality typically suffers when you use a radio transmitter like this, but if you find the quality high enough for you, this is an easy way of getting the music from your iPod to your stereo.

Use Your iPod as an Audio Recorder

What You'll Need:

- iPods Covered: Third-generation, fourth-generation, iPod with video, second-generation iPod nano
- Hardware Required: iPod-compatible microphone
- Cost: $70 U.S. or less

If you attach a suitable microphone, regular iPods (those that contain hard drives) can record audio as well as play it back. Recording audio is very handy, because if you haven't packed the iPod full of songs, videos, and photos, you can record many hours of audio with no need to carry a separate recorder.

If you have an iPod with video or a second-generation iPod nano, you can record full-quality audio—for example, you could record your band at practice and have the recording sound as good as the band does. If you have a third- or fourth-generation iPod, you can record only low-fidelity audio because of limitations in the iPod's software. This quality is fine for creating voice notes or for recording spoken audio (such as interviews or lecture notes), but it's not good enough for recording music. If you need to record music on a third- or fourth-generation iPod, you can—but you must install Linux on the iPod, which is an advanced maneuver. See Project 23 for details.

The first-generation iPod nano, iPod mini, and iPod shuffle don't have recording capabilities.

Step 1: Get a Suitable Microphone

The first step in recording audio with your iPod is to get a suitable microphone. This section mentions some of the microphones that are available at this writing for current iPod models, but because many companies now produce iPod accessories, it's worth looking for other microphones as well. You'll find iPod accessories in Apple Stores and many other brick-and-mortar stores that sell iPods. Online, good sources include the following:

- Apple Store (http://store.apple.com)
- GadgetLocker.com (www.thinkdifferentstore.com)
- www.everythingipod.com (www.everythingipod.com)

iPod with video and Second-Generation iPod nano

The iPod with video and the second-generation iPod nano can record audio at 22.05 kHz in mono or at 44.1 kHz in stereo (full CD quality). To make the most of this capability, you need a good microphone that connects through the dock connector. At this writing, there are two main contenders for your money. Despite their names, both these microphones work with the second-generation iPod nano as well as the iPod with video.

Belkin TuneTalk Stereo for iPod with Video

The Belkin TuneTalk Stereo for iPod with video ($69.99 U.S.; www.belkin.com) contains two built-in omnidirectional microphones that let you record in stereo. The TuneTalk Stereo (see Figure 3-1) also includes an external microphone adapter, so you can plug in a high-quality microphone that you can position more easily. For example, you might plug in a tie-clip or headset microphone so that you can record audio with your hands free.

Figure 3-1

The Belkin TuneTalk Stereo for iPod with video lets you record in stereo using two omnidirectional microphones.

MicroMemo for iPod with video

MicroMemo for iPod with video (see Figure 3-2) from XtremeMac (www.xtrememac.com; $59.95 U.S.) includes a detachable microphone and a speaker. When you detach the microphone, you can plug in a high-quality microphone of your own that you can position freely.

Third- and Fourth-Generation iPods

Third- and fourth-generation iPods use a microphone that connects through the remote-control socket, the small socket with the rounded-rectangle shape near to the headphone, and the headphone socket. (The headphone socket includes a third contact ring that's used for recording. Headphones use only two contact rings and so bypass the headphone connector.)

Because these microphones plug into the headphone socket, you can't use the socket directly while the microphone is attached. Some microphones have a pass-through socket that allows you to use the headphones, which is useful for listening immediately to the voice memos you record. Other microphones include a tiny speaker that enables you to play back audio at very low volume.

Griffin iTalk

The Griffin iTalk (around $35 used from Amazon.com, eBay, or other sources) is a microphone with an integrated speaker. The iTalk (see Figure 3-3) includes a pass-through connector that lets you use an external microphone rather than the iTalk's built-in microphone, so you can attach a microphone on a lead, a throat mike, or whatever you need.

Figure 3-3

The Griffin iTalk lets you record audio directly onto a third- or fourth-generation iPod.

Belkin Universal Microphone Adapter

The Belkin Universal Microphone Adapter for iPod ($29.99 U.S.; http://store.apple .com) plugs into the headphone socket and lets you plug in an external microphone and a pair of headphones. If you have a microphone you want to use, the Universal Microphone Adapter (see Figure 3-4) is a good solution.

Figure 3-4

The Universal Microphone Adapter for iPod includes a gain control that lets you easily adjust the microphone sensitivity.

Belkin iPod Voice Recorder

The Belkin Voice Recorder for iPod ($49.99 U.S., www.belkin.com) is a microphone with an integrated tiny speaker that plugs into the headphone socket and remote-control socket of third- and fourth-generation iPods. Figure 3-5 shows the Voice Recorder for iPod.

Figure 3-5

The Voice Recorder for iPod is a compact microphone with a built-in speaker.

note   *The Voice Recorder doesn't have a pass-through for an external microphone or for headphones.*

Step 2: Record Audio via the Microphone

Recording audio on your iPod is easy once you have a suitable microphone. Follow these steps:

1. Connect the microphone to the iPod via the appropriate connector.

   - For an iPod with video or a second-generation iPod nano, connect the microphone via the dock connector port.

- For a third-generation or fourth-generation iPod, conne the microphone to the headphone socket and the remote-control sock on the top
of the iPod.

2. When your iPod recognizes the microphone, it automatically dis ys the
Voice Memo screen (shown next; these screens are from a third-ge ation
iPod). You can also access the Voice Memo screen manually by ch ing
Extras | Voice Memos | Record Now.

3. On an iPod with video or a second-generation iPod nano, set the rec ing
quality. Press the Menu button to go up to the Voice Memos screen. ll to
the Quality item, and then use the Select button to toggle between and
Low quality as needed. Select the Record Now button and pres Select
button to return to the Voice Memo screen.

4. To start recording, scroll to the Record item, and then press ect button. The recording starts, as shown here.

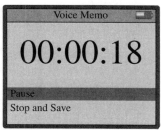

5. As the recording runs, the iPod shows ave it by using the ng time. You can
pause the recording by scrolling to the ing by the date and and then pressing
the Select button, or you can stop the
Stop And Save command. Your iPod
time—for example, 6/25 4:45 P.M.

s on the iPod

Step 3: Play Back and Delete V nt to check that the micro-
l. To do so, record a voice

If you're recording anything importar
phone is working and that it's reco
memo as described earlier, and th

To play a voice memo back, follow these steps:

1. Choose Extras | Voice Memos to display the Voice Memos screen.

2. Scroll down to the memo you want to play, and then press the Select button to display the screen for the memo (as shown here).

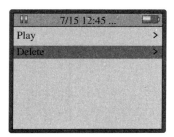

3. Scroll to the Play item, and then press the Select button to start the memo playing.

To delete a voice memo, follow these steps.

1. Choose Extras | Voice Memos to display the Voice Memos screen.

2. Scroll down to the memo you want to delete, and then press the Select button to display the screen for the memo.

3. Scroll down to the Delete item, and then press the Select button. The iPod displays the Delete Memo screen, as shown here.

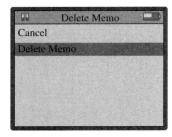

4. Scroll down to the Delete Memo item, and then press the Select button.

Step fer the Voice Memos to Your Computer

synchronize your iPod with iTunes, your voice memos are transferred
puter and added to the Voice Memos playlist. If iTunes prompts you to
nos to your Music Library, click the Yes button.

Once iTunes has copied the voice memos, you can access them through the Voice Memos playlist:

- You can simply play a memo back (for example, to transcribe it or take notes from it) and then delete it.

- You can use the Advanced | Convert Selection To *Format* command to convert a memo to a compressed format (such as AAC). You might want to do this if you want to put the voice memo back on the iPod as part of a playlist— for example, as lecture notes or language lessons for light listening.

Use Your iPod as an E-book Reader

What You'll Need:

- iPods Covered: Any iPod but the iPod shuffle
- Windows Software Required: iPod Library
- Mac Software Required: Book2Pod
- Cost: Free

Chances are that your iPod has become your permanent companion—in your car, on the street, and even in bed, though perhaps not in the shower or sauna. If you're taking your iPod everywhere, you probably want to make it do as much as possible. The iPod's bright, clear screen is great for displaying text, even if only a small amount at a time, so using your iPod as an e-book reader is a natural move. You can also read your e-mail on your iPod (see Project 5)—handy for those times when *War and Peace* must give way to the demands of work or your pressing social life.

To get text onto your iPod, you need to get a suitable document containing the text, and then use a utility to divide it up into iPod-sized bites and transfer it to your iPod.

These maneuvers work with any iPod but the iPod shuffle, which has no screen on which to display text.

Step 1: Find Your Text

First, you'll need a text, preferably one that you can copy legally. You'll find plenty on the Internet, though perhaps not as many as you might like—usually for reasons of copyright.

This isn't the place for a detailed examination of copyright, but if you're planning to download files from the Internet, you should know that almost all original written works are protected by copyright even if they don't contain an explicit statement detailing the copyright. Congress keeps extending the copyright period, largely to keep valuable intellectual property such as Mickey Mouse and Winnie the Pooh protected by copyright and bringing in money to the corporations that own them, so it can be hard to determine whether a work is still in copyright. The best way to proceed is to assume that all works are copyrighted unless they explicitly say that they're not. Some authors make their works freely available on the Internet even though the works qualify for copyright protection.

 To learn about copyright in the U.S., visit the U.S. Copyright Office (www.copyright.gov). For a brief and lively introduction, see Brad Templeton's "10 Big Myths About Copyright Explained" (www.templetons.com/brad/copymyths.html).

Buy E-Books Online

Because of copyright concerns, most e-books for sale online are available only in restricted formats that you can't use on the iPod. For example, sites such as Amazon.com (www.amazon.com) and eBooks.com (www.ebooks.com) sell e-books in formats such as MobiPocket Reader, Adobe eBook Reader, and Microsoft Reader, none of which you can transfer to the iPod.

Some sites do sell e-books in "open" formats such as HTML files, text files, or unlocked PDF files, but these are very much the exceptions.

Download Free E-Books from Project Gutenberg

Project Gutenberg (www.gutenberg.org) is a great source of electronic books that you can download for free. The majority of Project Gutenberg's works are in English, but the site also has a fair selection of works in other languages. Almost all of these books are out of copyright in the United States, most because the copyright has expired but some because the author has chosen to make the book freely available. When copyright expires, or when the author or other copyright holder waives copyright, a work enters what's called the *public domain*, which includes all works that do not have restrictions on their use and that anyone can (by and large) use freely.

caution *Copyright has somewhat different implementations in different countries. Project Gutenberg's works are out of copyright in the United States but may still be in copyright in other countries. If you live in a country other than the United States, it's technically a good idea to make sure that you can legally download works that are freely available on Project Gutenberg.*

Project Gutenberg typically offers works in one or more text formats, HTML format, and other formats such as Plucker (a format for reading on Palm OS handhelds). If you're planning to put a work on your iPod, you'll usually do best to get the plain text format with no particular encoding (no special set of characters).

Step 2: Prepare the Text for the iPod

To put the text onto your iPod, you need to convert it into notes. Each note is limited to a maximum of 4,000 characters, or about 600–700 words of average length. The iPod can hold up to 1,000 notes at a time, and the notes can be linked together to make them easy to navigate, so you can get plenty of text onto your iPod to keep you reading.

This step shows you how to use iPod Library to prepare notes on Windows and Book2Pod to prepare notes on the Mac. Both utilities embed links at the start and end of each note-size section so that you can navigate to the next section by pressing the Select button.

Prepare Notes on Windows Using iPod Library

iPod Library (freeware; www.sturm.net/nz) is a freeware utility for dividing text files, HTML text files, and PDF files into note-sized sections and loading them on the iPod.

Get and Install iPod Library

To get and use iPod Library, follow these steps:

1. Download the latest version of iPod Library from www.sturm.net/nz. Save the zip file to disk, and then click the Open button in the Download Complete dialog box to open a Windows Explorer window showing the file's contents.

2. Click the Extract All Files link in the Folder Tasks pane, and then use the Extraction Wizard to extract the files to a temporary folder. If you have bad memories of dentistry, you may prefer to open another Windows Explorer window to a suitable temporary folder and then simply drag the files from the first window to the second.

3. Either way, after you've extracted the files, double-click the setup.exe file to run the setup routine. Windows will probably display an Open File—Security Warning dialog box to let you know that the file doesn't have a valid digital signature.

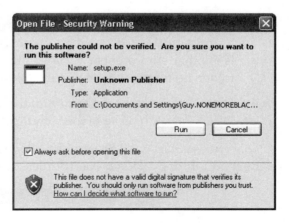

4. Normally, the lack of a digital signature is a red flag, but if you've just down-loaded the file from the website mentioned in step 1, it should be fine. Click the Run button if you want to proceed.

5. Follow through the setup routine, choosing a folder in which to put iPod Library (the default folder, an iPod Library folder inside your Program Files folder, is fine).

6. When the installation is complete, choose Start | All Programs | iPod Library to run iPod Library.

At this point, you may run into an error such as the "Component 'COMDLG32.OCX' or one of its dependencies not correctly registered: a file is missing or invalid" message shown here:

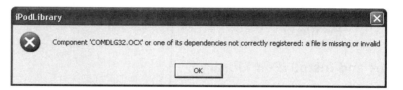

If this happens, don't worry. COMDLG32.OCX is an ActiveX control (a standard Windows control) that's almost guaranteed to be on your computer already. The problem is that iPod Library can't find it. To fix the problem, click the OK button, and then follow these steps:

1. Choose Start | Run to open the Run dialog box. In the Open text box, type **%windir%\system32** and press Enter (or click the OK button) to open a Windows Explorer window to the System32 folder in your Windows system folder. (If you're wondering, %windir% is an environment variable, or placeholder, that tells Windows to use the name of your Windows folder, no matter what the folder happens to be actually called.)

2. Click in the document window (where the long list of files is) and type **comd** at a good speed to jump to the comdlg32.ocx file. Press CTRL+C or choose Edit | Copy to copy it to the Clipboard.

3. Press ALT+D to select the contents of the Address Bar, and then type **%programfiles%** to switch to your Program Files folder. (%programfiles% is another environment variable that gives you access to the Program Files folder, no matter what name the folder actually uses.)

4. Double-click the iPod Library folder to open it, then press CTRL+V (or choose Edit | Paste) to paste in the comdlg32.ocx file.

Now choose Start | All Programs | iPod Library again. This time, you may well see the iPod Library dialog box error message shown here:

Click the OK button, and iPod Library appears (see Figure 4-1).

Figure 4-1

The iPod Library page of iPod Library lets you manage the books you've installed.

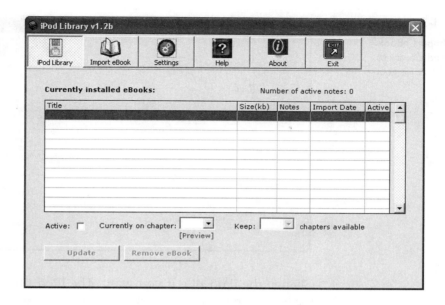

Click the Settings button, and then use the iPod Drive drop-down list to select the drive that represents your iPod. If you've just plugged the iPod in and it doesn't appear in the list, click the [Refresh] button.

To make sure your iPod knows how to handle HTML files, click the Setup button. iPod Library sets up the iPod, and then displays a message box telling you that it has done so.

In the Default Keep Chapters Available Setting drop-down list, specify how many chapters to keep available on your iPod. The standard setting is [All], but you may want to set a limit. The choices are 20, 40, 60, and 80. You can override this default setting for each book on the iPod Library page.

Import an E-Book with iPod Library

To import an e-book with iPod Library, follow these steps:

1. Click the Import eBook button to display the Import eBook page (see Figure 4-2).

2. Click the Browse button to display the Choose eBook To Import dialog box. This is a standard Windows Open dialog box with the name changed. Navigate to the folder that contains the file, select the file, and then click the Open button. iPod Library enters the file's path and name in the eBook File text box, the file's name (minus the extension) in the Library Title text box, and an abbreviated version of the title in the iPod Title text box.

3. Change the library title if you want. The library title is the name you see for the book in iPod Library.

Figure 4-2

Use the Import eBook page of iPod Library to import a book for your iPod.

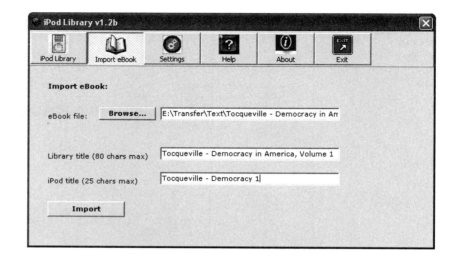

4. Change the iPod title if you want. The iPod title is the name under which the book appears on your iPod. The title can be up to 25 characters long, but shorter is usually better.

5. Click the Import button to import the file and transfer it to your iPod. iPod Library displays the Import Complete dialog box when it has finished:

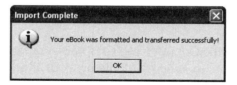

Manage E-Books with iPod Library

Once you've added books to your iPod Library (and thus to your iPod), you can manage them from the iPod Library page (see Figure 4-3). Follow these steps:

1. In the Currently Installed eBooks list box, select the book you want to affect. This list shows each book's title, size in kilobytes, number of notes, the date you imported the book, and whether the book is active (whether it's loaded on your iPod).

2. To change the Active status of the selected book, select or clear the Active check box.

3. To set the current chapter, use the Currently On Chapter drop-down list. You can click the Preview link to display a preview of that chapter's text inside the window.

Figure 4-3

Use the iPod Library page to manage your books.

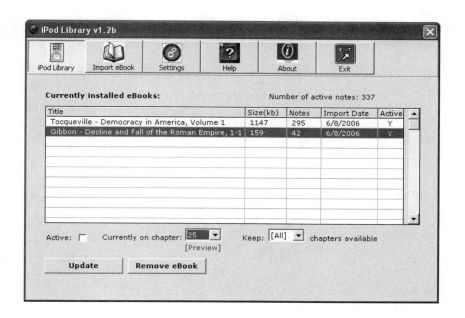

4. To control how many chapters are available for the book, choose [All] or the appropriate number (20, 40, 60, or 80) in the Keep Chapters Available drop-down list.

5. Click the Update button to apply the changes you've made.

6. To remove an e-book from your library, select it, click the Remove eBook button, and then click the OK button in the confirmation message box:

Prepare Notes on the Mac Using Book2Pod

On the Mac, use the freeware tool Book2Pod (www.tomsci.com/book2pod) to divide a text file into pieces the right size for iPod notes. Book2Pod enables you to get around the 1,000-note limitation by letting you load and unload books even after you've split them up into pieces. Book2Pod requires Mac OS X 10.2 or later and iPod firmware 2 or higher (if you've got an iPod with video or an iPod nano, you'll be fine).

To prepare notes using Book2Pod, follow these steps:

1. Download the latest version of Book2Pod from TomSci.com (www.tomsci .com/book2pod), open the disk image, and drag the Book2Pod file to your Applications folder.

2. Double-click the Book2Pod file in your Applications folder to start Book2Pod (see Figure 4-4).

Figure 4-4

Start Book2Pod.

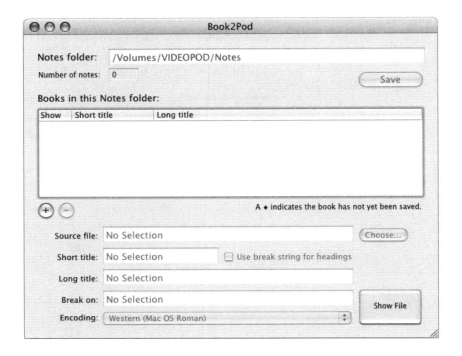

3. Look at the Notes Folder readout and make sure that Book2Pod has detected the iPod you want to use:

    ● If you have two or more iPods connected, and Book2Pod has chosen the wrong iPod, choose Source | Choose Notes Folder Manually. In the resulting dialog box, click the iPod, click the Notes folder, and then click the Open button.

    ● If Book2Pod hasn't detected the iPod, choose Source | Automatically Detect iPod to place a check mark by the Automatically Detect iPod command. If that doesn't work, choose Source | Choose Notes Folder Manually, click the iPod, click the Notes folder, and then click the Open button.

4. Click the Add A New Book button (the round button bearing a plus sign) to display an Open sheet.

5. Navigate to the text file, select it, and then click the Open button. Book2Pod adds the book to the Books In This Notes Folder list box (see Figure 4-5). The Source File box shows the name of the file you just selected. You shouldn't need to change this, but if you do, click the Choose button and use the resulting dialog box to select the right file.

Figure 4-5

Each book you add appears in the Books In This Notes Folder list box.

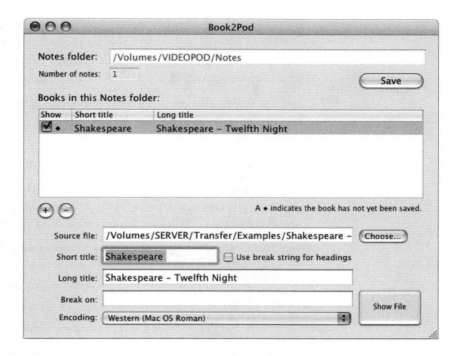

The check mark in the Show check box makes the book appear in the Notes folder. The diamond symbol next to the Show check box means that the book hasn't yet been saved.

6. In the Short Title box, enter the short title you want to use for the book. The short title is the one you see on the iPod, so make it descriptive. Book2Pod enters the first part of the file name here, but you'll often want to change it. In the example, Book2Pod has entered *Shakespeare*, which isn't helpful; *Twelfth Night* would be better.

7. In the Long Title box, enter the long title you want to use for the book. The long title is the one you use in Book2Pod. Book2Pod enters the full file name here (minus the extension). You may not need to edit this text.

8. In the Break On text box, you can type a string of text that recurs in the book to tell Book2Pod where to break the text into separate documents:

   ● What you'll most often want to enter here is **^Chapter**, which tells Book2Pod to break at a line break followed by the word "Chapter"—for example, a line beginning "Chapter 2."

   ● Select the Use Break String For Headings check box if you want Book2Pod to create heading names based on the break string.

   ● You can also leave the Break On text box blank to have Book2Pod break the files as needed to make them fit on the iPod.

9. If you know that the text file uses a special encoding, choose it in the Encoding drop-down list. For example, some text files downloadable on the Internet use the Unicode (UTF-8) encoding. For general use, stick with Western (Mac OS Roman) unless you find it's giving you strange characters (see the next step).

10. Click the Show File button to display the beginning of the text file in a new panel at the bottom of the Book2Pod window.

11. Check that the text looks okay. If it doesn't, select another encoding in the Encoding drop-down list until the text looks normal.

12. To display the text as it will appear on your iPod, select the Show As On iPod check box. To display a page readout and page breaks (as lines), select the Show Page Marks check box. Here's an example showing both these options:

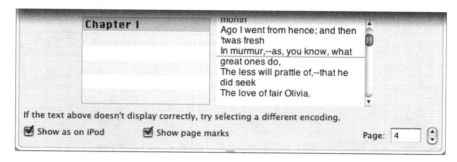

13. Click the Save button to divide the file up into notes and save it to your iPod.

Step 3: Read the Text on Your iPod

To read the text on your iPod, go to the main menu and choose Extras | Notes. On the Notes screen, select the name of the note containing the text you want, and then press the Select button. If you use Book2Pod on the Mac to prepare your notes, you'll find the books in the Book2Pod Data folder.

note *The first time you access the Notes category after adding the notes, your iPod has to build an index of the notes it contains. If there are nearly 1,000 notes, building the index takes several minutes. Once the index is built, accessing the notes is quick.*

When you reach the end of one note and see the >> link or Next link, press the Select button to "click" the link and move to the next chapter.

Read Your E-mail on Your iPod

What You'll Need:

- iPod Required: Any iPod but the iPod shuffle
- Windows Software Required: iPodSync
- Mac Software Required: iPDA
- Cost: $25 U.S. or less

Using your iPod as an e-book reader (as described in the previous project) is great, especially if you've got a long commute or you tend to get stuck places with only your iPod for entertainment. But there's no reason you need to stay with e-books. If you want to get things done and process as much input as possible in your downtime, you probably hanker to put e-mail on your iPod—and you can. This project shows you how to put e-mail from Outlook (Windows), Entourage (Mac), and Mail (Mac) on your iPod.

Before you dive in, there's one restriction you need to know—but you probably know it already. For text, your iPod is read-only: there's no way yet to compose e-mail on your iPod, other than by recording voice memos using a microphone (see Project 3). What you can do very effectively is triage your Inbox when you can't be using your computer—for example, on a bus or train—or catch up on newsletters that you haven't found time to read at your desk. You may also want to carry around important messages for reference; for example, in case you have a bright idea for which you need to refer to specifics in a message.

Step 1: Load Your E-mail on Your iPod

To load your e-mail on your iPod, you need a custom utility. This section introduces you to the best utility for Outlook (Windows) and Entourage and Mail (Mac).

Windows: iPodSync

At this writing, the best utility for putting e-mail messages from Outlook on your iPod is iPodSync. iPodSync can also put your contacts, calendars, notes, and more on your iPod if you need to bring these along with you too.

Download and Install iPodSync

You can download a trial version of iPodSync from the iPodSync website (www.ipod-sync.com). The trial version is fully functional for 15 days, after which you have to pay $14.95 U.S. for the full version. That should give you plenty of time to see whether iPodSync works well enough for you to want to keep using it.

After downloading the iPodSync distribution file, open it. For example, if you've used Internet Explorer to download the file, click the Run button in the Download Complete dialog box.

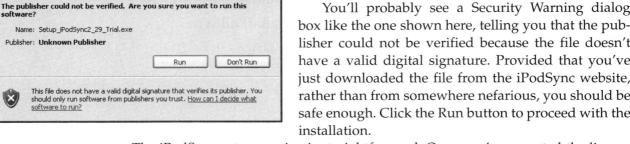

You'll probably see a Security Warning dialog box like the one shown here, telling you that the publisher could not be verified because the file doesn't have a valid digital signature. Provided that you've just downloaded the file from the iPodSync website, rather than from somewhere nefarious, you should be safe enough. Click the Run button to proceed with the installation.

The iPodSync setup routine is straightforward. Once you've accepted the license agreement, the setup routine lets you choose between a Typical installation and a Custom installation. The Typical installation installs iPodSync to a folder called iPodSync in your Program Files folder (which is as good a place for it as any) and creates an iPodSync group on your Start menu (which is also pretty normal). If you want to change either of these default settings, go with the Custom installation. Otherwise, use the Typical installation.

Once the installation is finished, double-click the iPodSync shortcut on the Desktop or choose Start | All Programs | iPodSync | iPodSync to launch iPodSync. When you do, iPodSync displays the message box shown here, telling you that you need to enable disk mode on your iPod so that iPodSync can access it.

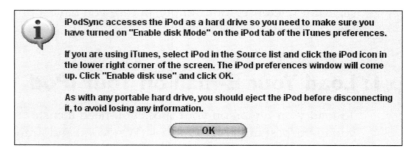

If you've already set up your iPod for manual management of songs and playlists, you're already using disk mode and don't need to make any changes.

Turn On Disk Mode

To turn on disk mode, follow these steps:

1. Connect your iPod to your PC if it's not already connected.

2. Start iTunes if it's not already running.

3. Click the iPod's entry in the Source pane.

4. On the Summary tab, select the Enable Disk Use check box. iTunes displays the following dialog box to warn you that you will need to eject the iPod manually when using disk mode.

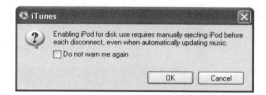

5. Click the OK button to close the message box, and then click the Apply button to apply the change to your iPod.

Configure iPodSync to Synchronize the Items You Want

Once you've turned on disk mode, iPodSync can access your iPod. Figure 5-1 shows the iPodSync window with its Advanced tab's iPodSync subtab displayed.

You now need to tell iPodSync which items you want it to synchronize. Most of these options are easy to understand—for example, to synchronize your Outlook contacts, click the Contacts tab (shown on the next page), select the Synchronize Contacts

Figure 5-1

To set up iPodSync, display the tab that contains the options you want to use, and then choose settings.

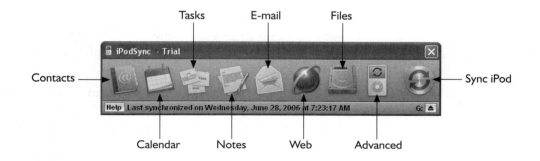

check box, and select the check box for each option you want to apply, such as Include Birthday In Notes Field.

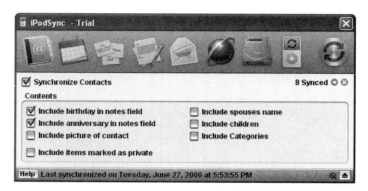

To carry your e-mail around with you, you'll need to set options on the E-mail tab and the Advanced tab. Follow these steps:

1. Click the E-mail tab to display it, as shown here.

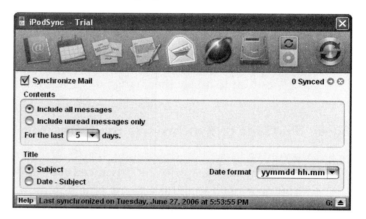

2. Select the Synchronize Mail check box.

3. In the Contents group box, select the Include All Messages option button or the Include Unread Messages Only option button, depending on whether you want to take all your messages with you or just those you haven't read. In the For The Last *NN* Days drop-down list, specify how many days' worth of messages to include.

4. In the Title group box, specify how you want iPodSync to title the messages by selecting the Subject option button or the Date – Subject option button. Date – Subject is useful for keeping your messages sorted by date. Choose the date format in the Date Format drop-down list: month and date only (mmdd), including the hour and minute (mmdd hhmm), or including the year, hour, and minute (yymmdd hhmm).

5. Click the Advanced tab, and then make sure the iPodSync subtab is selected, as shown here.

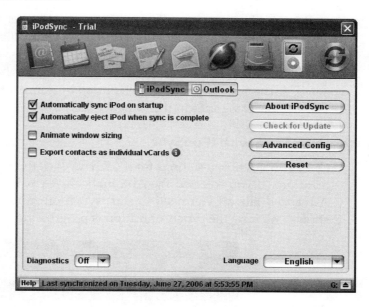

6. If you want to synchronize your iPod automatically when you launch iPodSync, select the Automatically Sync iPod On Startup check box. You can also select the Automatically Eject iPod When Sync Is Complete check box if you want to be able to make a quick departure from your desk as soon as synchronization is finished.

7. Click the Outlook subtab button to display the subtab, as shown here.

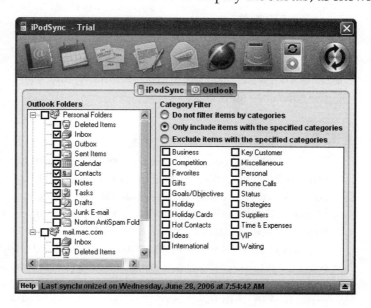

8. In the Outlook Folders pane, select the check box for each folder you want to sync. iPodSync automatically selects the most popular folders for you.

9. In the Category Filter area, decide whether you want to filter the items by categories. By default, the Do Not Filter Items By Categories option button is selected, so iPodSync doesn't filter items. To filter, select the Only Include Items With The Specified Categories option button or the Exclude Items With The Specified Categories option button, and then select the check boxes for the categories in the category list.

Synchronize Data with iPodSync

Once you've chosen settings for iPodSync, click the Sync iPod button to start synchronization. (If you selected the Automatically Sync iPod On Startup check box on the Advanced tab, all you need to start synchronization is launch iPodSync.) iPodSync shows you how the synchronization is progressing, as shown here.

If you selected the Automatically Eject iPod When Sync Is Complete check box on the Advanced tab, iPodSync tells you when you can disconnect your iPod, as shown here.

Otherwise, eject your iPod manually, and you'll be ready to read your e-mail on the road (see step 2).

Mac: iPDA

The best utility for putting e-mail messages from Mail (Apple Mail, if you will) or Microsoft Entourage on your iPod is iPDA. Apart from e-mail, iPDA also lets you copy contacts, notes, tasks, and calendar information from Entourage or information from Stickies, Address Book, and iCal. iPDA also supports downloading news headlines from Google, weather forecasts, and directions.

To get started with iPDA, you can download a mostly functional trial version that lets you put individual categories of data (for example, mail or contacts) on your iPod manually but not synchronize all your data. To get one-touch synchronization, you must buy the full version of iPod, which costs $19.95 U.S.

Download and Install iPDA

To download and install iPDA, follow these steps:

1. Steer your browser to the ZappTek website (www.zapptek.com/ipda/), and then download the trial version of iPDA.

2. Double-click the zip file to extract the disk image file.

note *Depending on how you've configured Mac OS X, the OS may automatically unzip the zip file, mount the image file, open a Finder window showing the file's contents, and trash the zip file for you.*

3. Double-click the disk image file to mount it on the Desktop.

4. Double-click the disk image to open a Finder window showing its contents.

5. Drag the iPDA item to your Applications folder.

6. Right-click the disk image and choose Eject from the shortcut menu.

7. Drag the zip file to the Trash to get rid of it. (You may also want to trash the disk image file. If not, store it somewhere convenient in case you need it again.)

To start iPDA, double-click the iPDA item in your Applications folder.

Turn On Disk Mode

To enable iPDA to transfer data to your iPod, you must turn on disk mode. Otherwise, iPDA displays the dialog box shown here to warn you of the problem.

To turn on disk mode, follow these steps:

1. Connect your iPod to your Mac if it's not already connected.

2. Start iTunes if it's not already running.

3. Click the iPod's entry in the Source pane.

4. On the Summary tab, select the Enable Disk Use check box. iTunes displays the following dialog box to warn you that you will need to eject the iPod manually when using disk mode.

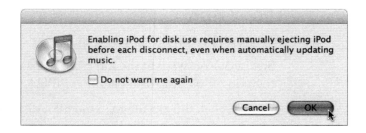

5. Click the OK button to close the message box, and then click the Apply button to apply the change to your iPod.

Configure iPDA to Synchronize the Items You Want

The first time you launch iPDA, the application displays its Preferences dialog box (see Figure 5-2).

Figure 5-2

Start by setting General preferences and telling iPDA which applications you want to synchronize with your iPod.

In the General area of the Preferences dialog box, you can set iPDA up to quickly synchronize your iPod and eject it. You can also choose to maintain formatting on the files you transfer.

- **Maintain Formatting**   Select this check box to make iPDA maintain formatting on text rather than stripping it down to plain text.

- **Auto Sync On Launch**   Select this check box if you want iPDA to synchronize your iPod automatically when you launch the application.

- **Quit After Sync** Select this check box to make iPDA close after completing the synchronization.

- **Eject iPod On Quit** Select this check box to make iPDA automatically eject the iPod when you close the application.

In the Sync area, select the check box for each item you want to synchronize. For example, to synchronize your e-mail messages from Mail, select the Mail check box in the Apple area. To synchronize your Entourage e-mail messages, select the Mail check box in the Entourage area.

If you need to use a proxy server for web services, select the Proxy Server check box and enter the host and port. For a typical home Internet connection, you won't normally need to specify a proxy server.

Click the OK button to close the Preferences dialog box. You then see the iPDA interface (see Figure 5-3), which allows you to configure synchronization for each category of item, run synchronization, and eject your iPod.

Figure 5-3

Here, only Mail in the Apple area is set to synchronize—as shown by the check mark.

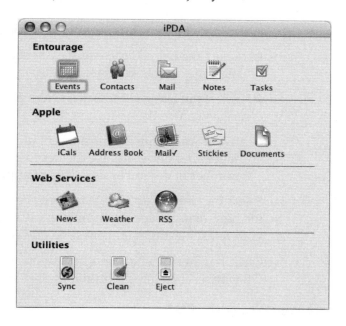

Click an item you've set to synchronize, and then choose settings in the dialog box that appears. Figure 5-4 shows the dialog box for Mail, in which you work as follows:

1. In the Messages area, choose which mailboxes to transfer:

   - Select the Transfer All Messages option button if you want to transfer messages from all mailboxes.

   - If you want messages from only some mailboxes, select the Transfer Messages From Selected Mailboxes option button, and then select the check box for each mailbox you want to include.

Figure 5-4

Use the Messages dialog box to specify which e-mail messages iPDA should transfer to your iPod.

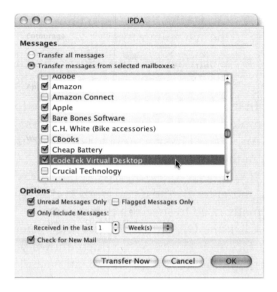

2. In the Options area, choose which messages to get from those mailboxes:

   ● Select the Unread Messages Only check box if you want to include only messages you haven't read (or that you've marked as unread).

   ● Select the Flagged Messages Only check box if you want only those messages you've flagged.

   ● If you want only the most recent messages, select the Only Include Messages check box and use the Received In The Last controls to specify the number of days or weeks—for example, "2 Day(s)" or "1 Week(s)."

3. Select the Check For New Mail check box if you want to force iPDA to check for new mail before synchronizing. (Checking for new mail like this puts your latest messages on your iPod and is usually a good idea.)

4. Click the Transfer Now button if you want to transfer the messages now. Otherwise, click the OK button to close the dialog box.

Synchronize Data with iPDA

Once you've set up iPDA as described in the previous section, you can synchronize your data by clicking the Sync button in the Utilities area.

To eject your iPod, click the Eject button in the Utilities area.

Step 2: Read Your E-mail on Your iPod

To read your e-mail on your iPod, scroll to the Extras menu, and then press the Select button. Scroll down to the Notes item, and then press the Select button to access your notes. You'll find the mailboxes and messages you transferred inside the Notes folder.

You're all set to read your e-mail on your iPod. Now, cue some music and stroll right out of the office to somewhere more pleasant.

Clean Up Your Songs, Tags, and Album Art

What You'll Need:

- **iPods covered: Any iPod**
- **Windows software required: Tag&Rename (optional), iTunesKeys (optional), Total Audio Converter (optional)**
- **Mac software required: MP3 Rage (optional), iTunes Catalog (optional)**
- **Cost: $50 U.S. or less**

By now, you probably have a music library that's burgeoning—or maybe even bursting at the seams. But are all the songs fit for your listening, or do some of them need some work to bring them up to scratch? This project shows you how to take care of problems with songs.

First, iTunes offers a quick and easy fix for any song that has a beginning or ending that you want to skip: you can simply tell iTunes not to play the part you don't like. If you want to actually get rid of that part of the song, you can remove it using iTunes itself or other software.

What's usually more of a problem is songs with missing, incomplete, or incorrect tags that prevent you from finding the songs you want or sorting them. You can fix the tags on a song or album manually, but if you need to retag many songs, you can save time and effort by having a program do most of the work for you. What you will need to do manually is rate your songs (by giving one to five stars to each), because only you know how much you like each song. Rating songs lets you build playlists based on which songs you like and helps you cull the duds from your music library.

What about art? Do all your songs have at least the cover of the CD or album to which they belong? Could you use a hand from a utility that automatically adds art to songs that are missing it? Sure you could. And are you sure that there aren't any duplicate songs in your music library? Chances are that some unplanned twins are wasting precious space on your computer and iPod.

Last, do you have any songs that are in formats that iTunes can't handle, such as Ogg Vorbis or FLAC? This project shows you how to make good citizens of such songs too so that they can take their place in your music library.

Step 1: Trim Bad Outros and Intros from Songs

Your first step in fixing your songs is to trim off any intros or outros that you don't like. Ever find yourself reaching for the mouse so that you can skip those 30 seconds of garbled phone call that must have seemed so hilarious to the artist when she dubbed it onto the end of a song? What about having to skip the first few minutes of a Pink Floyd song to get to the good part?

You're not alone. iTunes can help, or you can use third-party software.

Trim a Song Using iTunes

iTunes offers you two ways to deal with song beginnings and endings that you prefer not to hear:

- You can simply tell iTunes to start playing the song a certain number of seconds after the beginning, or stop playing it a certain number of seconds before the end. The advantage of this method is that it's easy to do and you don't actually make any changes to the song file, just to the way that iTunes handles it. So if you want to play the whole of such a song to one of your friends, you can do so.

- You can crop off the parts of the song you don't want to hear. Cropping changes the song file permanently, but the only way you can crop in iTunes is to create a new song file, so you still have the original song file.

Tell iTunes Not to Play the Beginning or End of a Song

To tell iTunes not to play the beginning or end of a song, follow these steps:

1. Select the song, and then open the Song Information dialog box in one of these ways:

   - Press CTRL-I (Windows) or ⌘-I (Mac).

   - Right-click or CTRL-click (Mac) the song and choose Get Info from the shortcut menu.

   - Choose File | Get Info.

note *The Song Information dialog box's title bar shows the song's name rather than "Song Information."*

Figure 6-1

Use the Start Time and Stop Time boxes to tell iTunes not to play the beginning or end of a song.

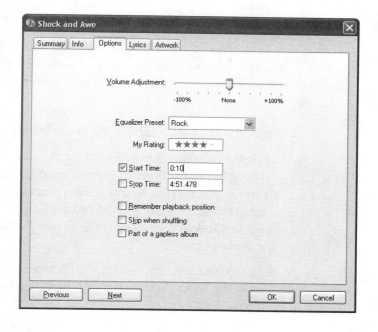

2. Click the Options tab to display it (see Figure 6-1).

3. To cut off the beginning of the song, click in the Start Time text box, and then change the default start time (0:00 minutes and seconds) to tell iTunes how far into the song you want it to start play. For example, type 0:34 to start 34 seconds into the song. When you type in the Start Time text box, iTunes automatically selects the Start Time check box for you, so you don't need to click it to select it.

4. To cut off the end of the song, click in the Stop Time text box, and then change the default stop time. Normally the default stop time is the very end of the song, which iTunes shows in minutes, seconds, and thousandths of seconds—for example, 4:58.328, as in Figure 6-1. Type your new stop time in minutes and seconds—for example, **2:25**. iTunes automatically selects the Stop Time check box when you type in the Stop Time text box, so you don't need to select it manually.

5. While you've got the Song Information dialog box open, make any other adjustments needed on this page. For example, drag the Volume Adjustment slider to boost or lower the volume, choose an equalizer preset, or apply a star rating to the song.

6. Click the OK button to close the Song Information dialog box.

Now when you play the song, iTunes automatically starts it and stops it at the times you indicated. This change carries over to your iPod, so you won't suffer the unwanted intros and outros when you're out and about.

Create a Shortened Version of a Song with iTunes

Once you've marked the points at which you want iTunes to start and stop playing a song, you can create a new file that contains only the parts of the song that you've specified should play. To do so, you use the Convert Selection command. Follow these steps:

1. Mark the start and stop points as described in the previous list.

2. Click the Advanced menu, look at the Convert Selection To command, and verify that iTunes is set to use the encoder you want. The Convert Selection To command's name shows the current encoder: Convert Selection To AAC, Convert Selection To MP3, Convert Selection To Apple Lossless, Convert Selection To WAV, or Convert Selection To AIFF. To change the encoder, follow these steps:

   - On Windows, choose Edit | Preferences to open the iTunes dialog box. On the Mac, choose iTunes | Preferences to open the Preferences dialog box.

   - Click the Advanced tab to display its contents.

   - Click the Importing subtab to display its contents.

   - In the Import Using drop-down list, choose the encoder you want to use—for example, choose AAC Encoder if you want to create AAC files. Use the Setting drop-down list to choose the bitrate for the encoder to use. For example, for the AAC encoder, High Quality (128 Kbps) is a good choice for all but the most demanding ears.

note   *The AAC format is usually the best bet for iTunes and the iPod, as it provides high audio quality with a relatively small file size (for example, encoded at the 128 Kbps bitrate). MP3 files offer marginally lower audio quality at the same file size. Apple Lossless Encoding files are much larger but have full audio quality. WAV and AIFF files are larger still, because they contain uncompressed audio at full quality.*

3. Select the song you want to shorten, and then choose Advanced | Convert Selection To *Encoder*, where *Encoder* is the name of the encoder iTunes is set to use. For example, choose Advanced | Convert Selection To AAC. iTunes exports a shortened version of the song in that format.

note   *If the Convert Selection To command specifies the same encoder as the original song uses, iTunes doesn't actually perform a conversion; instead, iTunes just creates a shorter version of the song. Not converting the song is in fact better if the original song uses a compressed format (AAC, MP3, or Apple Lossless Encoding), because you lose audio quality when you convert a compressed song and then reencode it in a different format.*

4. Play the shortened version of the song to make sure that it starts and ends exactly where you wanted it to.

5. Decide whether to keep or delete the original version of the song. You might want to keep it but remove it from your music library so that Party Shuffle or a Smart Playlist doesn't play it for you—or so that you don't play it by mistake.

> **note** *You can also use the technique described in this section to divide a single song into two or more songs. For example, to divide a four-minute song into two two-minute songs, first set a start time of 2:01, and then use the Convert Selection To command to export the second part of the song to a new file. Then change the start time on the original song to 0:00, set a stop time of 2:00, and use the Convert Selection To command to export the first part of the song to another new file.*

Step 2: Fix Tags So That You Can Sort Your Songs

You've probably noticed by now that iTunes is really a database of all your music. And it's a pretty good database: it makes searching as simple as typing a few letters or a phrase in the Search text box. Or you can browse your songs in various ways—for example, by selecting the Rock genre in the Browser pane, and then clicking the My Rating column heading once to produce a descending sort (five stars first, four stars next, and so on).

But—as you'll know if you've ever dealt with a bureaucracy that has the wrong information about you—a database is only as good as the data it contains. To work properly, iTunes needs all your songs to have reliable tag information so that it can sort them by artist and album and slice and dice them by Smart Playlist. If the tag information is wrong or incomplete, iTunes can't arrange your songs as you need it to. Worse, iTunes doesn't even transfer to your iPod any song whose tag doesn't have artist, album, and track name, because the iPod won't be able to deal with it.

> **tip** *You can force iTunes to load untagged songs on your iPod by assigning them to a playlist and loading the playlist. The iPod gives the song a temporary name consisting of its filename (without the extension), so you can access it either through the playlist to which it belongs or through the Songs list.*

Know How Tags Work

Compressed audio formats such as AAC, MP3, and Apple Lossless Encoding include containers for a full set of tag information about the song the file contains. The tag information lets you sort, organize, and search for songs on iTunes and enables your iPod to organize the songs.

Your main tool for tagging song files should be iTunes, because it provides solid if basic features for tagging one or more files at once manually. But if your music library contains many files that don't have tags or have incorrect tag information, you may need a heavier-duty application. This section shows you how to tag most effectively in iTunes and then presents two more powerful applications—Tag&Rename for Windows, and MP3 Rage for the Mac.

Tag Songs Effectively with iTunes

If you want to keep your music library organized (and you should), try to make sure each song is tagged correctly when you add it to iTunes. If you check tags relentlessly on admission, your music library remains fully tagged, and you'll have no problems with sorting.

But that's easier said than done, and if you're building the mother of all music libraries, you'll probably run into times when you need to add song files to your music library without checking the tags on each one. For example, you find a CD containing a backup of songs you thought you'd lost from your old computer. You copy the songs to your laptop—but then it's time to head out the door on a business trip. Better to take the songs with you and have the chance of checking them on the plane than to leave them and forget about them…but then you never get around to plowing through the tags to make sure they're complete and accurate.

Anyway, sooner or later, even the best-organized music library will tend to have its fair share of songs with tags that are wanting. Songs distributed for free on the Internet—legally or illegally—tend to be worse offenders than most of the songs that are for sale, if only because purchasers normally demand at least the semblance of a quality product.

Running a Reality Check on CDDB

As you'll know by now, the easiest way to add tag information to songs you rip from your CDs to your music library is to allow iTunes to look each CD up on CDDB, the database of CD information. CDDB lookups are wonderful—but you should always check the tag information that CDDB supplies, because (even with the best will in the world) it's not always accurate.

You've probably found yourself catching gross ID errors such as suggesting that (say) *Born To Run* is actually a compilation called *Undead* containing Gothic-rock "masterpieces," but it's the insidious errors that tend to sneak through the reality filter. A close look often reveals misspellings, miscapitalizations, and even misreadings of song names, all of which you'll want to correct. And wait, who in the name of the City of Angels decided that Concrete Blonde was Blues music?

When tagging an artist who has had many bands, you may want to standardize on the artist's name to reduce the complexity of your music library. That way, only the artist's entry appears in iTunes and on the iPod, and the interfaces are easier to navigate.

When you need to change the tag information for a whole CD's worth of songs, proceed as follows:

1. In iTunes, select all the song files you want to affect.

2. Right-click or CTRL-click (Mac) the selection and choose Get Info from the shortcut menu to display the Multiple Song Information dialog box (see Figure 6-2). Alternatively, choose File | Get Info or press CTRL-I on Windows or ⌘-I on the Mac. (If iTunes displays a message box confirming that you want to edit the information for multiple songs, select the Do Not Ask Me Again check box, and then click the Yes button.)

Figure 6-2

Use the Multiple Song Information dialog box to enter common tag information for all the songs in one fell swoop.

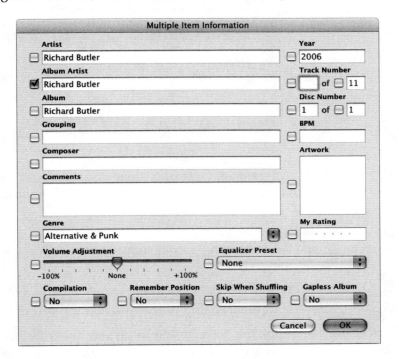

3. Enter as much common information as you can: the artist, year, album, total number of tracks, disc number, composer, comments, and so on. If you have the artwork for the CD available, drag it to the Artwork pane.

4. Click the OK button to apply the information to the songs.

5. Click the first song to clear the current selection. Right-click (or CTRL-click on the Mac) the song and choose Get Info from the shortcut menu to display the Song Information dialog box for the song. Click the Info tab to display it if iTunes doesn't display it automatically. Figure 6-3 shows the Mac version of the Song Information dialog box for the song "Post Blue." The song's title appears in the title bar of the dialog box.

Figure 6-3

Use the Song
Information dialog
box to add song-specific
information.

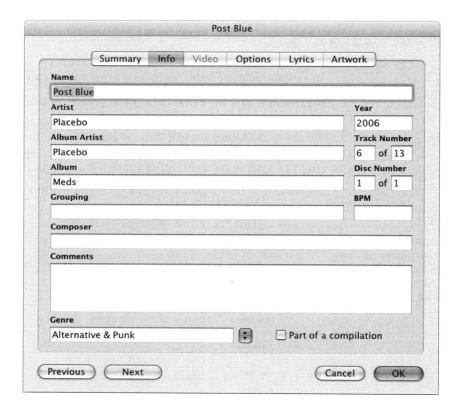

6. Add any song-specific information here: the song name, the track number, and so on.

7. If you need to change the song's relative volume, equalizer preset, rating, start time, or stop time, work on the Options tab.

8. Click the Next button to display the information for the previous song or next song, and then work through each song in turn.

9. Click the OK button to close the Song Information dialog box when you've finished adding song information.

Tag Songs on Windows with Tag&Rename

Tag&Rename, from SOFTPOINTER, Ltd., is a powerful tag-editing application for various types of files, including AAC and MP3. You can download a free 30-day evaluation version from www.softpointer.com/tr.htm and from various other sites on the Internet. The full version costs $29.95 U.S.

Tag&Rename can derive tag information by breaking down a file's name into its constituents. For example, if you set Tag&Rename on the file Aimee Mann – Lost in Space – 06 – Pavlov's Bell.mp3, Tag&Rename can derive the artist name (Aimee Mann), the album name (*Lost in Space*), the track number (06), and the song name ("Pavlov's Bell") from the file, and apply that information to the tag fields.

It can also derive tag information from the folder structure that contains an MP3 file that needs tagging. For example, if you have the file 06 – Pavlov's Bell.mp3 stored in the folder Aimee Mann\Lost in Space, Tag&Rename will be able to tag the file with the artist name, album name, track name, and track number.

Figure 6-4 shows Tag&Rename in action, working on the ID3 tags of some MP3 files.

Figure 6-4

Tag&Rename can edit multiple ID3 tags at once.

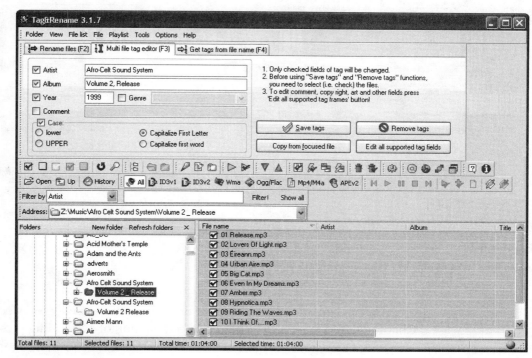

note   *Another powerful tagging utility for Windows is Super Tagging, which is part of Musicmatch Jukebox Plus ($19.99 U.S. for lifetime upgrades; www.musicmatch.com). Musicmatch Jukebox Plus is a competitor for iTunes, but it has such powerful tagging capabilities that you might consider buying it for that alone—especially as it costs less than Tag&Rename.*

Tag Songs on the Mac with Media Rage

Media Rage, from Chaotic Software (www.chaoticsoftware.com), is an impressive bundle of utilities for tagging, organizing, and improving your MP3 files. The tagging features in Media Rage include deriving tag information from filenames and folder paths (see the left screen in Figure 6-5) and changing the tags on multiple files at once (see the right screen in Figure 6-5).

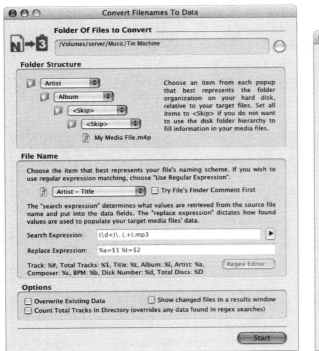
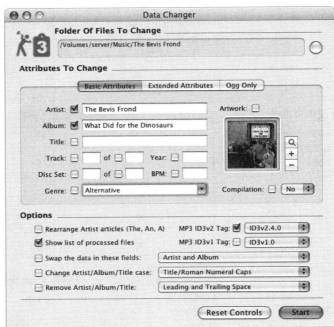

Figure 6-5

Media Rage includes powerful tagging among many other features.

You can download a fully functional evaluation version of Media Rage from the Chaotic Software website. The registered version of Media Rage costs $29.95 U.S.

Step 3: Apply Ratings to Songs

Rating provides a cross-genre means of defining roughly how much you like a song. iTunes and your iPod let you assign a rating of one star to five stars to each song in your music library; you can also assign no stars, but this leaves the song unrated, as if you've applied no rating at all.

Your first reaction to iTunes' ratings may be to shake your head at the effort involved in applying ratings to even a few hundred songs, let alone to a full music library consisting of many thousands of songs. Rating the songs takes a while, but having each song rated can be really helpful in managing your music library:

- You can more easily identify which songs you like the most.

- You can also identify which songs you like the least. When pressed for space, you might decide to remove all the one-star and two-star songs from your music library.

● You can use the rating as part of your Smart Playlists. For example, to keep the quality of a Smart Playlist high, you might specify that it include only songs to which you've given four- or five-star ratings.

iTunes and your iPod let you apply a rating in any of these ways:

● Click in the My Rating column. iTunes displays five dots in the column. Click the dot that represents the number of stars you want to assign (counting from the left). If the My Rating column doesn't appear in the iTunes window, right-click any column heading, and then click the My Rating item on the submenu to place a checkmark next to it.

● Right-click a song (CTRL-click on the Mac), choose My Rating from the shortcut menu, and select the appropriate number of stars from the submenu.

● Use the My Rating box on the Options tab of the Song Information dialog box (press CTRL-I on Windows or ⌘-I on the Mac, or choose Get Info from the File menu or the shortcut menu) to specify the number of stars.

● On your iPod, press the Select button twice from the Now Playing screen while the song is playing, scroll left or right to select the appropriate number of stars, and then press the Select button again. iTunes picks up the rating the next time you synchronize your iPod.

Step 4: Add Art to Songs That Don't Have It

Art—in songs? Who needs it?

These days, everyone wants it, even if they don't need it. In the old days of iPods, having each song's art stored with the song used to benefit only iTunes: you could use the Now Playing feature to display the song's artwork either in the artwork pane or in a separate window. You can still do that, of course, but now that all iPods except the iPod shuffle can display the art in full, glorious color on the screen, art is much more desirable. Both on the iPod and on your computer, art helps you more quickly identify which song is playing.

Some third-party widgets for playing iTunes (see "Step 2: Control iTunes with a Widget" in Project 10) can automatically display a pop-up containing the art for a few seconds as each song starts. This is a great way of keeping tabs on which song is playing without having the iTunes window take up a serious amount of your desktop's real estate.

Getting Suitable Art

The easiest way to get art in your songs is to buy the songs with art already present. Most songs you buy from the iTunes Music Store include the appropriate artwork—for example, the cover of the single, EP, album, or CD that includes the song. For other songs, you can add artwork either manually, via a semi-automated process (on Windows), or automatically (on the Mac).

The second easiest way is to have iTunes automatically add art to songs for you. iTunes 7 and later versions automatically check an online database for cover art when encoding a song you're importing from CD or converting from another format (for example, WAV). If iTunes finds the cover art for the song, it adds it automatically. This feature requires an Internet connection, of course, but it works well.

You can apply any image you want to a song, provided that it is in a format that QuickTime supports. (QuickTime's supported formats include JPG, GIF, TIFF, PNG, BMP, and PhotoShop.) For example, you might download album art or other pictures from an artist's website, and then apply those to the song files you ripped from the artist's CDs. Or you might prefer to add images of your own to favorite songs or to songs you've composed yourself.

tip *Amazon.com (www.amazon.com) has cover images for millions of CDs and records. For most music items, you can click the small picture on the item's main page to display a larger version of the image. Another source is Allmusic (www.allmusic.com), a service that requires registration.*

Add Artwork to Songs Manually

You can add artwork to songs manually by using either the artwork pane in the iTunes window or the Artwork box in the Song Information dialog box or the Multiple Song Information dialog box. The artwork pane is usually easiest.

To add artwork manually, follow these steps:

1. Open a Windows Explorer window (Windows) or a Finder window (Mac) to the folder that contains the image you want to use for the artwork, or open a browser window to a URL that contains the image. For example, open an Internet Explorer window to Amazon.com and navigate to the image you want.

2. Arrange iTunes and the Windows Explorer window, Finder window, or browser window so that you can see them both.

3. In iTunes, select the song or songs you want to affect:

   ● SHIFT-click to select a contiguous range of songs: click the first song, then hold down SHIFT as you click the last song in the range.

   ● CTRL-click (Windows) or ⌘-click (Mac) to select noncontiguous songs: click the first song, then hold down CTRL (Windows) or ⌘ (Mac) while you click each of the other songs to add them to the selection.

4. To use the artwork pane, follow these steps:

   ● If the artwork pane isn't displayed (below the Source pane), display it by clicking the Show Or Hide Song Artwork button, pressing CTRL-G (Windows) or ⌘-G (Mac), or choosing View | Show Artwork.

- If the title bar of the artwork pane says Now Playing, click the title bar to change it to Selected Song.

- Drag the image to the artwork pane and drop it there.

5. To use the Song Information dialog box or the Multiple Song Information dialog box, follow these steps:

    - Display the Song Information dialog box or the Multiple Song Information dialog box by right-clicking and choosing Get Info from the shortcut menu, choosing File | Get Info, or press CTRL-I (Windows) or ⌘-I (Mac).

    - If you've opened the Song Information dialog box, click the Artwork tab to display its contents.

    - Drag the image to the Artwork box in the Multiple Song Information dialog box or the open area on the Artwork tab of the Song Information dialog box.

    - If you're using the Song Information dialog box, add further images as needed. To change the order of the images, drag them about in the open area (see Figure 6-6). You may need to reduce the zoom by dragging the slider to get the pictures small enough to rearrange.

6. Add further images to the song or songs if you want while you have them selected.

Figure 6-6

The Song Information dialog box lets you add multiple images to a song and rearrange them into the order you want.

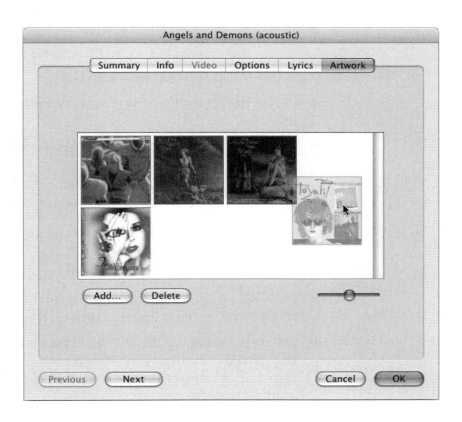

Most CD cover images are relatively small in dimensions and are compressed, so their file size is fairly small. Adding an image to a song increases its file size a little, but not normally enough to cause a problem. If you add a large image to a song, iTunes uses a compressed version of the image rather than the full image.

Add Artwork Automatically As You Play Songs on Windows

iTunesKeys (discussed in "Control iTunes on Windows with iTunesKeys" in Project 10) can automatically download the art for the current song, if the art is available on Amazon.com. This is a great way of gradually adding art to your music library as you play songs.

Add Artwork to Songs Semi-Automatically on Windows or the Mac

The art4itunes.com website (www.art4itunes.com) can search for as many artwork items as are available for your music library. You then must add the artwork items manually to the songs. This works on either Windows or the Mac.

To use art4itunes.com:

1. In iTunes, select your music library in the Source pane. If you want to get art for only some songs, create a playlist containing those songs, and then select the playlist in the Source pane.

2. Choose File | Export Song List to display the Save As dialog box (Windows) or the Save: iTunes dialog box (Mac).

3. Specify the filename for the list, and choose the folder in which to store it.

4. Make sure iTunes is set to save the file as text:

    ● On Windows, verify that Text Files is selected in the Save As Type drop-down list.

    ● On the Mac, verify that Plain Text is selected in the Format drop-down list.

5. Click the Save button to save the file.

6. Open a web browser window to the art4itunes website (www.art4itunes.com), and follow the instructions to upload your library listing, choose an image size, and start the search.

7. From the resulting page, drag an image to iTunes to apply it to songs:

    ● On Windows, select the songs you want to affect, display the artwork pane, and drop the image in the artwork pane. Figure 6-7 shows an example.

    ● On either Windows or the Mac, select the songs you want to affect, choose File | Get Info to display the Multiple Song Information dialog box, and then drag the image to the Artwork box. Click the OK button to close the Multiple Song Information dialog box.

Figure 6-7

The art4itunes website finds as much artwork as possible for the songs in your music library.

Add Artwork to Songs Automatically on the Mac

If you're using the Mac and you're prepared to pay a few dollars, you can add artwork to your songs automatically by using iTunes Catalog from KavaSoft ($24.95 U.S.; www.kavasoft.com). You can use the trial edition to see how well iTunes Catalog finds the images for artists with names starting A, B, C, D, and E.

Enjoy the Art You've Added—Or Remove It

When you've added two or more pictures to the same song, the artwork pane displays a Previous button and a Next button for browsing from picture to picture.

You can display the current picture at full size by clicking it in the artwork pane. Click the Close button (the X button) to close the artwork window.

To remove the artwork from a song, right-click (or CTRL-click on the Mac) the song and choose Get Info from the shortcut menu. Click the Artwork tab of the Song Information dialog box, click the picture, and then click the Remove button.

Step 5: Remove Duplicate Songs from Your Music Library

Even if your music library is a modest size, you can easily get duplicate songs in it, especially if you add folders of existing song files as well as rip and encode your CDs and other audio sources. Duplicate songs waste disk space, particularly on your iPod, so iTunes offers a command to help you identify them.

1. In the Source pane, click your library. If you want to confine the duplicate-checking to a playlist, click that playlist in the Source pane.

Figure 6-8

Use the View | Show Duplicates command to display a list of songs that may be duplicates.

2. Choose View | Show Duplicates. iTunes displays a list of duplicate songs. Figure 6-8 shows an example on the Mac.

> **note** *Often many of the "duplicates" identified simply have the same artist and album names but are different versions rather than being actual duplicates—so check carefully before you delete a song.*

3. Where you have duplicate copies of a song (rather than different versions of the same song by the same artist), decide which copy to keep. To find out where a song is stored, right-click it (or CTRL-click on the Mac) and choose Show Song File from the shortcut menu. You'll see a Windows Explorer window or a Finder window that shows the contents of the folder that includes the song file.

> **note** *If your music library contains various file formats, you may find it helpful to display the file type in iTunes so that you can see which song is in which format. For example, when you have duplicate files, you might want to delete the MP3 files rather than the AAC files. Right-click (or CTRL-click on the Mac) the heading of the column after which you want the Kind column to appear, and then select the Kind item from the shortcut menu.*

4. To delete a song, select it and press DELETE (Windows) or BACKSPACE (Mac). Click the Yes button in the confirmation dialog box; select the Do Not Ask Me Again check box first if you want to turn off the confirmation.

5. If the song file is stored in your iTunes Music folder, iTunes prompts you to move it to the Recycle Bin (Windows) or to the Trash (Mac). Click the Yes button or the No button as appropriate.

Once you've finished pruning your duplicates, click the Show All button at the bottom of the iTunes window or choose View | Show All to return to your full music library.

Step 6: Convert Songs from Formats iTunes Can't Handle

Advanced Audio Coding (AAC) is a very appealing music format for iTunes users and iPod owners because it delivers high audio quality in a small file size. But AAC has far less appeal to anyone using Windows Media Player, iTunes' major competitor on Windows, because Microsoft has chosen not to let Windows Media Player play AAC files at all. Instead, Windows Media Player uses Microsoft's own Windows Media Audio (WMA) format, and most users go with this default setting. Like AAC, WMA provides higher audio quality than MP3 at the same bitrates; also like AAC, WMA supports digital rights management (DRM), which means that music creators can set limitations on how you can play the songs you buy from them.

Similarly, AAC isn't strong on Linux, whose devotees tend to favor either the open-source Ogg Vorbis (Ogg) format (which gives similar quality to AAC) or the lossless Free Lossless Audio Codec (FLAC), which gives similar quality to Apple Lossless Encoding.

So if you receive an audio file from a Windows user who's not running iTunes, or from a Linux user, it's likely to be either an MP3 or a format that iTunes can't play. That doesn't mean you can't add the song to your music library: It just means that you must convert it first.

Converting WMA Files to AAC or MP3

iTunes itself can convert WMA files to AAC or MP3. Just drag a WMA file to your music library, and iTunes automatically converts it to the format specified on the Importing subtab of the Advanced tab in the iTunes dialog box (Windows) or the Preferences dialog box (Mac).

Converting Ogg Vorbis Files

If you receive a song in the Ogg Vorbis format, you can convert it either via a two-step process using the freeware sound editor Audacity (discussed in detail in Project 9) or via a one-step process using software for which you have to pay.

Using Audacity to Convert Songs from Ogg Vorbis Format

To convert a song from Ogg Vorbis format to a format iTunes can play using Audacity:

1. Use Audacity to convert the Ogg file to a WAV file.

2. Drag the WAV file to your music library.

3. Right-click or CTRL-click (Mac) the WAV file in iTunes and choose Convert Selection To *Format* from the shortcut menu, where *Format* is the format currently set in your Importing preferences.

4. Once the conversion is complete, delete the WAV file.

5. Right-click or CTRL-click (Mac) the new file, choose Get Info from the shortcut menu, and use the Song Information dialog box to tag the new file.

Using Another Audio Converter

To convert Ogg Vorbis songs to AAC or MP3 in a single step on Windows, use a tool such as Total Audio Converter ($19.90 U.S.; www.coolutils.com/TotalAudioConverter).

Converting Songs from FLAC

If you receive a song in the FLAC format, use a tool such as Total Audio Converter ($19.90 U.S.; www.coolutils.com/TotalAudioConverter) on Windows.

note *Anyone who creates song files in the FLAC or Ogg Vorbis formats almost certainly has an audio program that could create MP3 files for you instead.*

By now, your music library should be in tip-top condition, with each song trimmed of unnecessary intro or outro twiddling, fully tagged, and complete with its cover art. You've even eliminated all duplicate songs that don't have a genuine reason for taking up space on your computer and your iPod.

It's time to sort out your videos. To learn more about this see the next project.

Put Your Home Videos and DVDs on Your iPod

What You'll Need:

- **iPods Covered: iPod with video**

- **Windows Software Required: iTunes, Windows Movie Maker, DVD43, DVD Shrink, Videora iPod Converter**

- **Mac Software Required: iTunes, iMovie, HandBrake, Instant Hand-Brake, MacTheRipper**

- **Cost: $30 U.S. or less**

Your iPod (with video) can play videos, either on its sharp little screen or on a TV to which you've connected it (see Project 1).

You can buy iPod-format videos from the iTunes Store: music videos, TV shows, and some movies. The selection is still relatively modest, and the prices could bear to be lower.

An encouraging number of other sites are making videos available in iPod-compatible formats, but what you'll almost certainly want to do is put your own videos and DVDs on your iPod. This project shows you how to do so.

Step 1: Understand the Legal Issues Involved

Before you start putting your videos and DVDs on your iPod, you should understand the copyright and decryption issues involved. The essential points are as follows:

- If you created the video (for example, it's a home video or DVD), you hold the copyright to it, and you can do what you want with it—put it on your iPod, release it worldwide, or whatever.

- If someone has supplied you with a legally created video file that you can put on your iPod, you're fine doing so. For example, if you download a video in an iPod-friendly format from the iTunes Store, you don't need to worry about legalities.

- If you own a copy of a commercial DVD, you need permission to rip (extract) it from the DVD and convert it to a format your iPod can play. Even decrypting the DVD in an unauthorized way (such as creating a file rather than simply playing the DVD) is technically illegal.

Step 2: Save Home Videos in iPod-Friendly Formats

If you make your own movies with a digital video camera, you can easily put them on your iPod. Use an application such as Windows Movie Maker (Windows) or iMovie (Mac) to capture the video from your digital video camera and turn it into a home movie.

Create iPod Video Files Using Windows Movie Maker

The version of Windows Movie Maker included with Windows XP can't export video files in an iPod-friendly format, so what you need to do is export the video file in a standard format (such as AVI) that you can then convert using another application.

To save a movie as an AVI file from Windows Movie Maker, follow these steps:

1. With your movie open in Windows Movie Maker, choose File | Save Movie File to launch the Save Movie Wizard. The wizard displays its Movie Location screen.

2. Select the My Computer item, and then click the Next button. The wizard displays the Saved Movie File screen.

3. Enter the name and choose the folder for the movie, and then click the Next button. The wizard displays the Movie Setting screen (shown in Figure 7-1 with options selected).

4. Select the Other Settings option button, and then select the DV-AVI item in the drop-down list.

note *The DV-AVI item appears as DV-AVI (NTSC) or DV-AVI (PAL), depending on whether you've chosen the NTSC option button or the PAL option button on the Advanced tab of the Options dialog box.*

5. Click the Next button to save the movie in this format. The wizard displays the Completing The Save Movie Wizard screen.

6. Select the Play Movie When I Click Finish check box if you want to test the movie, and then click the Finish button. If you selected the check box, the wizard launches Windows Media Player (or your default movie player) and starts the movie playing.

Figure 7-1

Click the Show More
Choices link to make
the Other Settings
option button available.

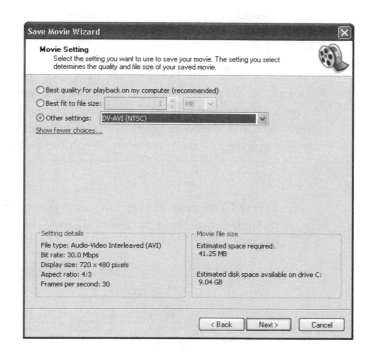

Now that you've created an AVI file, use Videora iPod Converter (discussed later in this chapter) to convert it to an iPod-friendly format.

Create iPod Video Files Using iMovie

To create iPod-friendly video files from iMovie, follow these steps:

1. With the movie open in iMovie, choose File | Share to display the Sharing sheet.

2. Click the QuickTime button to display its tab (shown here).

Put YouTube Videos on Your iPod

At this writing, one of the best sources of interesting video content on the Internet is YouTube (www.youtube.com). If you're a YouTube user, you may wonder if you can put YouTube videos on your iPod. You can, by using utilities such as iTube (Windows) or PodTube (Mac). See the Epic Empire web site (www.epicempire.com/software/youtube-to-ipod.html) for details.

3. In the Compress Movie For drop-down list, choose Expert Settings, and then click the Share button to display the Save Exported File As dialog box (shown here).

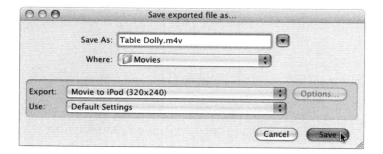

4. Type the name for the file in the Save As text box, and specify the folder in which to save it.

5. In the Export drop-down list, select the Movie To iPod (320×240) item.

6. Click the Save button, and then wait while iMovie creates the compressed file.

Step 3: Create iPod Video Files from Your Existing Video Files

If you have existing video files (for example, files in the AVI format or QuickTime movies), you can convert them to iPod format in a couple of ways. The easiest way is by using the capabilities built into iTunes—but unfortunately, these work only for some video files. The harder way is by using QuickTime Pro, which can convert files from most known formats but which costs $30.

On Windows, you can also use Videora iPod Converter, discussed later in this chapter.

Create iPod Video Files Using iTunes

To create an iPod-friendly video file using iTunes, follow these steps:

1. Add the video file to your iTunes library in either of these ways:

   ● Open iTunes if it's not running. Open a Windows Explorer window (Windows) or a Finder window (Mac) to the folder that contains the video file. Arrange the windows so that you can see both the file and iTunes. Drag the file to the Library item in iTunes.

   ● In iTunes, choose File | Add File To Library (Windows) or File | Add To Library (Mac), use the Add To Library dialog box to select the file, and then click the Open button (Windows) or the Choose button (Mac).

2. Select the movie in the iTunes window, and then choose Advanced | Convert Selection For iPod. You can also right-click or CTRL-click (Mac) and choose Convert Selection For iPod from the shortcut menu.

If the Convert Selection For iPod command isn't available for the file, or if iTunes gives you an error message, you'll know that iTunes can't convert the file.

Create iPod Video Files Using QuickTime

QuickTime, Apple's multimedia software for Mac OS X and Windows, comes in two versions: QuickTime Player (the free version) and QuickTime Pro, which costs $29.99. On Mac OS X, QuickTime Player is included in a standard installation of the operating system; and if you've somehow managed to uninstall it, it'll automatically install itself again if you install iTunes. Likewise, on the PC, you install QuickTime Player when you install iTunes, because QuickTime provides much of the multimedia functionality for iTunes. The "Player" name isn't entirely accurate, because QuickTime provides encoding services as well as decoding services to iTunes—but QuickTime Player doesn't allow you to create most formats of video files until you buy QuickTime Pro.

QuickTime Player is a crippled version of QuickTime Pro, so when you buy QuickTime Pro from the Apple Store, all you get is a registration code to unlock the hidden functionality. To apply the registration code, choose Edit | Preferences | Register in Windows to display the Register tab of the QuickTime Settings dialog box. On the Mac, choose QuickTime Player | Registration to display the Register tab of the QuickTime dialog box.

caution *When you register QuickTime, you must enter your registration name in the Registered To text box in exactly the same format as Apple has decided to use it. For example, if you've used the name John P. Smith to register QuickTime, and Apple has decided to address the registration to Mr. John P. Smith, you must use* **Mr. John P. Smith** *as the registration name. If you try to use* **John P. Smith**, *registration fails, even if this is exactly the way you gave your name when registering.*

Create iPod Video Files from Your TiVo

If you have a TiVo DVR, chances are that it contains content you'd like to transfer to your iPod. To do so:

- On the PC, use DirectShow Dump (http://prish.com/etivo/tbr.htm) to convert the shows from the TiVo format to MPEG. Then use another application (for example, QuickTime) to convert the MPEG file to iPod video format.

- On the Mac, if you have a TiVo DVR, use TivoTool (www.tivotool. com; donationware) to create iPod video files from TiVo content.

To create an iPod video file from QuickTime, follow these steps:

1. Open the file in QuickTime, and then choose File | Export to display the Save Exported File As dialog box.

2. Specify the file name and folder as usual, and then choose Movie To iPod (320×240) in the Export drop-down list. Leave the Default Settings item selected in the Use drop-down list.

3. Click the Save button to start exporting the video file.

Step 4: Create iPod Video Files from Your DVDs

If you have DVDs (and who doesn't?), you'll probably want to put them on your iPod so that you can watch them without a DVD player. This section shows you how to create iPod-friendly files, first on Windows, and then on the Mac.

Rip DVDs on Windows

If you type **DVD ripper Windows** into a search engine, you'll turn up a wide variety of programs that can do the job. Some are freeware, others shareware, and most commercial. This section shows you how to get the job done with three freeware programs: DVD43, DVD Shrink, and Videora iPod Converter.

Get and Install the Programs

To get and install DVD43, DVD Shrink, and Videora iPod Converter, follow these steps:

1. Open your browser and use it to download the three programs:

   - **DVD43** Go to the DVD43—Download Sites page (http://www.dvd43 .com) and follow the links.

- **DVD Shrink**   The DVD Shrink website (www.dvdshrink.org) has links to commercial download sites (ones that charge you to download free software), but if you use a search engine, you can find the program on free sites as well.

- **Videora iPod Converter**   Go to the iPod Converter page on the Videora Holdings site (www.videora.com/en-us/Converter/iPod/download.php) and follow the download link.

2. Double-click the DVD43 setup program to run it. If the program isn't signed with a digital signature (as the file used here isn't signed), Windows displays the Open File—Security Warning dialog box shown here. Click the Run button if you're confident that you've downloaded the program from a trustworthy source.

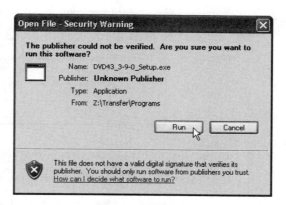

3. At the end of the DVD43 setup routine, restart Windows. DVD43 appears as an icon in the notification area—a yellow face (shown here on the left) when it detects no DVD, and a green smiley face (shown here on the right) when it does detect a DVD.

4. Extract the DVD Shrink setup file from the zip file, and then double-click the setup file to run it. Follow through the setup routine, which includes accepting the license agreement, choosing the installation folder, and deciding whether to create shortcuts on the Desktop and on the Quick Launch toolbar.

5. Double-click the Videora iPod Converter setup file, and then follow through the setup routine.

Configure DVD Shrink

To configure DVD Shrink, follow these steps:

1. Double-click the DVD Shrink shortcut on your Desktop, or choose Start | All Programs | DVD Shrink | DVD Shrink, to start DVD Shrink. The DVD Shrink window opens (see Figure 7-2).

2. Choose Edit | Preferences to open the DVD Shrink Preferences dialog box. Click the Preferences tab (shown here) if it's not automatically displayed.

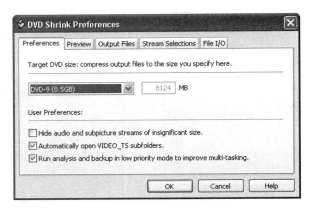

3. In the Target DVD Size drop-down list, choose DVD-9 (8.5GB).

4. Click the Output Files tab to display its contents (shown here).

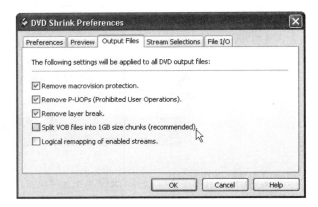

5. Select the Remove Macrovision Protection check box, the Remove P-UOPs (Prohibited User Operations) check box, and the Remove Layer Break check box. Clear the Split VOB Files Into 1GB Size Chunks check box.

6. Click the OK button to close the DVD Shrink Preferences dialog box.

Leave DVD Shrink open so that you can keep working with it in the next section.

Figure 7-2

After installing DVD
Shrink, configure it
to extract the DVD
content to a single file.

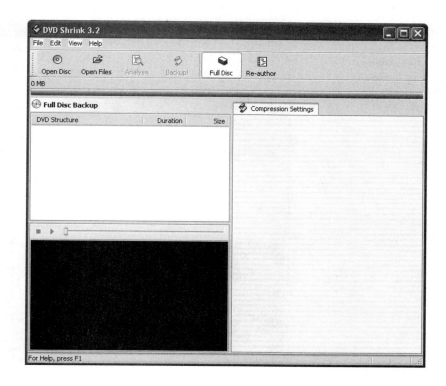

Rip a DVD with DVD Shrink and DVD43

To rip a DVD with DVD Shrink and DVD43, follow these steps:

1. Make sure that DVD43 is running (look at the notification area to see if the DVD43 face appears). If not, choose Start | All Programs | DVD43 | DVD43 to start DVD43.

2. Insert the DVD in your DVD drive and verify that DVD43 notices it. The DVD43 icon in the notification area displays its green smiley face.

3. Click the DVD Shrink button on the taskbar to activate DVD Shrink, and then click the Re-Author button in the toolbar. The Re-Author controls appear (see Figure 7-3).

4. Double-click the item that represents your DVD drive. DVD Shrink displays the DVD's contents (see Figure 7-4).

5. From the list in the DVD Browser, drag the item you want to rip to the Re-Authored DVD pane on the left. For example, to rip the movie itself from a movie DVD, drag the Title 1 item from the Main Movie section.

6. In the text box at the top of the Re-Authored DVD pane, type the title you want to give the file.

7. Click the Compression Settings tab to display its contents (see Figure 7-5).

8. Choose No Compression in the Video drop-down list.

Figure 7-3

On the DVD Browser subtab of the Re-Author controls, double-click your DVD drive to display the disc's contents.

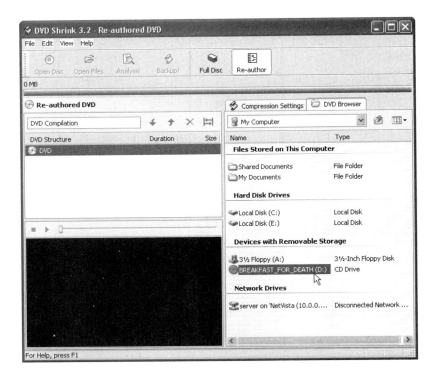

Figure 7-4

Normally, you'll want to drag the Title1 item from the Main Movie area to the left pane.

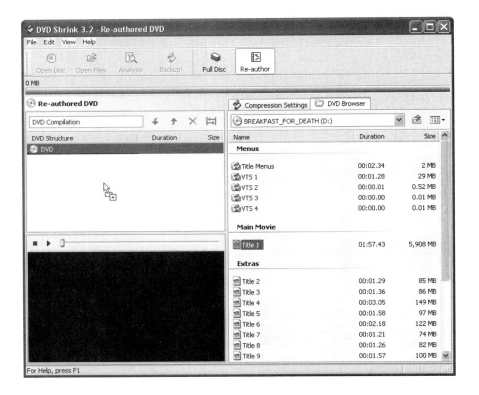

Figure 7-5

On the Compression Settings tab, choose No Compression in the Video drop-down list.

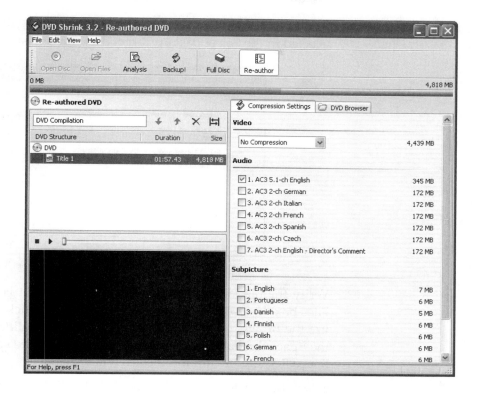

9. In the Audio area, select the check box for the audio track you want to include—for example, AC3 5.1-ch English. Clear all the other check boxes in the Audio area.

10. In the Subpicture area, clear all the subtitle language check boxes.

11. Choose File | Backup or click the Backup! button on the toolbar. DVD Shrink analyzes your DVD (as shown here), and then displays the Backup DVD dialog box.

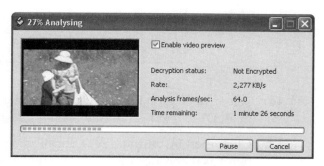

12. On the Target Device tab (shown next), make sure that Hard Disk Folder is selected in the Select Backup Target drop-down list.

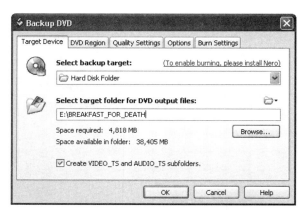

13. Verify the file location shown in the Select Target Folder For DVD Output Files box. If necessary, type a different path, or click the Browse button and use the Browse For Folder dialog box to select a different folder. Make sure the Space Available In Folder readout shows more space available than the Space Required readout indicates will be needed.

14. Select the Create VIDEO_TS And AUDIO_TS Subfolders check box.

15. Click the DVD Region tab to display its contents (shown here).

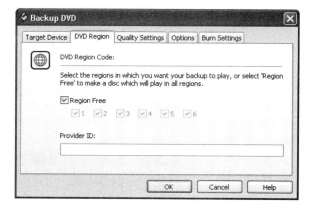

16. Select the Region Free check box to make sure that the ripped file is playable in all DVD regions rather than being restricted to only one or more regions.

17. Click the OK button. DVD Shrink displays the Encoding window (shown here) as it encodes the file. Clear the Enable Video Preview check box if you don't want to see a video preview of what DVD Shrink is working on.

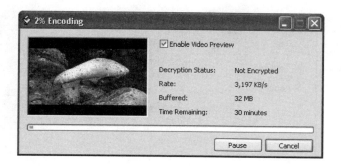

18. When DVD Shrink displays the Backup Complete dialog box (shown here), you can click the link to open a Windows Explorer window to the folder containing the DVD output files. Otherwise, click the OK button to close the dialog box.

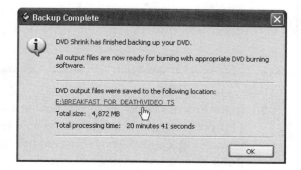

Configure Videora iPod Converter

To configure Videora iPod Converter, follow these steps:

1. Double-click the Videora iPod Converter icon on your Desktop (if you let the setup routine create one) or choose Start | All Programs | Videora iPod Converter | Videora iPod Converter to launch Videora iPod Converter.

2. In the left pane, click the Setup item to display the Setup controls (see Figure 7-6).

3. In the One-Click Profile drop-down list, choose the H264/320×240/640 kbps Stereo/128 kbps item. This is the best choice for encoding videos for use on your iPod.

4. In the Output Videos To text box, specify the folder in which you want Videora iPod Converter to save files. The default folder is a Videos folder in the VideoraiPodConverter folder in your Program Files folder. You'll probably prefer a folder that's easier to access. Make sure the folder is on a drive that has plenty of free space.

Figure 7-6

On the Setup tab's Settings subtab, choose your one-click encoding profile, output folder, and process priority.

5. In the Process Priority drop-down list, tell Windows how much effort to devote to processing the video. If you're able to leave your computer to work on the processing, choose AboveNormal or High. If you'll be working on your computer during the processing, choose Normal. The higher the level, the quicker the processing will happen, but other applications will be less responsive.

6. Click the Save button to save your profile.

Leave Videora iPod Converter running so that you can start encoding with it, as described next.

Encode Videos with Videora iPod Converter

To encode videos with Videora iPod Converter, follow these steps:

1. In the left pane, click the Convert item to display the Convert controls (shown in Figure 7-7 with some settings chosen).

2. Click the Transcode New Video button to open the Select A Video File dialog box.

3. Navigate to the file you want to convert, select the file, and then click the Open button. Videora iPod Converter adds the file to the New Transcoding Job text box.

4. In the Quality Profile drop-down list, make sure the H264/320×240/640 kpbs Stereo/128 kbps item is selected.

5. Click the Start button to start the transcoding.

Figure 7-7

Use Videora iPod
Converter to
transcode a file
ripped from a DVD
to a format your iPod
can play.

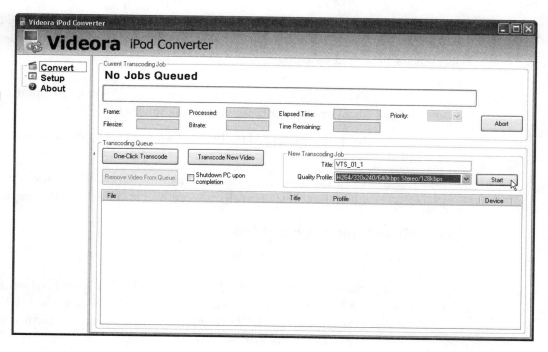

Rip DVDs on the Mac

To rip DVDs on the Mac, you need either HandBrake or Instant HandBrake. Hand-Brake is a long-established DVD ripper that gives you close control over the files you create. Instant HandBrake is a stripped-down version of HandBrake designed for users of the iPod with video and the PlayStation Pro.

You may also need MacTheRipper if either HandBrake or Instant HandBrake can't rip a particular DVD. All these three tools are freeware, so you may want to get them all.

Download and Install Instant HandBrake and HandBrake

To download and install Instant HandBrake and HandBrake, follow these steps:

1. Download Instant HandBrake and HandBrake from the HandBrake website (http://handbrake.m0k.org/).

2. If you get a warning that the disk image contains an application, as shown here, click the Continue button.

3. Double-click the disk image file to mount the disk image on your Desktop.

Depending on the security settings you've chosen in Safari or your default browser, Mac OS X may automatically expand the disk image file for you, mount it on the Desktop, and open a Finder window showing its contents.

4. Double-click the disk image on your Desktop to open a Finder window showing the contents of the disk image file.

5. Drag the Instant Handbrake item or the HandBrake item to your Applications folder.

6. Drag the disk image to the Trash to unmount it. Either drag the disk image file to the Trash as well, or store it in a folder for safe keeping.

Rip a DVD with Instant HandBrake

To rip a DVD with Instant HandBrake, follow these steps:

1. Insert the DVD in your DVD drive. If DVD Player runs automatically, choose DVD Player | Quit DVD Player (or press ⌘-Q) to close DVD Player. (If you want to prevent DVD Player from running automatically when you insert a DVD, see the nearby sidebar.)

2. Click the Finder icon on the Dock, choose Go | Applications, and then double-click the Instant HandBrake item to launch the application. The Instant Hand-Brake dialog box opens, as shown here.

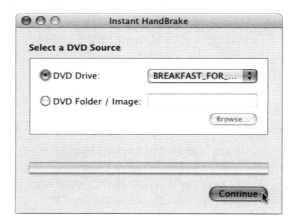

3. In the Select A DVD Source box, select the DVD Drive option button and make sure that Instant HandBrake has identified the DVD.

If Instant HandBrake can't rip a DVD, use MacTheRipper (discussed in the sidebar "Perform Heavy-Duty Ripping with MacTheRipper" toward the end of this project) or a similar tool to rip it to a file or a disk image. If you've ripped the DVD to a DVD image or a folder, select the DVD Folder/Image option button in the Instant HandBrake dialog box. Instant HandBrake displays an Open sheet. Select the folder or the DVD image, and then click the Open button.

4. Click the Continue button. The Instant HandBrake window appears (see Figure 7-8).

note *Instant HandBrake picks the longest of the DVD's "titles" (content items) as the one you're most likely to want to convert. The other titles are extras, such as bonus episodes, outtakes, or behind-the-scenes interviews.*

5. In the Select DVD Features list box, select the check box for each of the items you want to convert.

6. In the Settings group box, choose suitable settings:

   ● **Save Converted Files To**   Choose the folder in which you want Instant HandBrake to place the files. The default folder is your Movies folder. To change folder, click the drop-down list, choose Other, and then select the folder in the resulting sheet.

   ● **File Format**   Choose iPod 5G (H.264) in this drop-down list for best results on the iPod with video. You can also choose iPod 5G (MPEG-4), but the H.264 setting usually gives better results. Instant HandBrake also offers an encoding for the PlayStation Pro, but you won't want to use this setting for your iPod.

   ● **Picture Format**   Choose Fullscreen in this drop-down list unless you want the original format (in which case, choose Original).

Figure 7-8

The Instant HandBrake window.

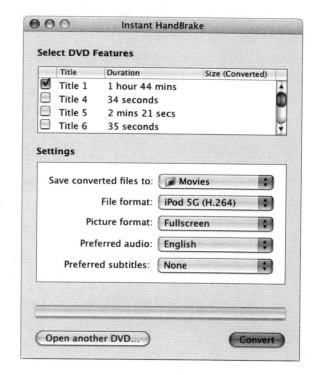

- **Preferred Audio**   Choose the language (for example, English) in this drop-down list.

- **Preferred Subtitles**   Choose None to omit subtitles. If you want subtitles, choose the language from the drop-down list.

7. Click the Convert button to rip the DVD and create the file. The bar at the bottom of the window shows you the progress and gives a readout of how much more time is needed.

8. When Instant HandBrake has finished converting the file, you can click the Open Another DVD button to open another DVD. If you've finished with Instant HandBrake, choose Instant HandBrake | Quit Instant HandBrake or press ⌘-Q to close Instant HandBrake.

9. Open a Finder window to the folder in which you saved your files. Arrange the Finder window and the iTunes window so that you can see both, and then drag the movie files to your iTunes music library or directly to your iPod's entry in the Source pane.

Rip a DVD with HandBrake for Greater Control

If you need greater control than Instant HandBrake gives you, use HandBrake itself. HandBrake gives you many more options than Instant HandBrake. For example, you can choose exactly which chapters of the DVD to rip; you can adjust the picture size; and you can specify the bitrate to use for encoding the video file.

Prevent DVD Player from Running Automatically When You Insert a DVD

When you insert a movie DVD, Mac OS X automatically launches DVD Player, switches it to full screen, and starts the movie playing. This behavior is great for when you want to watch a movie, but not so great when you want to rip it.

To prevent DVD Player from running automatically when you insert a DVD, follow these steps:

1. Choose Apple | System Preferences to open System Preferences.

2. In the Hardware section, click the CDs & DVDs item.

3. In the When You Insert A Video DVD drop-down list, you can choose Ignore if you want to be able to choose freely which application to use each time. If you always want to use the same application, choose Open Other Application, use the resulting Open sheet to select the application, and then click the Choose button.

4. Choose System Preferences | Quit System Preferences or press ⌘-Q to close System Preferences.

To rip a DVD with HandBrake, follow these steps:

1. Insert the DVD in your DVD drive.

2. Open your Applications folder and double-click the HandBrake item to run the application. HandBrake displays an Open sheet, as shown here.

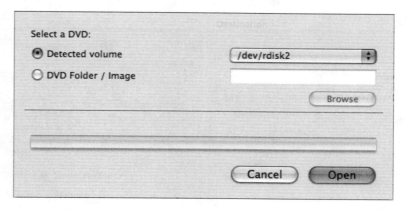

3. If you're ripping a DVD, make sure the Detected Volume option button is selected. The drop-down list shows the device, using the Unix name—for example, /dev/rdisk2. If you have only one DVD drive, you shouldn't need to change this setting. If you're ripping from a folder or a DVD image, select the DVD Folder/Image option button, click the Browse button, use the resulting dialog box to select the folder or image, and then click the Open button.

4. Click the Open button in the Open sheet. HandBrake scans the DVD and then displays its details in the main HandBrake window (shown in Figure 7-9 with settings chosen).

5. In the Source area, choose which parts of the DVD to rip.

   - Select the title (the content element) in the Title list. HandBrake selects the longest title on the basis that this is the one you likely want. The Duration readout shows how long the title is.

   - Use the two Chapters drop-down lists to specify which chapters of the title you want to rip—for example, from Chapter 2 to Chapter 6. HandBrake selects all the titles for you by default.

6. In the Destination area, specify the file format, codecs, and filename to use:

   - In the File Format drop-down list, choose MP4 File.

   - In the Codecs drop-down list, select AVC/H.264 Video/AAC Audio. These settings will give you the highest quality at the smallest file size.

   - In the File text box, change the default file name that HandBrake assigns. You may also want to change the folder.

Figure 7-9

HandBrake lets you choose which chapters of the DVD to rip.

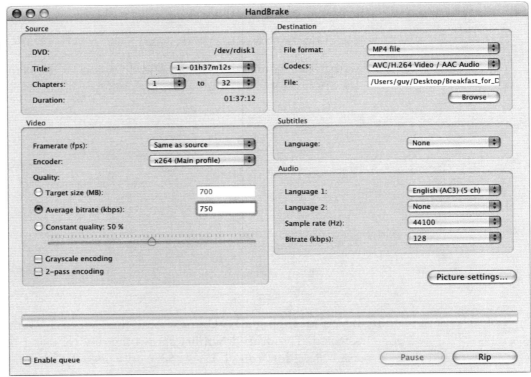

7. In the Subtitles area, use the Language drop-down list to specify any subtitles you want. The default setting is None.

8. In the Video area, choose video-encoding settings as follows:

   ● In the Framerate (fps) drop-down list, select Same As Source.

   ● In the Encoder drop-down list, choose x264 (Baseline Profile).

   ● In the Quality area, select the Average Bitrate (Kbps) option button, and then type **750** in the text box.

   ● Make sure the Grayscale Encoding check box and the 2-Pass Encoding check box are cleared.

9. In the Audio area, choose audio encoding settings as follows:

   ● In the Language 1 drop-down list, choose the language you want—for example, English (AC3) (5 ch).

   ● In the Language 2 drop-down list, choose None unless you want a second language.

   ● In the Sample Rate (Hz) drop-down list, choose 44100.

   ● In the Bitrate (Kbps) drop-down list, choose 128.

Figure 7-10

Use the Picture
Settings dialog box
to change the picture
size to 320×240
pixels.

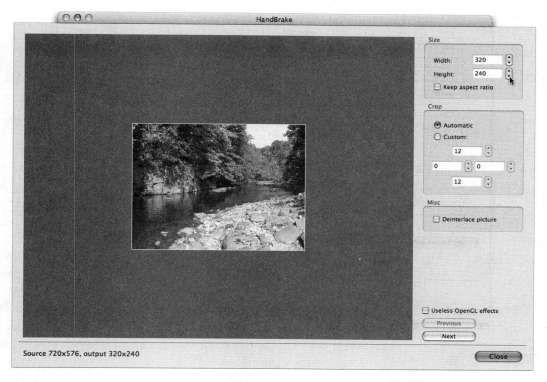

10. Click the Picture Settings button to display the Picture Settings dialog box
(see Figure 7-10).

11. Clear the Keep Aspect Ratio check box, reduce the figure in the Width text
box to 320, and reduce the figure in the Height text box to 240. In the Crop
area, leave the Automatic option button selected.

12. Click the Close button to close the Picture Settings dialog box and return to
the main HandBrake window.

13. Click the Rip button to start ripping. The bar across the bottom of the Hand-
Brake window shows the progress, the current and average speed in frames
per second, and the estimated time left, as shown here.

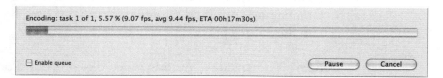

14. When you've finished encoding, choose HandBrake | Quit HandBrake or
press ⌘-Q to close HandBrake.

Perform Heavy-Duty Ripping with MacTheRipper

If you find that Instant HandBrake or HandBrake can't rip a particular DVD, try MacTheRipper instead. Open Safari and go to VersionTracker.com (www .versiontracker.com). Search for **MacTheRipper** in the Mac OS X category. Follow the link to the download site, and then download the file, unzip it, and install it in your Applications folder.

In your Applications folder, double-click MacTheRipper to start the program. The first time you run MacTheRipper, you have to agree to a disclaimer by which you accept responsibility for all your actions using MacTheRipper and declare you're not a member of a law and enforcement agency or the Motion Picture Association of America. Once you've taken this step, you see the MacTheRipper interface.

MacTheRipper is easy to use—you can get good results by accepting the default settings and clicking the Go! button—but it also has plenty of options for configuring regional coding and user operation prohibitions (UOPs), the restrictions that most DVD producers feel obliged to foist on DVD users (for example, not being able to skip the FBI warnings or trailers at the beginning of a DVD). MacTheRipper comes with a comprehensive help file that explains how to use these options.

Step 5: Add Your New Video Files to Your iPod

To add your new video files to your iPod, follow these steps:

1. Open iTunes if it's not already running.

2. Open a Windows Explorer window (Windows) or a Finder window (Mac) to the folder in which you saved your files.

3. Arrange the Windows Explorer window or the Finder window and the iTunes window so that you can see both.

4. Drag the movie files to your iTunes music library. Alternatively, if you're managing your iPod's contents manually, drag the files to your iPod's entry in the Source pane.

If there's a downside to putting video files on your iPod, it's the amount of space that they take up—a 60GB iPod can hold enough songs to play for the best part of two months nonstop, but only enough video for a few days. Never mind: a little self-restraint will do you no harm. The easiest way to manage video content on your iPod is to create a video playlist, set the iPod to synchronize that playlist automatically (on the Videos subtab of the iPod tab of the iTunes dialog box or the Preferences dialog box), and then add to that playlist the video files you want to take with you. Once you've finished with a file, remove it from the playlist to free up space on your iPod.

Use Your iPod as Your Car's Stereo Source

What You'll Need:

- iPods Covered: Any iPod
- Hardware Required: Cassette adapter, docking adapter, or RF adapter
- Cost: $25–$400 U.S.

If you love music, you'll want to play it in your car. Your car probably came with some form of stereo—a CD player, a cassette player, or maybe only a radio—but all the songs you want to listen to are now stored on your iPod. Your mission (and you've chosen to accept it) is to get the iPod to play through your car stereo, preferably so that it sounds really good. You get bonus points for a neat solution.

This project walks you through the main options for connecting an iPod to your car stereo, starting with the connection that's easiest but that you're least likely to have— a connection that's already built into your car—and moving on to third-party iPod-integration systems, direct wiring connections, cassette adapters, and radio frequency transmitters. Apart from the third-party iPod-integration systems, this project assumes that you're going to use your existing system and speakers, and that the challenge of this project is to get the music from your iPod to your car's stereo system rather than replace the stereo system itself—although you may sometimes want to take the latter approach.

Step 1: Use a Built-in iPod Connection

If your car has a built-in connection for an iPod, you're all set: pop the iPod in the dock or slot provided, maybe connect a plug to its dock connector or headphone socket, and you'll be ready to play music and put your foot to the floor. In most such setups, the controls on the car's stereo system take command of the iPod, so you use the stereo system's controls to start and stop play and to navigate from song to song. Only in the most basic setups do you need to use the iPod's controls once it's connected to a built-in system.

Given the popularity of the iPod family, it's no surprise that more and more car manufacturers are building iPod connections into their cars, but even so, only a tiny minority of cars on the road have iPod connections as of Fall 2006. Table 8-1 shows the manufacturers and cars that have iPod integration—oh, and motorbikes: Harley-Davidson has gotten in on the act too.

Manufacturer	Models
Acura	MDX, RL, TL
Audi	A3, A4, Allroad
BMW	All models
Chrysler	Pacifica, Sebring, Town & Country
Dodge	Caravan, Grand Caravan, Neon, Ram, Stratus Sedan
Harley-Davidson	Models including Street Glide
Honda	Accord, Civic, CR-V, Element, Odyssey, Pilot, Ridgeline, S2000
Jeep	Liberty, Wrangler
Mercedes-Benz	C-Class, CLK, CLS, E-Class, SLK, M-Class, R-Class
MINI	Cooper, Cooper S
Nissan	Armada, Frontier, Pathfinder
Scion	xA, xB, tC
Suzuki	Aerio SX, Grand Vitara
Volkswagen	Beetle, Jetta, Golf, GTI, Passat, Touareg
Volvo	S40, S60, S80, V50, V70, XC70, XC90

Table 8-1   Cars with iPod Integration.

To see the latest list of cars with integrated iPod connections, point your web browser at www.apple.com/ipod/ipodyourcar/. The list includes manufacturers whose iPod integration is "coming soon"; at this writing, this category includes Ford, GM, Mazda, Ferrari, and Infiniti. As of 2007, most new Fords, all GM models, and all Mazda models will have iPod integration.

A cursory glance at Table 8-1 suggests that the more you pay for your car, the more likely the car is to feature iPod integration—but it's encouraging to see Dodge, Honda, Volkswagen, and Volvo including iPod integration in more affordable models of car as well. The addition of Ford, GM, and Mazda will also even up the distribution.

Step 2: Add a Built-in iPod Connection to Your Car

Maybe one day all cars will come with iPod integration—but if your current car isn't one of the fortunate few, that's neither help nor consolation to you right now. To the rescue come assorted third-party manufacturers with iPod-integration units for cars that not only let you play back music from the iPod through the car's stereo and control the iPod using the stereo system's controls, but also let you display the song information from the iPod on the stereo's display, making it easier to see what you're listening to.

Short of buying a new car that features iPod integration, getting an integrated unit is the most expensive way of connecting your iPod to your car stereo—so unless dollars are a dime a dozen to you, you have to weigh up whether integration is worth the extra cost over a more modest solution such as those discussed later in this chapter. Being able to control your iPod through your car stereo can be great, especially if your car has easy-to-access controls for the stereo, such as volume controls and basic play controls built into the steering wheel or the driver's side of the dashboard. But it comes at a cost.

How severe is that cost? It depends on what you're getting. Here are a couple of examples:

- **Car stereo replacement unit**   If the iPod-integration system involves replacing your existing car stereo with a custom unit, you're probably looking at a price north of $250 U.S.—more if you have the unit installed professionally, which is usually a good idea unless you're technically proficient. The good news is that most such units are a standard size, so they fit any car. The bad news—well, the cost, and the fact that you can no longer use your existing car stereo.

- **Custom iPod interface add-on**   If the iPod-integration system is simply a unit that adds an iPod interface to your existing car stereo, you're probably looking at a price in the $50 U.S. to $200 U.S. range, depending on the manufacturer involved. Apart from cost, the upside is that you won't need to replace your car stereo, just patch the interface into it. The downside is that you will most likely need a specialized unit that works only with your car's stereo system and that you won't be able to use the same unit in a different car. There are some exceptions, such as the Harman Kardon Drive + Play, which works with all dock connector–equipped iPod models and with most car stereos. The Drive + Play includes a small monitor for displaying the iPod's screen, will run off either your car's accessory socket or the car's stereo wiring, and will set you back around $200 U.S. (http://store.apple.com).

Step 3: Wire Your iPod Directly to Your Car Stereo

If you haven't got a car stereo with iPod integration, your next best bet is to use a wired connection between your iPod and your car stereo. A wired connection gives you the best audio quality and is inexpensive—provided that your car stereo has an input that you can use:

- If your car stereo is one of the few that has a miniplug input built in, get a miniplug-to-miniplug cable and you'll be in business.

- If your stereo is built to take multiple inputs—for example, a CD player (or changer) and an auxiliary input—you may be able to simply run a wire from unused existing connectors. Plug your iPod into the other end, press the correct buttons, and you'll be ready to rock-and-roll down the freeway.

- If no unused connectors are available, you or your local friendly electronics technician may need to get busy with a soldering iron.

If none of these options is available, a wired connection probably isn't a good choice. The only exception is if you're looking to buy a new car stereo and can choose one that has an auxiliary input you can use for your iPod. But even in this case, you'll normally do better to buy an iPod-integrated car stereo (as discussed in step 2) to make sure that the stereo is fully iPod-aware, can control the iPod, and can display information from the iPod on its screen.

Step 4: Connect Your iPod to Your Car Stereo via a Cassette Adapter

If your car stereo has a cassette deck, your easiest option is to use a cassette adapter to play audio from your iPod through the cassette deck. There are two kinds of such adapters: conventional and iPod-specific.

Get a Conventional Cassette Adapter

A conventional cassette adapter is shaped like a cassette and uses a playback head to input analog audio via the head that normally reads the tape as it passes. A wire runs from the adapter to your iPod. Figure 8-1 shows an example of a cassette adapter.

Figure 8-1

You can buy a conventional cassette adapter for between $10 and $20 U.S. from most electronics stores or from an iPod specialist.

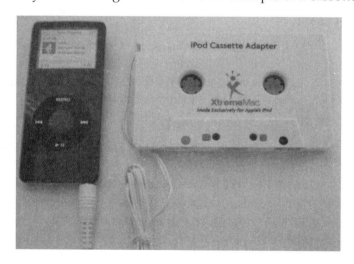

A cassette adapter can be an easy and inexpensive solution, but it has a couple of disadvantages. First, the audio quality can be poor, because the means of transferring the audio to the cassette player's mechanism is less than optimal. If the cassette player's playback head is dirty from playing cassettes, audio quality will be that much worse. To keep the audio quality as high as possible, clean the cassette player regularly using a cleaning cassette.

 If you use a cassette adapter in an extreme climate, try to make sure you don't bake it or freeze it by leaving it in your car.

Get an iPod-Specific Cassette Adapter

A conventional cassette adapter is a great tool to have on hand because it allows you to put almost any audio source through your car stereo (or any other stereo system that can play cassettes—for example, a boombox). But you need to control the songs from the iPod and control the volume from the car stereo, which is less than optimal.

Enter the second category of cassette adapter: the iPod-specific cassette adapter. At this writing, this is a small category, populated solely by the SmartDeck from Griffin Technology ($29.95 U.S.; www.griffintechnology.com). The SmartDeck (see Figure 8-2) connects to your iPod via the dock connector and lets you control your iPod's play by using the controls built into the cassette deck. You can't navigate the iPod's screens from the cassette deck, so what you do is choose the music using the iPod's controls, and then use the controls on the cassette deck to start play, stop it, move to the previous or next song, or eject the iPod (to pause the iPod).

Figure 8-2

The Griffin SmartDeck lets you use the controls on your cassette deck to play any iPod that has a dock connector: iPod with video, iPod nano, iPod photo, fourth-generation regular iPod, or iPod mini.

Step 5: Use a Radio Transmitter to Play Your iPod Through Your Car Stereo

If your car stereo doesn't have a cassette deck, or you scorn analog technology, consider using a radio transmitter to play music from your iPod through your car stereo. This device plugs into your iPod and broadcasts a signal on an FM frequency to which you then tune your radio to play the music. Basic radio transmitters have only a single frequency, while better radio transmitters offer a choice of frequencies to allow you easy access to both the device and your favorite radio stations.

Radio transmitters are simple to use and can deliver reasonable audio quality. If possible, try before you buy by asking for a demonstration in the store. Take a portable radio and headphones along with you so that you'll be able to judge whether the quality will be acceptable for your needs.

Radio transmitters are usually relatively inexpensive (many cost between $15 and $50 U.S.) and are easy to use. Depending on the model of radio transmitter, you may be able to put your iPod out of sight (for example, in the glove compartment—provided it's not hot enough there to bake the iPod) without any telltale wires to help the light-fingered locate it.

On the downside, most of these devices need batteries (others can run off the accessory outlet or cigarette-lighter socket), and less expensive units tend not to deliver the highest sound quality. The range of these devices is minimal, but at close quarters, other radios nearby may be able to pick up the signal—which could be embarrassing, entertaining, or irrelevant, depending on the circumstances. If you use the radio transmitter in an area where the airwaves are busy, you may need to keep switching the frequency to avoid having the transmitter swamped by the full-strength radio stations.

If you decide to get a radio transmitter, you'll need to choose between getting a model designed specifically for the iPod and getting one that works with any audio source.

The Power and the Law

Low-power radio transmitters are legal in the United States, but some other countries don't permit them. If you don't know whether your country permits radio transmitters, check before buying one.

Where transmitters are legal, you'll usually want to get the most powerful model you can. Many users' leading complaint about radio transmitters is that the signal is not powerful enough for the car radio to pick it up cleanly, especially in metropolitan areas where the airwaves are busy.

Signal strength is a concern because many cars use an antenna outside the passenger cabin rather than an antenna integrated into the stereo unit to improve reception for conventional radio signals. With an external antenna, your transmitter inside the car is at a disadvantage. If the stereo unit is relying on an external antenna rather than an internal one, you may find you get better results by moving the transmitter nearer to the aerial (for example, by putting it on the dash) rather than nearer to the car's stereo.

When buying a radio transmitter in a store, test the transmitter's range to make sure that the signal will be powerful enough for your car. In the store, you won't be able to simulate conditions in your car, but you should be able to compare the relative strengths of different models of transmitters on offer. When buying online, check other buyers' reviews of products to get an idea of how powerful the signal is and of other problems (such as poor audio quality or flimsiness) of which you should be aware.

Radio transmitters designed for the iPod and car use often double as a dock for the iPod, keeping it anchored even when the brakes squeal.

Criteria for Choosing a Radio Transmitter for Your Car

Many models of radio transmitters are available, some designed especially for iPods and others for general use. When choosing a radio transmitter for your car, consider the following questions:

- **Do you want a transmitter only for your car, or for general use as well?**   This decision will affect which model you buy. Radio-frequency transmitters work with all radios, so you can use one to play music through your stereo system—or someone else's—or through another system, such as a hotel alarm clock or television. Typically, if a transmitter is designed specifically for use in a car, it may be awkward in general use. For example, if the transmitter has a plug to draw power from the car's accessory socket and a mounting to fit into a cup-holder, it will be larger and less pocketable than a general-purpose unit.

tip   *You may also want to connect a radio-frequency transmitter to your PC or Mac and use it to broadcast audio to a portable radio. This is a great way of getting streaming radio from the Internet to play on a conventional radio.*

- **Does the transmitter have the type of mounting you need for the car?**   Some transmitters mount in a cup holder, others on a neck that plugs into the accessory socket to draw power, and others yet on the dash.

- **Does the transmitter draw power from the car, and if so, can it power your iPod?**   Having the iPod recharge from the car as you play songs is a great convenience. At your destination, you can head off for work or play with your iPod fully charged instead of partially depleted.

- **Does the transmitter fit only one model of iPod, or will it work for any device?**   You may find that the choice is between a transmitter designed to fit only your current model of iPod or a less stylish transmitter that will work with any iPod—or indeed any sound source.

- **How does the transmitter connect to the iPod?**   For any current iPod except an iPod shuffle, your best bet is a transmitter that connects via the dock connector. Not only does the dock connector provide higher-quality sound than the headphone socket and use a constant volume rather than a variable volume, but it also allows remote control of the iPod.

- **Is the transmitter powerful enough for your needs?**   Even among low-power transmitters that are legal for unlicensed use, power and range vary widely.

● **How many frequencies can the transmitter use?**   Some transmitters are set to broadcast on a single frequency, which means you're out of luck if a more powerful local station happens to be using that frequency. Many transmitters offer several preset frequencies among which you can switch. Some transmitters provide a wide range of frequencies.

tip   *Check out the CNET Reviews section to get the latest opinions on a radio transmitter you're considering.*

Examples of Radio Transmitters for Cars

You can find radio transmitters for cars at your local electronics paradise, but you'll find a better selection of iPod-specific models at iPod specialist sites such as these:

● Apple Store (http://store.apple.com)

● everythingiPod.com (www.everythingipod.com)

● Gadget Locker (http://thinkdifferentstore.com)

Radio Transmitters for the iPod

Here are three examples of radio transmitters that are popular with iPod users:

● **Podfreq**   The Podfreq from Sonnet Technologies ($99.95 U.S.; www.podfreq .com) is a relatively powerful radio transmitter that's built in the shape of an iPod case. The iPod slips inside the Podfreq (see Figure 8-3), and the Podfreq's aerial extends past the top of the iPod. The Podfreq offers a full range of digital tuning from 88.3 to 107.7 MHz, enabling you to avoid other stations even if the airwaves are jammed. You can get Podfreq models for the iPod video, the fourth-generation iPod, the iPod nano, and the iPod mini.

Figure 8-3

The Podfreq is one of the larger radio transmitters built for the iPod—and one of the most powerful.

● **TuneBase FM for iPod** The TuneBase FM for iPod from Belkin Corporation ($79.99 U.S.; www.belkin.com) comes with interchangeable trays that let you connect the iPod video, the iPod nano, the fourth-generation iPod, and the iPod mini. The TuneBase FM (see Figure 8-4) has four programmable memory buttons that you can set anywhere from 88.1 and 107.9 FM, giving you a good range of frequencies to use.

Figure 8-4

The TuneBase FM comes with interchangeable trays that let you connect different models of iPod—useful if you want to use different types of iPods in your car.

● **iTrip and iTripmini** The iTrip family from Griffin Technology ($39.99 U.S. each; www.griffintechnology.com) consists of compact radio transmitters designed for the iPod video, the iPod nano, third- and fourth-generation iPods, and the iPod mini. The iTrip models for the iPod video and the iPod nano (see Figure 8-5) attach to the bottom of the iPod and let you set it to broadcast on any frequency between 87.7 and 107.9 FM, so you should be able to get the signal through even in a busy urban area. Earlier iTrip models sit on top of the third- and fourth-generation iPods and the iPod mini, connecting via the headphone port and the remote-control port, and they draw power from the iPod's battery rather than using batteries of their own.

note *At this writing, there are no radio transmitters designed specifically for the iPod shuffle. Instead, use one of the radio transmitters designed for all iPods.*

Figure 8-5

The iTrip family includes a version for the iPod nano.

Step 6: Dock and Power Your iPod in Your Car

If you chose an integrated solution or a radio transmitter that includes a dock and a power connection, you'll already have somewhere to put the iPod in your car. If you went with a dock-less radio transmitter or a cassette adapter, you may need a car dock to secure your iPod so that it doesn't try to leave the passenger cabin under enthusiastic cornering or braking. You may also prefer to power your iPod from your car's accessory socket rather than run down the iPod's battery.

You'll find a good selection of docks for the assorted iPod models at online sites such as the Apple Store (http://store.apple.com), Gadget Locker (http://thinkdifferentstore.com), and everythingiPod.com (www.everythingipod.com). Here are three docks to consider (but see also the flexibleDock in the list after this one):

- **Gripmatic**   The Gripmatic from everythingiPod.com ($29.99 U.S.; www.everythingipod.com) is a multiangle mount designed for use in the car. You can mount the Gripmatic either with screws or with adhesive (both of which are provided).

- **iGrip**   The iGrip ($8.99 U.S.; http://thinkdifferentstore.com) is an adhesive pad that you can use to secure your iPod to your car dashboard or another convenient location. Refreshingly low-tech, the iGrip will also stick to other objects, such as your mobile phone or the case for your shades.

- **iSqueez**   The iSqueez from Griffin Technology ($9.99 U.S.; www.griffin-technology.com) is a flexible iPod nest that mounts in your cup holder.

tip   *The iPod shuffle can be a great audio source for the car for two reasons. First, it's so easy to keep to hand: You can either hang it round your neck the way you would normally wear it, or stick it to the steering wheel or dash with adhesive tack (no, not chewing gum) or adhesive tape and be fairly secure in the hope that it won't come unstuck during ambitious cornering. Second, you won't be tempted to take your eyes off the road to look at the iPod's screen, because it has none.*

Here are three models of power connectors to consider:

- **XtremeMac RoadShow Car Audio/Video Cable** If you need to deliver video as well as audio from your iPod to your car's entertainment system, the RoadShow ($49.99 U.S.; http://store.apple.com) may be the device you need. One cable connects to your car's accessory socket, delivering power to run and charge the iPod with video; another cable connects to the iPod's dock connector; and the third cable ends in three RCA jacks that deliver audio and video to the entertainment system.

- **Ten Technology flexibleDock for iPod** The flexibleDock ($49.95 U.S.; http://store.apple.com) combines a dock with a charger, plugging into your car's accessory socket (to charge any iPod equipped with a dock connector) and positioning the iPod on a flexible arm that you can move as needed. The flexibleDock is a good choice if you're using a cassette adapter to connect your iPod to your car stereo.

- **DLO AutoPod Intelligent Car Charger for iPod shuffle** The AutoPod Intelligent Car Charger for iPod shuffle ($19.99 U.S.; www.everythingipod. com) lets you run and charge your iPod shuffle from the accessory socket. The AutoPod has a coiled cable, allowing you to put the iPod somewhere handy when it's connected and includes status lights to show you whether the AutoPod is getting power and whether the iPod shuffle is charging.

At this point, you should be all set to get your motor running, fire up your iPod, and rock on down the highway. Happy trails!

Put Your Vinyl Records on Your iPod and iTunes

What You'll Need:

- iPods Covered: Any iPod
- Hardware Required: Turntable, cables
- Windows Software Required: Audacity
- Mac Software Required: Audacity
- Cost: $75–150 U.S.

If you've been buying music for many years, chances are that you have a stack of vinyl records gathering dust in a box somewhere. Or perhaps you've been playing them front and center in your living room to teach the younger generation that vinyl isn't solely for house siding and fetishes.

Either way, isn't it about time you ripped your records so that you can listen to them on your iPod? You may even want to dig out your old cassettes so that you can rip them too.

caution *Before you start, there's one potential pitfall of which you should be aware. Technically, you may need permission to create audio files that contain copyrighted content. If you hold the copyright to the audio, you can copy it as much as you want. If not, you need specific permission to copy it, unless it falls under a specific copyright exemption. For example, the Audio Home Recording Act (AHRA) personal use provision lets you copy a copyrighted work (for example, an LP) onto a different medium so you can listen to it—provided that you use a "digital audio recording device," a term that doesn't cover computers.*

Step 1: Connect Your Record Player to Your Computer

Record player? Check. Computer? Check. Cables to connect them? Uh-oh.

Look at the back of your record player to see what kind of connection it uses. The odds are pretty good that it'll be two RCA jacks, but it might also have some form of DIN socket.

Next, look at your computer's sound card or other audio input. You're looking for the line-in socket, preferably one separate from the microphone socket. The symbols on many sound cards and computer chassis are notoriously hard to decipher, particularly in dim light at the back of your desk, but you can usually pick out some or all of the following:

- Microphone socket: microphone symbol; usually red if color coded

- Line-in socket: sound-input symbol; often blue if color coded

- Digital input socket: sound-input symbol; often black if color coded

- Line-out socket: sound-output symbol; usually green if color coded

In those descriptions, "usually" means more frequently than "often" but not "invariably." Here's an example of a typical sound card for a desktop PC:

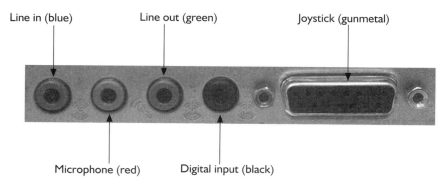

Laptops are often more economical with ports, sometimes combining microphone and line-in sockets like this:

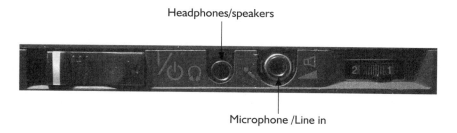

Choose a suitable cable to connect the ports you've found. For example, if your record player has two RCA plugs and your soundcard has a standard line-in socket, get a cable with two RCA plugs at one end and a stereo miniplug at the other:

If your sound card has a line-in port and a mic port, use the line-in port. If your sound card has only a mic port, turn the source volume down to a minimum for the initial connection, because mic ports tend to be sensitive.

Some computers—mostly Macs, but some PCs have followed this oddball path—don't have an audio input. As long as the computer has a USB port, the lack of an audio input doesn't mean you're sunk: it just means that you need to use a USB input instead of an analog input. There are two choices here:

- Get an analog-to-USB audio input such as the Griffin iMic ($39.99 U.S.; www .griffintechnology.com). The iMic has a stereo miniplug input that doubles for microphone input and line-in input; you move a switch to toggle between the two modes. The iMic also provides speaker output via the USB socket, which can be useful for quick connections.

- If you don't have a record player but plan to buy one so that you can rip your records, get a direct-to-USB record player such as the Ion ITTUSB ($199 U.S.; many stockists, including Amazon.com). Such a record player gives you the greatest convenience if not the highest quality, but it should be more than adequate unless you're a serious audiophile. Figure 9-1 shows the Ion ITTUSB.

Figure 9-1

The Ion ITTUSB turn-table connects directly to your computer via USB, eliminating all issues with cabling and audio conversion.

Start by connecting the audio source to your computer with a cable that has the right kinds of connectors for the audio source and your sound card. For example, to connect a typical cassette player to a typical sound card, you'll need a cable with two RCA plugs at the cassette player's end (or at the receiver's end) and a male-end stereo miniplug at the other end to plug into your sound card. If the audio source has only a headphone socket or line-out socket for output, you'll need a miniplug at the source end too.

note *Because record players produce a low volume of sound, you'll almost always need to put a record player's output through the Phono input of an amplifier before you can record it on your computer.*

Step 2: Get Your Records and Turntable into Shape

If you've been playing your records, you're probably ready to start recording them on your computer. But if they've been sitting in a dusty basement or attic for a while, they probably need some TLC.

Clean Your Records

To clean vinyl records:

1. Wet a soft cloth with an isopropyl alcohol solution up to 20 percent strong (20 percent is one part isopropyl alcohol in four parts of water).

 caution *Don't use isopropyl alcohol on shellac records (for example, 78 rpm records), because it will dissolve them. Instead, dissolve a small amount of dish soap in water. Wipe the record as described in step 2, and then rinse it with clear water.*

2. Starting at the center of the record, wipe in a spiral motion out to the edge.

3. Use a clean, antistatic cloth to pat the record dry.

4. If you can still see specks of dust on the record, use a fine camel-hair paint brush to dab them off.

 If your records are really dirty, consider buying a special-purpose vacuum cleaning machine for records.

Unwarp Your Records

If your records are badly warped, they may not play at all on your turntable. If they do play, they'll probably sound pretty bad, as the warping distorts the electrical signal generated as the stylus bumps its way through the record's grooves.

To straighten out a warped record, follow these steps:

1. Get two clean sheets of medium-heavy glass that are larger than the record. For example, get 12-inch squares of glass if you need to straighten out an LP.

2. Place the warped record flat (or as flat as it will go) between the two sheets of glass.

3. Turn the oven on low (less than 140 degrees Fahrenheit) and bake the record. As the vinyl softens a fraction, the weight of the glass presses it flat.

4. Remove the glass and the record from the oven, and let them cool to room temperature together.

note *A more exciting method of straightening warped records is to get two thin but strong plates of clean, smooth metal and a clothes iron. Put the record between the plates of metal, turn the iron on low, and get pressing. This method gives quicker results, but it's easier for you to over-heat the record and wreck it.*

Clean Your Stylus and Turntable Mat

Wait—don't put that record on your grubby turntable. Is the turntable mat about to load dust on the underside of the record the moment you put it down? And is the stylus dragging a baby dust bunny on its tip?

Clean the mat if it's dirty. Usually, the best method is to vacuum the mat gently. If the mat is made of felt, be sure not to wash it, as you'll probably ruin it. If the mat is made of rubber, clean it with a cloth.

Check the stylus and clean it if necessary. Some people recommend using a paint-brush dipped in isopropyl alcohol to brush the stylus clean, but the alcohol can un-stick the diamond tip from the stylus. A custom stylus cleaning kit is much safer, although it will set you back around $20 U.S.

Step 3: Set Up Windows or Mac OS X for Recording

So far, so good. Now tell Windows or Mac OS X which audio source you'll be recording from.

Specify the Audio Source for Recording in Windows

To set Windows to accept input from the source so you can record from it, follow these steps:

1. If the notification area includes a Volume icon, double-click this icon to display the Volume Control window. Otherwise, choose Start | Control Panel to display the Control Panel and then open the Volume Control window from there. For example, in Windows XP, click the Advanced button in the Device Volume group box on the Volume tab of the Sounds And Audio Devices Properties dialog box.

note   *Depending on your audio hardware and its drivers, the Volume Control window may have a different name (for example, Play Control).*

2. Choose Options | Properties to display the Properties dialog box. Then select the Recording option button to display the list of devices for recording (as opposed to the devices for playback). The left screen in Figure 9-2 shows this list.

3. Select the check box for the input device you want to use—for example, select the Line-In check box or the Microphone check box, depending on which you're using.

4. Click the OK button to close the Properties dialog box. Windows displays the Record Control window, an example of which is shown on the right in Figure 9-2. (Like the Volume Control window, this window may have a different name—for example, Recording Control.)

Figure 9-2

Click the Recording option button in the Properties dialog box (left) to display the Record Control window (right) instead of Volume Control.

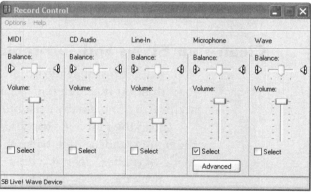

5. Select the Select check box for the source you want to use.

6. Leave the Record Control window open for the time being so you can adjust the input volume on the device if necessary.

Specify the Audio Source for Recording on the Mac

To specify the source on the Mac, follow these steps:

1. Choose Apple | System Preferences to display the System Preferences window.

2. Click the Sound item to display the Sound preferences sheet.

3. Click the Input tab to display it (see Figure 9-3).

Figure 9-3

Configure your sound source on the Input tab of the Sound window.

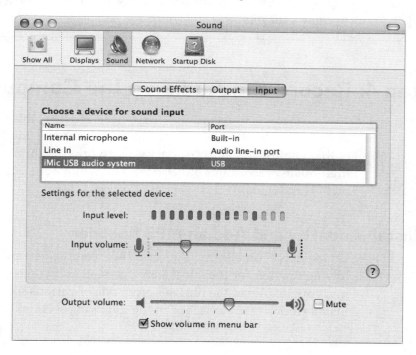

4. In the Choose A Device For Sound Input list box, select the device to use (for example, Line In).

5. Start some audio playing on the sound source. Make sure that it's representative of the loudest part of the audio you will record.

6. Watch the Input Level readout as you drag the Input Volume slider to a suitable level.

Recording with Sound Recorder (Windows) or iMovie (Mac)

If you're reluctant to use Audacity, your computer probably already has software that you can use to record audio.

Windows includes an applet called Sound Recorder (choose Start | All Programs | Accessories | Entertainment | Sound Recorder to launch it), which works okay. On Windows XP, Sound Recorder can record only up to 60 seconds unless you trick it by creating a longer file and recording over that file. See *How to Do Everything with Your iPod and iTunes* (also published by Osborne/McGraw-Hill and available from any bookstore worth patronizing) for details.

Most Macs come with iMovie, a powerful video-editing application that you also use to record and edit audio on its own. Again, see *How to Do Everything with Your iPod and iTunes* for details.

Step 4: Record the Audio on the Computer

The next step is to record the audio from the turntable to the computer. This section shows you how to record with the freeware application Audacity, which works on both operating systems. (Audacity also works on Linux.) Audacity not only produces high-quality recordings but also lets you remove clicks, pops, and hiss from them (see Step 5 for details).

Install Audacity and Add an MP3 Encoder

Go to SourceForge (http://audacity.sourceforge.net) and download Audacity by following the link for the latest stable version and your operating system. At this writing, you download the file itself from one of various software-distribution sites. Then install Audacity as described in the following sections.

note *Internet Explorer may try to block you downloading Audacity. If nothing happens when you click the download link, click the Information Bar (the yellow bar that appears between the lowest toolbar and the top of the window) to display a menu that allows you to circumvent the blocking.*

Keep your browser open for the moment, and go back to the Audacity page. You'll need to download another file in a minute.

Install Audacity on Windows

To install Audacity on Windows, follow these steps:

1. Run the file you've downloaded. For example, if you're using Internet Explorer, click the Run button in the Download Complete dialog box.

2. If Internet Explorer warns you that "the publisher could not be verified," click the Run button. As long as you've downloaded Audacity via Source-Forge, the file should be fine, even though it has not been signed with a digital certificate.

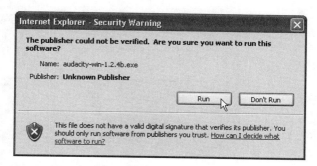

3. Accept the license agreement.

4. Specify where to install Audacity. The default location, in an Audacity folder inside your Program Files folder, is fine unless you particularly want to put it somewhere else.

5. On the Select Additional Tasks screen, choose whether to create a desktop icon (you may find it useful) and create Windows file associations with the Audacity project file extension (.aup; usually a good idea).

6. On the Completing the Audacity Setup Wizard screen, leave the Launch Audacity check box selected so that the wizard launches Audacity for you.

Install Audacity on the Mac

On the Mac, expand the downloaded file, and then drag the resulting Audacity folder to your Applications folder.

Set Up Audacity

The first time you run Audacity, choose the language you want to use—for example, English. You then see Audacity. Figure 9-4 shows Audacity on Windows.

After you install Audacity, you'll need to add an MP3 encoder if you want to be able to create MP3 files with Audacity. (Instead of adding the MP3 encoder, you can create WAV files with Audacity and then use iTunes to create MP3 files or AAC files.)

Follow these steps to add an MP3 encoder to Audacity:

1. Download the latest stable version of the LAME encoder from the LAME Project home page (www.mp3dev.org) or another site. The Audacity home page maintains a link to a site that provides LAME downloads.

Figure 9-4

Audacity is a great freeware application for recording audio and fixing problems with it.

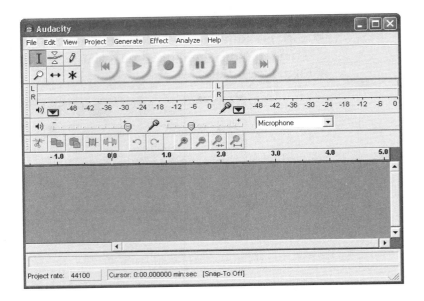

note *Internet Explorer may try to block this download as well. Click the Information Bar to display a menu that allows you to download the file.*

2. Extract the LAME file from the download package:

    ● In Windows, extract the lame_enc.dll file and put it in the System32 folder in your Windows folder. The easiest way to open a Windows Explorer window to this folder is to choose Start | Run, type **%windir%\system32**, and press ENTER. Windows may try to hide the contents of the System32 folder from you. If so, assert yourself by clicking the Show The Contents Of This Folder link.

    ● On the Mac, extract the LameLib file and put it in a folder of your choosing, such as your ~/Library/Audio folder.

3. Display the Audacity Preferences dialog box by pressing CTRL-P or choosing Edit | Preferences on Windows or by pressing ⌘-COMMA or choosing Audacity | Preferences on the Mac.

4. Click the File Formats tab to display its contents (see Figure 9-5).

5. Check the MP3 Export Setup area. If the MP3 Library Version readout says "MP3 exporting plugin not found," you need to add an MP3 encoder.

Figure 9-5

Use the File Formats
tab of the Audacity
Preferences dialog box
to add an MP3 encoder
to Audacity.

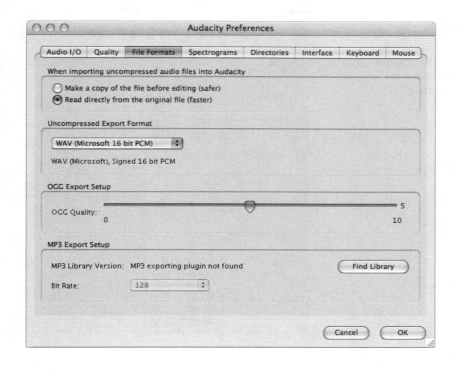

6. Click the Find Library button. Audacity displays the Export MP3 dialog box, which explains that you need to supply the LAME MP3 encoder and asks if you want to provide it:

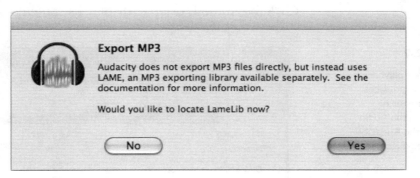

7. Click the Yes button and use the resulting dialog box to find lame_enc.dll (Windows) or LameLib (Mac) in the folder to which you extracted it in step 2.

8. Click the Open button. Audacity adds the LAME version to the MP3 Library Version readout (see Figure 9-6).

9. In the Bit Rate drop-down list, select the bitrate at which you want to export MP3 files. For example, choose 128 Kbps if you want acceptable-quality audio at small file sizes (so that you can cram more songs onto a low-capacity iPod) or choose 320 Kbps for maximum quality at the expense of file size.

Figure 9-6

Once you've added the LAME encoder, you can choose the bitrate to use for exporting MP3 files.

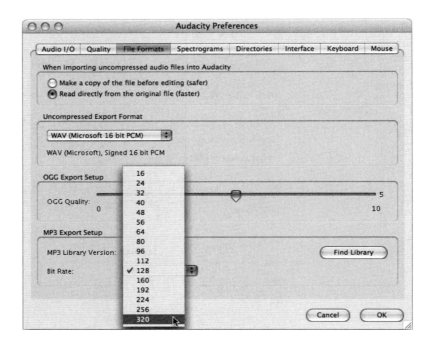

Configure Input/Output and Quality Settings

With the Audacity Preferences dialog box still open, configure the audio input/output settings and the quality settings:

1. Click the Audio I/O tab to display its contents (see Figure 9-7).

Figure 9-7

Choose your playback and recording devices, and the number of channels, on the Audio I/O tab of the Audacity Preferences dialog box.

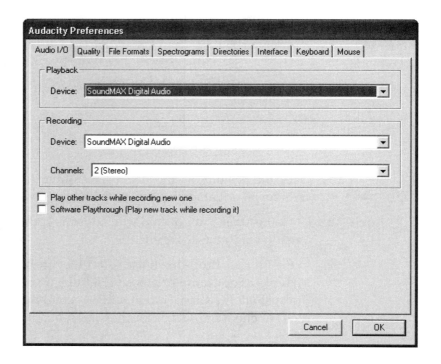

2. Select your playback device, recording device, and the number of channels—for example, 2 (Stereo). You can also choose whether to play existing tracks while recording a new track (which you won't need to do if you're recording a single audio track, such as a song) and whether to play the new track that's being recorded (this can help you stop the recording at the appropriate point).

3. Click the Quality tab to display its contents (see Figure 9-8).

Figure 9-8

Choose the default sample rate on the Quality tab of the Audacity Preferences dialog box.

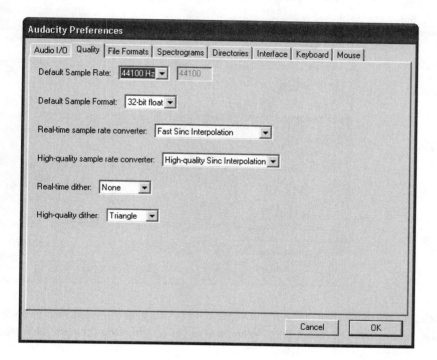

4. In the Default Sample Rate drop-down list, select the sample rate you want to use. If you don't know the rate you want, use 44100 Hz. Leave the other settings on the Quality tab at their defaults unless you know you need to change them.

5. Click the OK button to close the Audacity Preferences dialog box.

Vinyl—Stylus—Action!

After all that preparation, recording the audio with Audacity is almost an anticlimax. Follow these steps:

1. Start Audacity if it's not already running.

2. If necessary, choose a different sound source in the Input Source drop-down list on the right-hand side of the window.

3. Place your clean record reverently on your clean turntable, and then drop the clean stylus in the groove before the song you want to record.

4. Click the Record button to start the recording (see Figure 9-9).

Figure 9-9

Recording at last! Adjust the input volume if the signal is too low or too high.

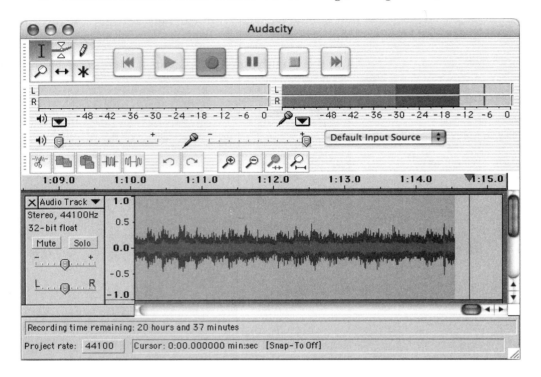

note   *If necessary, change the recording volume by dragging the Input Volume slider (the slide with the microphone at its left end). When you've got it right, stop the recording, create a new file, and then restart the recording.*

5. Click the Record button again to stop recording.

6. Choose File | Save Project to open the Save Project As dialog box, specify a filename and folder, and then click the Save button.

Now that you've saved the project, you can leave it where it is while you record the other songs from the album. But let's assume that you want to clean up the file (as described in the next step) and then export it as a WAV file or an MP3 file.

Step 5: Remove Clicks, Pops, and Hiss from Audio Files

Even if you got a good signal from your record player and recorded it at a suitable volume, you may also have got some clicks and pops in the file from scratches on the record. Or there may be background hum caused by electrical noise along the connection that you're not able to remove.

note *You can use the technique described here to remove hiss from audio recordings you've made from other analog sources. For example, even if you use a noise-reduction system such as Dolby, audio cassettes tend to hiss as the tape moves across the playback head.*

All these noises—very much part of the analog audio experience and actually appreciated as such by some enthusiasts—tend to annoy people accustomed to digital audio. The good news is that Audacity can remove the scratches and hiss for you.

To remove scratches and hiss using Audacity, follow these steps:

1. In Audacity, open the project containing the song. (If you've come here straight from the previous section, you should already have the song's project open.)

2. Select a part of the recording with just noise—for example, the opening few seconds of silence (except for the stylus clicking and popping along).

3. Choose Effect | Noise Removal to open the Noise Removal dialog box:

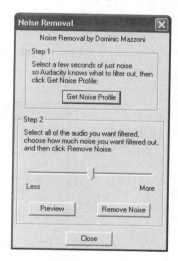

4. Click the Get Noise Profile button. The Noise Removal system analyzes your sample and applies the corresponding noise profile.

5. Select the part of the recording that you want to affect:

   ● To affect all the recording, choose Edit | Select | All. This is usually the easiest approach.

   ● To affect only part of the recording, drag through it. For example, you might want to affect only the end of the recording if this is where all the scratches occur.

6. Choose Effect | Noise Removal to open the Noise Removal dialog box again. This time, drag the slider in the Step 2 box along the Less–More axis to specify how much noise you want to remove. Click the Preview button to get a preview of the effect this will have, and adjust the slider as needed. When you're satisfied with the effect, click the Remove Noise button to remove the noise.

7. Choose File | Save to save your project.

tip *If you have a lot of records and tapes that you want to copy to digital audio files, consider buying an audio-cleanup application that includes recording capabilities instead of an application whose strengths lie mainly in recording. For example, applications such as Magix's Audio Cleaning Lab and Steinberg's Clean Plus focus mainly on audio cleanup (removing crackle, pops, hiss, and other defects) but include more-than-adequate recording capabilities.*

Step 6: Export Your Songs from Audacity to WAV or MP3 Files

By this point, your song project should be ready for export. Follow these steps:

1. Choose the appropriate command from the File menu—for example, File | Export As WAV or File | Export As MP3. The Save WAV (Microsoft) File As dialog box or the Save MP3 File As dialog box opens.

2. Type the name for the song, specify the folder, and then click the Save button.

3. If you're saving the song as an MP3 file, Audacity displays the Edit The ID3 Tags For The MP3 File dialog box (see Figure 9-10).

Figure 9-10

Apply tags to your MP3 file.

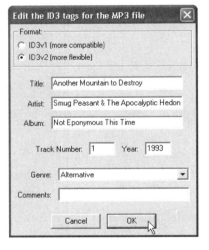

note *When you export an MP3 file from Audacity, apply tags to it immediately so that it doesn't become one of the great unnamed in your music library. ID3v2 tags are a better choice than ID3v1 tags, although iTunes and the iPod can read both types.*

4. Choose the tag format, type the tag information, and then click the OK button.

Step 7: Import Your Songs into iTunes and Convert Them

Now, you'll all set to import the songs you've recorded into iTunes. If you chose to create MP3 files with Audacity, importing them is all you need do. If you chose to create WAV files (or AIFF files), you'll need to use iTunes to convert the songs to your preferred format (for example, AAC or Apple Lossless Encoding), and then delete the WAV files (or AIFF files).

To import the songs, either use the File | Add File To Library command (Windows) or the File | Add To Library command (Mac), or follow these steps to add the files via drag-and-drop:

1. Open a Windows Explorer window or a Finder window to the folder that contains the song files.

2. Arrange iTunes and the Windows Explorer window or Finder window so that you can see your Library icon.

3. Select the songs, and then drag them to the Library icon.

If you created MP3 files, you're all set once iTunes has copied the songs (if you've chosen to copy all songs you add to your music library) or added their details (if you've chosen not to copy songs). If you created WAV files, follow these additional steps to convert them:

1. Select all the songs belonging to the same album in iTunes.

2. Right-click the selection and choose Get Info to display the Multiple Song Information dialog box, apply common tag information to all the songs, and then click the OK button.

3. Right-click the first song and choose Get Info to display the Song Information dialog box, apply song-specific tag information (song name and track number) to each song in turn, and then click the OK button.

4. Select all the songs in the album, right-click the selection, and then choose Convert Selection To AAC from the shortcut menu.

5. When the conversion is complete, check the AAC files, and then delete the WAV files from iTunes.

6. When iTunes prompts you to delete the song files, choose whether to do so:

   ● If these song files are copies of the original WAV files that iTunes created when you added the songs to your music library, you will probably want to delete them.

   ● If these song files are the originals you recorded, you will probably want to keep them. But you may want to burn them to a CD so that they don't waste valuable space on your hard disk.

Once you've recorded all your records, box them up carefully and store them safely. Soon, they'll be valuable antiques.

Part II
Challenging

Become an iTunes Expert

What You'll Need:

- iPods Covered: Any iPod
- Windows Software: Yahoo! Widget Engine
- Mac Software: ByteController
- Cost: Free

By this point, you should be more than comfortable using iTunes—but are you longing to take your use of it to the next level? This project upgrades you to an iTunes pro.

iTunes has an easy-to-use graphical interface—but you don't need to use the mouse if you prefer to use the keyboard. Hidden behind iTunes' easy-to-use interface are a barrage of keyboard shortcuts that put the program's full power at your fingertips. By adding software, you can even control iTunes when you're working in another application, which means that you don't have to have iTunes taking up space on your screen while you're working.

Getting the most out of iTunes also means creating Smart Playlists that select music automatically according to the criteria you specify. And it means cranking the Visualizer up to the max to entertain yourself and your guests—even if you have to rope in your TV or a projector to help out your computer.

Step 1: Control iTunes from the Taskbar or Dock

First, is the iTunes window taking up too much space on screen? Even if you have a huge, high-resolution display, you probably don't want to devote a serious chunk of it to iTunes all the time.

Sure, you can choose Advanced | Switch To Mini Player (on Windows) or Window | Zoom on the Mac to shrink the iTunes window to the mini player (shown on the left here). And you can drag the lower-right corner of the mini player window to the left to reduce the mini player even further, at the expense of the song details, as shown on the right here:

That saves you a good deal of space, but it still leaves you dealing with the iTunes window. You don't need to. Instead, you can use the iTunes toolbar or the notification-area icon (on Windows) or the Dock icon (on the Mac).

Control iTunes from the Windows Taskbar or Notification Area

To control iTunes from the iTunes toolbar, minimize iTunes, right-click any open space in the taskbar (avoiding any application buttons on the taskbar) or anywhere in the notification area, and then choose Toolbars | iTunes from the pop-up menu. Up pops the iTunes toolbar, which offers basic play controls:

Click the button in the upper-right corner of the toolbar to restore iTunes to its previous nonminimized size and hide the toolbar. Click the button in the lower-right corner of the toolbar to display a menu that shows which song is playing and lets you change the rating, alter the repeat setting or shuffle the songs, or exit iTunes.

To reposition the toolbar on the taskbar, right-click the taskbar or the notification area and click to remove the check mark from the Lock The Taskbar item. You can then drag the dotted sizing handle at the left end of the iTunes toolbar to reposition it. Lock the taskbar again afterwards by right-clicking and choosing Lock The Taskbar to replace the check mark.

To get rid of the iTunes toolbar again, right-click the taskbar or notification area and choose Toolbars | iTunes from the shortcut menu again to remove the check mark from the iTunes item.

If you can't afford the space on the taskbar for the iTunes toolbar, you can control iTunes from the iTunes icon in the notification area instead.

● Hover the mouse pointer over the icon for a couple of seconds to display a pop-up showing the details of the current song:

● Right-click the icon and choose a command from the shortcut menu:

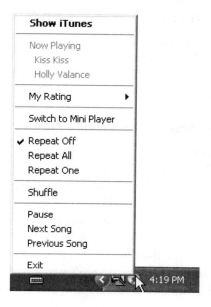

Control iTunes from the Mac Dock

On the Mac, you can control iTunes directly from the Dock icon, as shown in Figure 10-1.

Figure 10-1

Dock control is handy when you've hidden the iTunes window and need basic control of the music.

Step 2: Control iTunes with a Widget

If iTunes itself isn't appealing enough to you, you can control it with a widget instead. A *widget* is a miniature application that performs a specific function—in this case, controlling iTunes. Mac OS X comes with a few handfuls of built-in widgets, including an iTunes one. Windows XP doesn't have widgets, but you can add widgets easily enough by using Yahoo! Widgets. This section shows you how.

Get and Use an iTunes Widget on Windows

The easiest way to get started using widgets on Windows XP is to download the Yahoo! Widget Engine. The Yahoo! Widget Engine is free, and it works well, but it comes bundled with Yahoo! paraphernalia that you may prefer not to install, so you have to pay attention during the installation process.

Download and Install the Yahoo! Widget Engine

Steer your web browser to the Yahoo! Widgets website (http://widgets.yahoo.com) and follow the link for downloading the Yahoo! Widget Engine for Windows. Rather than downloading an entire package that might take a while over a slow connection, you download a small setup program, which you then run to download and install whichever of the remaining components you want.

When you click the Download link, your browser prompts you to decide whether to run or save the file. The easiest choice is to click the Run button to run the setup file from memory. If this doesn't work for some reason, try again, but this time click the Save button to save the file to your hard disk. The Save As dialog box opens to let you choose where to save the file. If you have a standard folder for saving downloaded files, save it there. Alternatively, save it to your Desktop, where it will be handy both to run and then to delete when you no longer need it. When the download is complete, your browser may prompt you to run the file. If so, click the Run button; if not, go to the folder in which you saved the file, and then double-click it to start the setup routine.

Your key decision when setting up the Yahoo! Widget Engine is choosing which Yahoo! paraphernalia to install. Figure 10-2 shows you the options on offer on the Choose The Products To Install screen. For most people, the best bet is to leave the Yahoo! Widget Engine check box selected (you can't clear it anyway—and this is the item you want) but clear all the other check boxes. Click the Next button, accept the license agreement, read the Yahoo! Privacy Policy if you care to, and then allow the setup routine to download the remaining components and install them. On the Install Complete screen, you can choose to launch the Yahoo! Widget Engine automatically. This lets you get started with the Yahoo! Widget Engine without even the minimal effort of launching it from the Start menu.

Figure 10-2

Setting up the Yahoo!
Widget Engine.

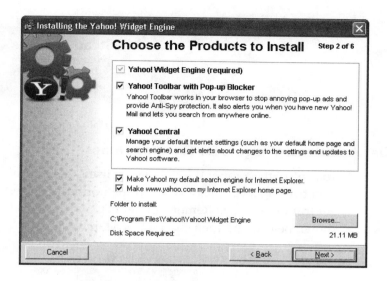

note *Unless you're sure you want to install the Yahoo! Toolbar With Pop-Up Blocker and Yahoo! Central, clear the check boxes for these features. Similarly, you'll probably want to clear the check boxes for making Yahoo! your default search engine and making Yahoo! your home page in Internet Explorer.*

When the Yahoo! Widget Engine starts, it leads you through some introductory screens and then opens a minor explosion of widgets (including clock, calendar, mail, photos, and weather widgets) for you to experiment with. You'll immediately need the two most important commands for widgets:

- **Close a widget** Right-click the widget and choose Close Widget from the shortcut menu.

- **Configure a widget** Right-click the widget and choose Preferences from the shortcut menu. The contents of the Preferences dialog box depend on the widget and its capabilities. Most widgets let you customize various aspects of the display, such as fonts, colors, and backgrounds.

When you close the introductory screen, the Yahoo! Widget Engine opens a Windows Explorer window to the My Widgets folder under your My Documents folder. The My Widgets folder is the folder in which widgets are installed. From here, you can run any widget by double-clicking it or delete a widget by selecting it and then pressing DELETE. The Yahoo! Widget Engine usually includes the iTunes Remote widget, so if this widget is present, double-click it to start it running. The widget is simplicity itself to use, as you can see here: Unshuffled/Shuffle and Display-The-Information buttons at the top, play controls in the middle, and a volume slider providing a twisted smile across the bottom:

Get Additional Widgets for Running iTunes

To control the Yahoo! Widget Engine itself, use the Yahoo! Widget Engine icon (a gray icon bearing a couple of cogs) in the notification area. To get a different iTunes widget from the iTunes Remote, either click or right-click this icon to produce the menu shown below, and then choose Get More Widgets.

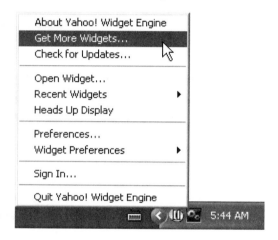

The Yahoo! Widget Engine opens the Yahoo! Widgets Gallery in your default browser (for example, Internet Explorer). Use the Search The Gallery box to search either for **iTunes** or **iPod** (some widgets use the iPod name rather than iTunes) or for a specific widget by name. (Two examples are coming right up.) When you find a widget you want, click the download link to download it. From the zip file, drag the widget to your My Widgets folder, and then double-click the widget to run it.

The Yahoo! Widgets Gallery offers various widgets for controlling iTunes. At this writing, two of the best are:

● **iTunes Bar**   iTunes Bar provides the key iTunes controls in a shallow bar that takes up a minimal amount of space on screen. You can apply different skins to change the widget's look. iTunes Bar displays the album art and can download lyrics to songs. iTunes Bar also lets you set hot keys for playing and pausing music, moving to the previous or next song, changing the volume, and opening iTunes. iTunes Bar is donationware.

- **iPod nano**   The iPod nano widget controls iTunes through an iPod nano–like interface. For example, you click the Play/Pause button to start or pause play, and click the Menu button to go up a level in the menu system. iPod nano is donationware.

Use the iTunes Widget on Mac OS X

If you're using Mac OS X Tiger, you can use the built-in iTunes widget to control iTunes from the Dashboard. To set the Dashboard to display the iTunes widget, follow these steps:

1. Click the Dashboard button on the Dock to display the Dashboard.

2. Click the + button superimposed in the lower-left corner of the screen to display the bar showing the available widgets.

3. Click the iTunes icon to display the iTunes widget.

4. Click the × button superimposed in the lower-left corner of the screen to close the widget bar.

You can then control iTunes by displaying the Dashboard and using the iTunes widget. Figure 10-3 shows the controls on the widget.

Figure 10-3

Mac OS X's built-in iTunes widget lets you control your music from the Dashboard.

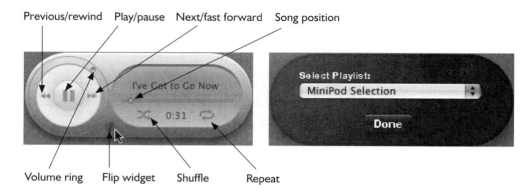

Previous/rewind   Play/pause   Next/fast forward   Song position

Volume ring   Flip widget   Shuffle   Repeat

> **tip** Apart from clicking the Dashboard button on the Dock, you can display the Dashboard by pressing the hot key assigned it on the Dashboard & Exposé sheet of System Preferences (choose Apple | System Preferences and then click the Dashboard & Exposé icon). On this sheet, you can also set an active screen corner for the Dashboard so that Mac OS X displays the Dashboard when you move the mouse pointer into that corner of the screen.

To open a playlist, click the Flip Widget button (the button showing the lowercase *i*). The iTunes widget rotates to show its other side. Select the playlist in the drop-down list and then click the Done button to flip the widget back to its regular position.

> **tip** If you find the iTunes widget doesn't suit you, you can get the Yahoo! Widget Engine for Mac OS X as well. For details, see the previous section.

Step 3: Control iTunes from the Keyboard

iTunes looks made for the mouse, so you might not guess that you can control it just as easily using the keyboard. Keyboard control lets you keep the music going—or stop it—without reaching for your mouse. It also enables you to issue commands that aren't even visible in the iTunes window—for example, when you've reduced the window to one of its smaller sizes.

> **note** The keyboard shortcuts shown in this section work only when iTunes is the active application—when it has the focus and so is receiving the input from the keyboard. You can change the focus by pressing ALT-TAB (Windows) or ⌘-TAB (Mac), clicking another window, or using the taskbar (Windows) or Dock (Mac). Keystrokes going to the application that has the focus is normal and usually convenient—you wouldn't want your e-mail program to suddenly start grabbing the keyboard input when you were working in Excel, for example. But when you have iTunes running in the background, you will often want to be able to pause or restart play, change song, or adjust the volume without moving the focus to it first. You can do so—but only by adding software. See "Control iTunes on Windows with iTunesKeys" and "Control iTunes on Mac OS X with ByteController," both later in this section, for details.

Figure 10-4

Press TAB to move to
the next element in the
iTunes interface.

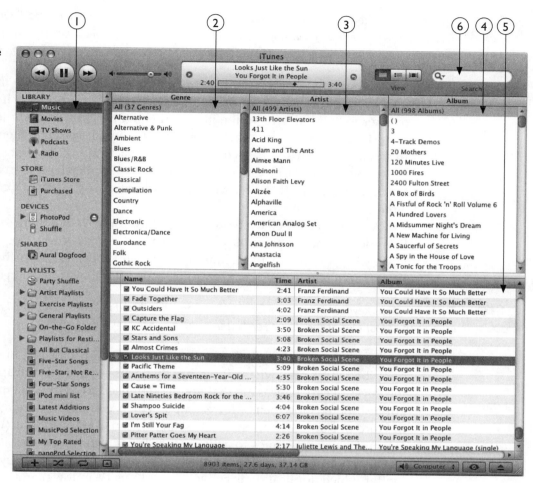

Move from One iTunes Element to Another Using Tabs and Arrow Keys

For basic navigation, you can move around the iTunes interface by using TAB and the arrow keys:

- Press TAB to move to the next element in the interface (details in a moment).

- Press SHIFT-TAB to move to the previous element in the interface.

- Press DOWN ARROW to move down to the next item in the current list.

- Press UP ARROW to move up to the previous item in the current list.

Exactly how this works depends on which item you're viewing (for example, your music library or the contents of a playlist) and so which iTunes elements are displayed. For instance, if you have the browser panes displayed, you can navigate to each of them in turn; if the browser isn't displayed, you navigate straight to the next element. Figure 10-4 shows the progression from element to element when you press TAB with the three browser panes displayed (including the genre pane).

> **note** *If you don't see the Genre pane, you can display it by choosing Edit | Preferences (Windows) or iTunes | Preferences (Mac), clicking the General tab, selecting the Show Genre When Browsing check box, and then clicking the OK button.*

Once you've reached the list you want, you can move down through it by pressing DOWN ARROW or back up through it by pressing UP ARROW. But if the list is long, it's quicker to "type down" to the item you want: type the first few letters of the item's name to jump to the first item beginning with those letters, and then press DOWN ARROW to scroll down further if needed. If you've reached an item that's playable, you can press SPACEBAR to start it playing. Items that are playable include an artist (start playing the first song in the first album in the list according to the way it's currently sorted), an album, a song, or a video.

You've just learned the basics of keyboard control—but there's far more. Table 10-1 lists the keyboard shortcuts you can use to control iTunes. Most of these shortcuts work with both the regular iTunes window and the mini player, but some work only for the mini player (see the "Controlling the Mini Player" section of the table).

> **note** *There are more keyboard shortcuts for the Visualizer than listed in Table 10-1. You'll meet them in "Get the Most Out of the Visualizer," later in this project.*

Being able to control iTunes from the keyboard is handy, but the shortcuts just described work only when iTunes has the focus—when it is the application receiving the keystrokes. Chances are that you'll often need to control the music when another application has the focus—for example, when you're grinding away at a document in Word or a spreadsheet in Excel. Sure, you could press ALT+TAB (Windows) or ⌘+TAB (Mac) one or more times to activate the iTunes window so that it would receive the keystrokes, but it's much more convenient if you can issue the keyboard shortcuts no matter which application is active. iTunesKeys (Windows) and ByteController (Mac OS X) let you do so.

Control iTunes on Windows with iTunesKeys

iTunesKeys is a small program that you can download from www.mattberube.com/software/ituneskeys/. iTunesKeys is donationware: If you like it, you can send the author financial encouragement via PayPal.

After you download the setup file, double-click it to run it. These are the main decisions in the installation process:

● Choose the folder in which to install iTunesKeys. Usually, the best choice is to accept the default installation folder, an iTunesKeys folder in your Program Files folder.

> **note** *If you're using Internet Explorer, when you double-click the iTunesKeys setup program, you'll probably see a Security Warning dialog box telling you that the publisher could not be verified. If you see this warning, it's because the setup file doesn't have a digital signature applied to it, which raises a red flag to Internet Explorer, as it implies the file might contain malware. But as long as you got the file from the website given here, it should be fine.*

Action	Windows Keystroke	Mac Keystroke
Controlling Playback		
Play or pause the selected song.	SPACEBAR	SPACEBAR
Skip to the next song.	RIGHT ARROW CTRL–RIGHT ARROW	RIGHT ARROW ⌘–RIGHT ARROW
Skip to the previous song.	LEFT ARROW CTRL–LEFT ARROW	LEFT ARROW ⌘–LEFT ARROW
Rewind the song.	CTRL-ALT–LEFT ARROW	⌘-OPTION–LEFT ARROW
Fast forward the song.	CTRL-ALT–RIGHT ARROW	⌘-OPTION–RIGHT ARROW
Skip to the next album in the list.	ALT–RIGHT ARROW	OPTION–RIGHT ARROW
Skip to the previous album in the list.	ALT–LEFT ARROW	OPTION–LEFT ARROW
Controlling the Volume		
Increase the volume.	CTRL–UP ARROW	⌘–UP ARROW
Decrease the volume.	CTRL–DOWN ARROW	⌘–DOWN ARROW
Toggle muting.	CTRL-ALT–UP ARROW CTRL-ALT–DOWN ARROW	⌘-OPTION–UP ARROW ⌘-OPTION–DOWN ARROW
Controlling the iTunes Windows		
Toggle the display of the iTunes main window (some versions only).	n/a	⌘-1
Toggle the display of the Equalizer window (some versions only).	n/a	⌘-2
Toggle between the mini player and full player.	CTRL-M	⌘-CONTROL-Z
Mac: Minimize iTunes.	—	CTRL-M
Move the focus to the Find box	CTRL-ALT-F	⌘-OPTION-F
Display the Open Stream dialog box.	CTRL-U	⌘-U
Controlling the Mini Player		
Increase the volume.	UP ARROW	UP ARROW
Decrease the volume.	DOWN ARROW	DOWN ARROW
Turn the iTunes volume to maximum.	SHIFT–UP ARROW	SHIFT–UP ARROW
Turn the iTunes volume down to minimum.	SHIFT–DOWN ARROW	SHIFT–DOWN ARROW
Controlling the Visualizer		
Toggle the Visualizer on and off.	CTRL-T	⌘-T
Toggle full-screen mode on the Visualizer.	CTRL-F	⌘-F

Table 10-1   Keyboard Shortcuts for iTunes

●   On the Select Additional Tasks screen, choose where you want to have iTunes-Keys icons by selecting or clearing the Create A Desktop Icon check box, the Create A Quick Launch Icon check box, and the Restore Tray Icon check box. (The notification area is also called the "system tray" or "tray.") Having one or more of these iTunesKeys icons can be useful for launching iTunesKeys easily, but you may also prefer to launch iTunesKeys automatically whenever you start Windows. See the "Run iTunesKeys on Startup" sidebar, later in this project.

●   On the final screen, select the Launch iTunesKeys check box to have the setup routine launch iTunesKeys automatically for you so that you can start using it.

Either let the setup routine launch iTunesKeys for you, or launch it yourself by clicking the Quick Launch toolbar icon, double-clicking the desktop icon, or choosing Start | All Programs | iTunesKeys | iTunesKeys. iTunesKeys displays itself as a no-tification-area icon that you can click to issue a command (more on this in a moment) or right-click to open the menu of commands and options shown in Figure 10-5.

Figure 10-5

Access the iTunesKeys commands and options by right-clicking the notification-area icon.

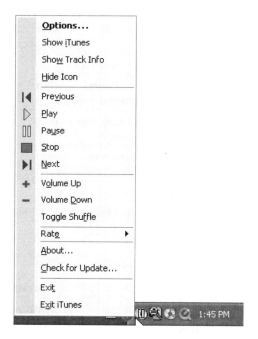

What you'll probably want to do first is configure iTunesKeys, so right-click the iTunesKeys notification-area icon and choose Options to open the iTunesKeys win-dow (see Figure 10-6). This lets you set the shortcut keys you want to use to control iTunes, make iTunesKeys display a pop-up of song info when each song starts, and tell the notification-area icon how to respond to clicks.

To set a keyboard shortcut, select the action in the list box on the left of the iTunes-Keys window, and then press the shortcut key you want. For example, you might select the Play/Pause command and press CTRL+ALT+P, as in the figure. The keys you press appear in the text box. To use the Windows Key as part of the key combination, don't press it, but select the Win Key check box instead. Once the text box shows the keyboard shortcut you want to use, click the Set button.

Figure 10-6

Configure keyboard
shortcuts for iTunes-
Keys and choose how
the notification-area
icon responds to clicks.

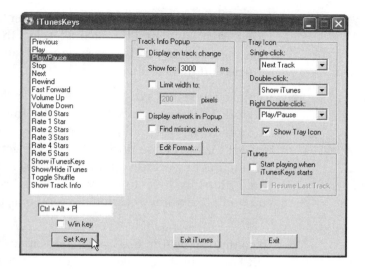

Repeat the process described in the previous paragraph for each of the keyboard shortcuts you want to set, and then turn your attention to the Track Info Popup group box:

● If you want to see a pop-up at the start of each song, select the Display On Track Change text box. In the Show For text box, type the number of milliseconds that the pop-up should appear for. The default setting is 3000 milliseconds—in other words, three seconds. This is enough for a quick glance at the notification area, but you might want to increase it to give yourself more time if you're not familiar with all the songs in your music library. Here's an example of a pop-up that includes a song's art:

- If you want to make sure the pop-up doesn't get too wide (to accommodate a long artist, song, or album name), select the Limit Width To check box and enter the width in pixels. The suggested setting is 200 pixels, but this setting is turned off by default.

- To make iTunesKeys display the song's art in the pop-up, select the Display Artwork In Popup check box. Usually this is a good idea, as it gives you a graphical representation as well as the text. To make iTunesKeys try to find art for songs that don't have any, select the Find Missing Artwork box. Adding missing art to your music library automatically is a great feature, so you'll probably want to select this check box. You might get a few pictures you don't like or the occasional wrong one, but you can deal with those easily enough.

- To configure the font used in the pop-up and the background color, click the Edit Format button, make your choices in the Edit Format dialog box, and then click the OK button to return to the iTunesKeys window.

In the Tray Icon group box, choose how you want the iTunesKeys notification-area icon to respond to single clicks, double-clicks, and right–double-clicks (a skill you may not have tried before). For example, you might choose Play/Pause in the Single-Click drop-down list, Next Track in the Double-Click drop-down list, and Show iTunes in the Right Double-Click drop-down list.

In the iTunes group box, select the Start Playing When iTunesKeys Start check box if you want iTunes to start playing music when you launch iTunesKeys. This instant-on setting doesn't suit everyone; you'll know whether you want it. In particular, beware of setting iTunesKeys to launch on login *and* making it start iTunes playing. Unless you're the only person within earshot of your computer when you start it, someone may get an earful of music unexpectedly.

If you select the Start Playing When iTunesKeys Starts this check box, iTunesKeys makes the Resume Last Track check box available. Select this check box if you want iTunes to start playing where you last stopped. Resuming with the last song is a nice feature—assuming that you want iTunes to start playing automatically.

When you've finished configuring iTunesKeys, click the Minimize button on the window's title bar to minimize iTunesKeys down to its notification-area icon. Don't click the Exit button—that closes iTunesKeys, which stops you from using the keyboard shortcuts you've configured. Don't click the Exit iTunes button, either, because if you close iTunes, you won't be able to play any music with iTunesKeys.

Control iTunes on Mac OS X with ByteController

iTunesKeys (discussed in the previous section) is great for keyboard control—but it runs only on Windows, not on Mac OS X. If you're using iTunes on the Mac rather than on Windows, you'll need another solution. Good news: ByteController will do the job admirably. Even better news: ByteController is free.

Run iTunesKeys on Startup

If you find iTunesKeys useful (and you probably will), add it to your Windows startup group so that Windows launches it automatically every time you log in. Running iTunesKeys automatically like this will save you from having to start it manually and from issuing keystrokes in vain when it's not running.

To add iTunesKeys to your Windows startup group, follow these steps:

1. Choose Start | All Programs | iTunesKeys to open the iTunesKeys submenu on the Start menu.

2. Right-click the iTunesKeys item and choose Copy from the shortcut menu.

3. Go up the All Programs menu to the Startup item, right-click it, and choose Open from the shortcut menu to open a Windows Explorer window to your Startup folder.

4. Right-click in the document area and choose Paste from the shortcut menu to paste in the iTunesKeys item.

5. Choose File | Close or click the Close button (the × button) to close the Windows Explorer window.

Now that you've added the iTunesKeys shortcut to your startup group, Windows starts iTunesKeys automatically when you log in. If you want to stop this behavior, choose Start | All Programs | Startup, right-click the iTunes-Keys item, and choose Delete.

To get ByteController, go to the Brainbyte Software & Design website (www .bytetastic.com). Follow the ByteController link in the Quick Downloads area to download the distribution file. Mac OS X usually unzips the distribution file automatically; if not, double-click the file to unzip it yourself. Double-click the resulting folder to open it, and then drag the ByteController icon to your Applications folder. Double-click the ByteController icon to start the application running. ByteController opens not as a window but as a tiny set of three buttons—Previous, Play/Pause, and Next—on the menu bar (see Figure 10-7).

Figure 10-7

ByteController appears as three buttons on the menu bar.

To configure ByteController, CTRL-click or right-click the menu bar icon and choose Preferences from the shortcut menu. The Preferences window opens.

On the General tab (see Figure 10-8), you can choose these two options:

● **Load At Startup**   Select this check box to make Mac OS X launch ByteController automatically each time you log in. This setting is very handy if you use iTunes every session. You can achieve the same effect by going to System Preferences, clicking the Accounts icon, and adding ByteController to the Login Items list for your accounts—but setting it in the Byte Controller Preferences window is much easier.

● **Show Only When iTunes Is Open**   Select this check box if you want to prevent ByteController from appearing on the menu bar when iTunes isn't running. This setting, too, is usually a good idea, because it helps you avoid trying to control the music via ByteController when iTunes isn't running.

Figure 10-8

The General tab of ByteController's Preferences window.

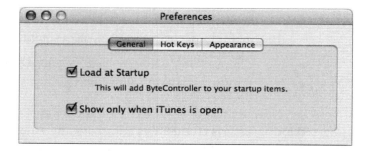

The Hot Keys tab (see Figure 10-9) lets you configure the keyboard shortcuts you use to control iTunes via ByteController. For each hot key you want to set, click in the

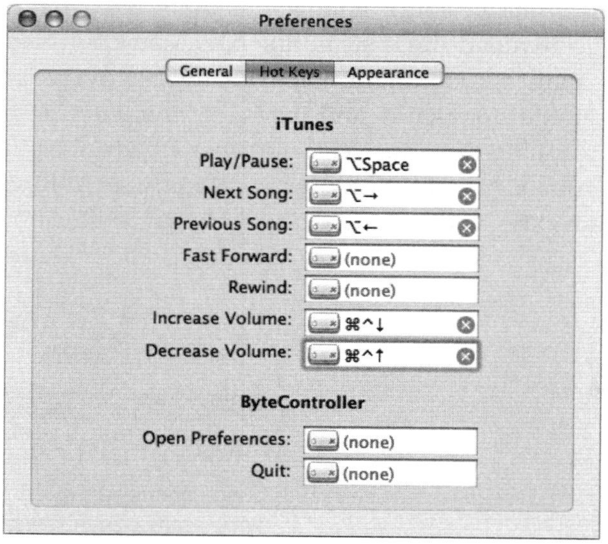

Figure 10-9

The Hot Keys tab of ByteController's Preferences window lets you define keyboard shortcuts for the major iTunes commands.

box for the command, and then press the keys that you want to use. For example, click in the box alongside Play/Pause and press OPTION-SPACEBAR if you want to use that key combination to start music playing and to pause it.

note　*You can also define keyboard shortcuts for opening the ByteController Preferences window and quitting ByteController, but you will probably not need to issue these commands often enough to make keyboard shortcuts worthwhile.*

The Appearance tab lets you choose which *skin* (graphical look) to use for Byte-Controller. The application includes several skins; you can find others on the Internet and then add them by clicking the Add button on the Appearance tab. If you're not particularly concerned about looks, leave the default set of buttons, which fit right in with Apple's icons on the Mac OS X Tiger menu bar.

Once you've finished configuring ByteController, click the Close button (the × button) to close the Preferences window. Start iTunes if it's not already running. You're now ready to use ByteController to run iTunes, either by clicking the buttons on the menu bar or by pressing the keyboard shortcuts you defined.

Step 4: Create Smart Playlists Tailored to Your Mood and Activities

Listening to songs by artist or album is great, but you'll often want to mix things up a bit. To help you do so, iTunes lets you create playlists and Smart Playlists:

● A *playlist* is simply a list of songs (or videos) that plays in the order in which you arrange them. You can change the play order by sorting the playlist by a different column; for example, you can sort the playlist by song name or artist name, or you can tell iTunes to shuffle it into a random order.

● A *Smart Playlist* is a playlist that iTunes creates for you based on criteria that you define. For example, you might tell iTunes to choose songs that you've rated with three stars or more and whose artists, albums, or song names include "faith." You can either create a Smart Playlist that contains a selection of songs that doesn't change after iTunes picks them or a Smart Playlist that automatically updates itself. Automatic updating lets you create Smart Playlists that adapt to the changes in your music library. For example, you might create a Smart Playlist that chooses songs from those you've added most recently.

Playlists are pretty straightforward to create, as you'll see next, but Smart Playlists have enough flexibility to give you outstanding results—provided that you know how to set them up. After the regular playlists, this section shows you how.

Create a Playlist

The normal way to create a playlist is by naming it and then adding songs to it. Here's how to proceed:

1. Click the + button below the Source pane, choose File | New Playlist, or press CTRL-N (Windows) or ⌘-N (Mac). iTunes adds a new playlist to the Source pane, names it *untitled playlist*, and displays an edit box around it. (If you already have a playlist named *untitled playlist*, iTunes uses the next available name, such as *untitled playlist 2*.)

2. Type the name for the playlist and then apply the name by pressing ENTER (Windows) or RETURN (Mac) or clicking anywhere other than in the name.

3. Click the Library item in the Source pane to display your songs. If you want to work by artist and album, click the Browse button (the button with the eye icon) in the lower-right corner of the iTunes window, press CTRL-B (Windows) or ⌘-B (Mac), or choose Edit | Show Browser, to display the Browser pane. (You can also work from Party Shuffle or from another playlist if you choose.)

4. Select the songs you want to add to the playlist and then drag them to the playlist's entry in the Source pane. You can drag one song at a time, multiple songs, a whole artist, a whole CD, or even an entire genre—whatever you find easiest. You can also drag an existing playlist to the new playlist.

5. Click the playlist's entry in the Source pane to display the playlist.

6. Drag the tracks into the order in which you want them to play.

> **note** *For you to be able to drag the tracks around in the playlist, the playlist must be sorted by the track-number column. If any other column heading is selected, you won't be able to rearrange the order of the tracks in the playlist, because iTunes continues to enforce the type of sorting you've specified.*

iTunes also provides a quick way to create a playlist from one or more songs that you've selected. This technique is useful when you've selected some songs from your music library (or from another playlist) so that you can add them to an existing playlist but then you realize that none of your existing playlists is suitable. Rather than deselect the songs, create the playlist, and then have to select the songs again so that you can add them to the playlist, you can create the new playlist in a single move.

Select the songs (you can be working anywhere—in your music library, in Party Shuffle, or in a playlist) and then take one of these actions:

● Drag the songs to an open space in the Source pane. Avoid any existing playlist, or else you'll simply add the songs to that playlist.

● With the songs selected, choose File | New Playlist From Selection or press CTRL-SHIFT-N (Windows) or ⌘-SHIFT-N (Mac).

Either way, iTunes creates a new playlist named *untitled playlist* (or the next free name) and adds the songs to it. iTunes displays an edit box around the provisional title so that you can change it immediately. Type the new name and press ENTER (Windows) or RETURN (Mac), or click elsewhere to apply the name. If necessary, drag the songs into the order in which you want them to play.

Create a Smart Playlist

As you've just seen, creating a regular playlist could hardly be easier. And regular playlists are great—as long as you either want to keep listening to the same selection of music or you're prepared to keep changing your playlists manually. But if you want to keep your playlists fresh and you prefer to let iTunes do the work for you, create Smart Playlists rather than regular playlists. A *Smart Playlist* is a playlist that iTunes creates automatically to fulfill certain criteria you set, such as music genre, artist names, or the years with which the songs are associated. iTunes can update each Smart Playlist for you so that it contains different songs each time you use it.

note   *Smart Playlist maintains playlists such as the My Top Rated playlist, the Recently Played playlist, and the Top 25 Most Played playlist, which iTunes creates by default.*

Here's how to create a Smart Playlist:

1. Press CTRL-ALT-N (Windows) or ⌘-ALT-N (Mac), or choose File | New Smart Playlist, to display the Smart Playlist dialog box. On the Mac, you can also OPTION-click the Add button.

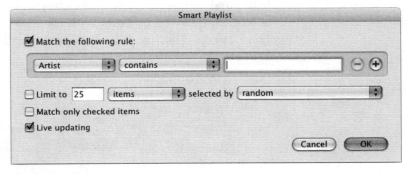

2. Select the Match The Following Rule check box. (Usually, iTunes selects this check box for you, because you can't specify any criteria if the check box is cleared.)

3. Describe your first condition using the controls in the first line:

   ● The first drop-down list offers an extensive range of choices: Album, Artist, Bit Rate, Comment, Compilation, Composer, Date Added, Date Modified, Genre, Kind, Last Played, My Rating, Play Count, Playlist, Sample Rate, Size, Song Name, Time, Track Number, and Year.

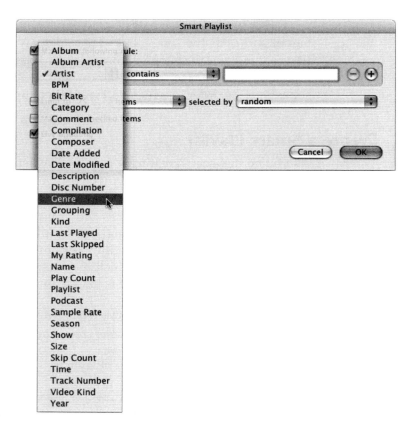

- The second drop-down list offers options suitable to the item you chose in the first drop-down list—for example, Contains, Does Not Contain, Is, Is Not, Starts With, or Ends With for a text field, or Is, Is Not, Is Greater Than, Is Less Than, or Is In The Range for the bitrate.

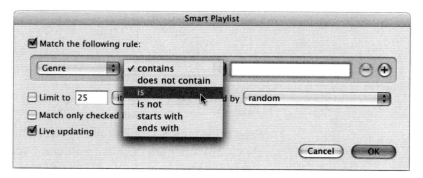

- The third box changes to offer suitable options for the choices you've made in the two drop-down lists. For example, if you choose Artist in the first drop-down list and Starts With in the second drop-down list, the third box is a text box into which you type the text for the condition (such as **sm** for artists beginning with those letters—for instance, Smashing Pumpkins). If you choose My Rating in the first drop-down list and

Is In The Range in the second drop-down list, you get two boxes of rating stars so that you can specify the range (for example, ★★★ to ★★★★★).

4. That's your first condition ready for action—but to create effective and subtle Smart Playlists that select only the songs you want, you'll usually need to create multiple conditions. To do so, click the + button at the end of the line. iTunes adds another line of condition controls, and changes the Match The Following Rule check box into a check box and drop-down list that offers the choices Match All Of The Following Rules and Match Any Of The Following Rules:

● For a playlist that will select a specific type of songs you have in mind, choose Match All The Following Rules. For example, to select early-'80s rock songs that you like, you can specify Year Is In The Range 1980 To 1985, My Rating Is Greater Than ★★★, and Genre Is Rock.

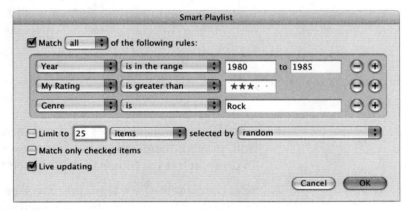

● For a playlist that will include various different types of songs, choose Match Any Of The Following Rules. For example, you may create a playlist where Genre Is Gothic Rock and Genre Is Industrial. In this case, you need to specify Match Any Of The Following Rules, because any song can have only one genre and choosing Match All The Following Rules would select no songs.

● To remove a condition, click the—button at the end of its line.

5. Often, you'll want to limit the playlist to a maximum number of songs, time, or disk space—for example, when you're creating a playlist for an iPod that has a limited capacity, or when you're creating a playlist to burn to CD. When you need to set a limit, select the Limit To check box, and then specify the limit and how iTunes should select the songs. For example, you could specify Limit to 950 MB Selected By Most Recently Added, Limit To 30 Songs Selected By Least Often Played, or Limit To 8 Hours Selected By Random.

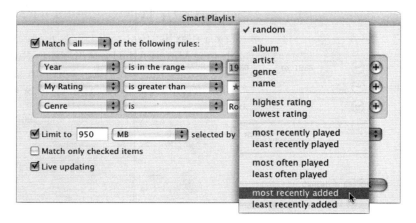

6. If you clear the check boxes for songs in your music library to prevent iTunes from playing them, you may want to exclude these songs from playlists too. To do so, select the Match Only Checked Items check box.

7. Select or clear the Live Updating check box to specify whether iTunes should update the playlist periodically according to your listening patterns. This is a great way of keeping playlists fresh and up-to-date.

8. Click the OK button to close the Smart Playlist dialog box. iTunes creates the playlist, assigns it a suggested name derived from the rule you specified, and displays an edit box around the name so you can change it.

9. Type the new name for the playlist and then press ENTER (Windows) or RETURN (Mac).

That's all fine in theory—but what about some examples of Smart Playlists? Table 10-2 gives six suggestions. You'll want to modify the specifics to suit your needs and tastes, and you'll probably want to use different names as well—but you get the idea.

Share a Playlist with a Friend

So you've made a killer playlist? Don't keep it to yourself: Share it with a friend or with the world instead. iTunes calls this "exporting" a playlist and makes it easy to do. Your friend can then "import" the playlist to add it to his or her library—or he or she can give you a playlist to import into your music library. You can also upload a playlist to the iTunes Music Store to share it with anyone who browses the store.

Playlist Name	Description	Rules and Details
New Music	Songs you've added to your music library in the last month	Match The Following Rule Date Added Is In The Last 1 Month Live Updating: On
Favorites for the Car	A CD's worth of favorite songs that you haven't played for a while	Match The Following Rule My Rating Is ★★★★ Limit To 74 Minutes Selected By Least Recently Played
nanoClassical	Classical music to fit on a 2 GB iPod nano—but leave any Bach out of it	Match All Of The Following Rules Genre Is Classical Composer Does Not Contain Bach Limit To 2 GB Selected By Random Live Updating: On
Unplayed Songs	Songs you've never played—and that you should decide whether to keep or delete	Match All Of The Following Rules Podcast Is False Play Count Is 0 Live Updating: On
All Songs But Classical	Songs that aren't classical music and that aren't movies or TV shows. Use this playlist as a basis for others (see the next example).	Match All Of The Following Rules Genre Is Not Classical Genre Is Not Movies Genre Is Not TV Shows Podcast Is False Live Updating: On
New Rock for iPod shuffle	Recently added songs from rock genres drawn from the All Songs But Classical playlist (described in the previous entry in this table) to avoid podcasts, movies, and TV shows. This playlist is limited to 400 MB to allow approximately 100 MB for data on a 512 MB iPod shuffle.	Match All Of The Following Rules Playlist Is All Music But Classical Date Added Is In The Last 1 Month Genre Contains Rock Limit To 400 MB Selected By Random Live Updating: On

Table 10-2 Examples of Creating Smart Playlists

note When you export a playlist, iTunes creates a small file that contains a text listing with the details of songs in the playlist, not a huge file that contains the songs themselves. Because the playlist file is small, you can send it easily via e-mail; and because it contains no music, you need have no concerns about copyright issues (as you would if you were sending the songs themselves). But the person with whom you share the playlist must have the songs in their music library to be able to play them.

To export a playlist, follow these steps:

1. Create the playlist as described in this project. Make sure it's perfect for distribution.

2. Right-click the playlist in the Source pane and choose Export Song List from the shortcut menu to display the Save As dialog box (Windows) or the Save: iTunes dialog box (Mac).

3. iTunes suggests using the playlist's name as the filename, which usually works well; change the name if needed. Choose the folder in which to store the playlist file. iTunes suggests your My Documents folder on Windows and your Documents folder on the Mac. These folders tend to get cluttered fast, so you might want to create a Playlists folder within one of these folders so that you can keep your playlists separate.

4. Choose the format for the file. Windows lets you choose between Text Files and XML Files. Mac OS X lets you choose among Plain Text, Unicode Text, and XML. Text Files or Plain Text is usually the best choice.

5. Click the Save button to save the playlist.

You can then share the playlist with someone else—for example, by sending it via e-mail.

Import a Playlist That a Friend Has Given You

When you receive a playlist, import it into iTunes so that you can see whether you like it. To import the playlist, follow these steps:

1. Choose File | Import to open the Import dialog box.

2. Select the playlist file, and then click the Open button (Windows) or the Choose button (Mac).

3. iTunes checks the playlist against your library and creates a playlist that contains as many of the songs as you have available. If one or more songs are unavailable, iTunes warns you, as shown here. Click the OK button.

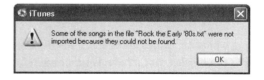

Upload a Playlist to the iTunes Music Store

Sharing a playlist with a friend can be great, but if you're convinced your playlist deserves a wider audience, you can share it with anyone who visits the iTunes Music Store. iTunes calls this an iMix and imposes a major limitation: Your iMix can include only songs that are available in the iTunes Music Store. You don't have to have bought the songs from the iTunes Music Store—you can have ripped them from your CDs or other audio sources—but the songs must be on the iTunes Music Store lists. This means that holes may appear in your carefully constructed playlist.

You must also have an Apple ID or an AOL screen name to be able to publish the iMix. You need one or other of these to buy music from the iTunes Music Store anyway, so if you've used the iTunes Music Store, you're all set.

To create an iMix, follow these steps:

1. Create the playlist as described in this project and make sure that it's fit for distribution.

2. Choose File | Create An iMix. iTunes opens a message box explaining what an iMix is.

3. Select the Do Not Show This Message Again check box, and then click the Create button. The Sign In To Publish Your iMix dialog box appears.

4. Enter your Apple ID and password or your AOL screen name and password, and then click the Publish button. iTunes compares the songs on your playlist to its database and then displays a screen showing you which of the songs are available.

5. Type a title and description for your iMix. As you might imagine, you're not allowed to use offensive words.

6. Click the Publish button. On the next screen, you can use the Tell A Friend button to notify your friends that the iMix is now available for their enjoyment.

Jump to a Particular Song on a Specific Playlist

Sometimes you may want to see which playlists contain a particular song. To do so, right-click the song and choose Show In Playlist from the shortcut menu. iTunes displays a submenu that shows you all the playlists that contain the song. Choose a playlist from the submenu to jump straight to where the song is in that playlist.

Delete a Playlist or a Smart Playlist

If you're sure you have no further use for a playlist, delete it. (You may want to export the playlist first, as described in the previous section, so that you can restore it effortlessly if you change your mind.) To delete a playlist, take one of these actions:

● Click the playlist's item in the Source pane, and then press DELETE (Windows) or BACKSPACE (Mac).

● Right-click the playlist's item in the Source pane, choose Clear from the shortcut menu, and then click the Yes button in the confirmation message box. You can turn off the confirmation from now on by selecting the Do Not Ask Me Again check box before you click the Yes button.

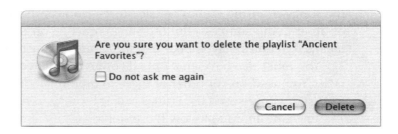

Are you sure you want to delete the playlist "Ancient Favorites"?

☐ Do not ask me again

Cancel   Delete

caution   *If you're a dedicated Mac user, you're probably familiar with pressing* OPTION *to modify the effect of a command—just as you can* OPTION-*click the Create A Playlist button to create a new Smart Playlist rather than a regular playlist. If you try pressing* OPTION *when you press* BACKSPACE *to delete a selected playlist, you may get a surprise, because this modified command deletes not only the playlist but all the songs it contains. iTunes prompts you for confirmation, so you shouldn't lose any songs unknowingly—but if you press* ⌘-OPTION-DELETE, *you suppress the confirmation and delete both the songs and the playlist. There may be times when you actually want to do this, but they're not likely to be frequent—so keep your fingers under control.*

Step 5: Get the Most Out of the Visualizer

If you've used iTunes more than a little, you've probably discovered the Visualizer, which lets you feast your eyes on stunning *visualizations*, graphical patterns generated automatically from the rhythm and the sounds of the music you're playing. But chances are that you haven't yet used it to the max. This section shows you how to do so.

Start the Visualizer

If you haven't discovered the Visualizer, here are the essentials:

- To start a visualization, press CTRL-T (Windows) or ⌘-T (Mac) or choose Visualizer | Turn Visualizer On. Press the same shortcut again to turn visualizations off.

- Press CTRL-F (Windows) or ⌘-F (Mac) to toggle between full-screen visualizations and windowed visualizations.

Display the Frame Rate or Song Info, or Change the Frame Rate

Apple sets iTunes up to run visualizations so that they look good to most people—but you may well want to customize the display to suit your tastes. There are two key settings: the frame rate and the song information.

- **Frame Rate**   This is the number of new images (frames) that the Visualizer generates every second. iTunes uses a maximum frame rate of 30 frames per second (fps), which is fast enough to give a smooth-looking display. If your computer's graphics card can't manage 30 fps, iTunes uses whichever rate your computer can manage. (You'll learn how to find out what frame rate iTunes is managing in a minute.) If your computer's graphics card can manage more than 30 fps, you can let it rip—at the expense of graphics performance on anything else you're doing. There's no benefit to displaying the frame rate beyond curiosity or getting a rough sense of how powerful your computer's graphics subsystem is.

tip *You'll usually get a faster frame rate by running the Visualizer full screen than running it at the Large size in a window. This is because when the Visualizer is running full screen, your computer can devote its full graphics capability to the Visualizer without having to render the windows of any other programs you're running.*

● **Song Information** As it starts playing each song, iTunes displays the song name, artist name, and album for a few seconds. You can choose to display the song information all the time, which is good for reference or publicity.

To change the options, follow these steps:

1. If iTunes is displayed at its small or minute size, click the Restore button (Windows) or the green button on the window frame (Mac) to return iTunes to a normal window.

2. Choose View | Visualizer | Options to display the Visualizer Options dialog box. Figure 10-10 shows the Visualizer Options dialog box for Windows on the left and the Visualizer Options dialog box for the Mac on the right.

Figure 10-10

The Visualizer Options dialog box (Windows, left; Mac, right) .

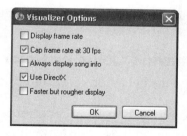
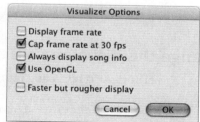

3. Select the Display Frame Rate check box if you want to make iTunes display the frame rate superimposed on the upper-left corner of the visualization.

4. Select the Cap Frame Rate At 30 fps check box if you want to limit the maximum frame rate to 30 frames per second. (This check box is selected by default to prevent the Visualizer from hogging all your computer's graphics capability and perhaps slowing down other applications.) Clear this check box if you want the Visualizer to crank out as many frames as possible.

tip *You can toggle the frame rate display at any time by pressing F. Similarly, you can toggle the frame-rate capping on and off by pressing T.*

5. Select the Always Display Song Info check box if you want to keep the song and artist information displayed all the time the Visualizer is running. Otherwise, leave this check box cleared, as it is by default.

tip *Press the letter i at any time to display the song information for 10 seconds. iTunes then hides the song information again.*

6. On the Mac, select the Use OpenGL check box if you want to let iTunes use the OpenGL graphics-rendering system to create the visualizations. This is usually a good idea, and this check box is selected by default. On Windows, select the Use DirectX check box to use the DirectX graphics-rendering system. This too is usually a good idea unless you find that your computer's graphics card can't handle DirectX. (Any modern graphics card should be able to handle DirectX.)

7. Select the Faster But Rougher Display check box if you want to increase the frame rate by lowering the quality of the visualizations. Usually, you'd want to select this check box only when your computer isn't powerful enough to run high-quality visualizations at full speed. In this case, the visualizations will look jerky rather than smooth, and you may prefer to have less-sharp visualizations running at a faster frame rate.

tip *You can also trigger most of these options from the keyboard while a visualization is playing, without displaying the Visualizer Options dialog box. Press F to toggle the frame rate display, T to toggle frame rate capping, I to toggle the display of song information, and D to restore the default settings.*

8. Click the OK button to close the Visualizer Options dialog box.

Change the Visualizer's Behavior, Color, or Color Theme

iTunes also lets you change the behavior, color, and color theme of the Visualizer:

● **Behavior** This controls the general appearance of the patterns that the Visualizer makes. The Visualizer has a wide range of behaviors with descriptive names such as Big And Banded, DT—Wild, A New Hope, Align, Critters, and many others. Press Q or W to move from the current behavior to another behavior.

● **Colors** This controls the color scheme the Visualizer is using. The Visualizer has a wide range of colors, too, with evocative names such as Tripping Hard, Wild Fire, Whoo! Whoo!, Whirlpool In The Waves, Warpo Tunnel, and Quantum Ripple. Press A to move to the next color; press S to move to the previous color.

● **Color Theme** This controls the overall mix of colors that the Visualizer uses. As with the behaviors and colors, the Visualizer has a slew of color schemes, each with a memorable name—for example, Muted Middle, Radioactive, QuickSilver, Blue Lightning, Purple Ghost, or Firestorm. Press Z to move to the next color theme and X to return to the previous color theme.

Save Visualizer Configurations and Display Them

When the Visualizer produces a really cool visualization, or when you produce one yourself by using the commands discussed in this section, you may want to save the configuration so that you can show it to someone else. To save a configuration, press SHIFT and one of the number keys: SHIFT+0, SHIFT+1, and so on up to SHIFT+9, giving you up to 10 saved configurations.

To load one of the configurations you've saved, press the number you assigned (without pressing SHIFT). For example, press 5 to load the configuration you saved by pressing SHIFT+5.

tip *While the Visualizer is running, you can still use the keyboard to control the volume (press ↑ to increase the volume or ↓ to decrease it) and move from song to song (press ← to go to the previous song and → to go to the next song).*

Randomize or Reset the Visualizer

You can also use keyboard shortcuts to randomize or reset the Visualizer:

- **Randomize** To switch to a new visualization at random, press R.
- **Reset to iTunes default** To delete all your custom Visualizer configurations and reset the visualizations to iTunes' default visualizations, press D. Use this shortcut with care if you've created custom configurations.

Go Big Screen

Visualizations look pretty good in a window and can look really great full screen, especially if you've got a large screen (for example, an Apple Cinema Display). But if you want to make iTunes the life and soul of a party, you'll need to crank up the visualizations to the max. There are two main ways to do so:

- Connect your computer to a large-screen TV
- Connect your computer to a projector

The following sections outline how to go about each of these ways of going big screen.

Connect Your Computer to a Large-Screen TV

If you've got a TV with a much bigger screen than your monitor, you can get some impressively large visualizations at high quality. The main challenge to connecting your computer to a TV is figuring out which cables to use. These depend on the type of outputs your computer offers and the type of inputs the TV uses. The following list shows the types of connection that are typically available, arranged in descending order of preference:

- **DVI**   Digital Visual Interface is a digital video standard primarily used for LCD displays (including LCD TVs) and digital projectors. DVI connectors come in several variations, including DVI-D (digital-only signal between source and monitor), DVI-A (analog only, for connecting a digital source to an analog monitor), and DVI-I (both digital and analog). The various DVI connectors have the same shape and size but have different arrangements of pins.

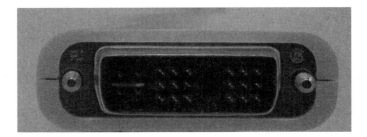

- **HDMI**   High-Definition Multimedia Interface is an interface for transferring uncompressed video and audio from a digital source to a digital monitor. At this writing, HDMI is mostly used for connecting DVD players, set-top boxes, and other high-quality video sources to digital televisions. Few PC graphics cards have HDMI outputs, but if you get the right kind of cable, you can connect a computer's DVI output to a HDMI port on a television. The next illustration shows an HDMI connector.

- **S-Video**   S-Video or Separate Video separates the brightness and color into two separate signals to avoid interference between them. S-Video doesn't have an audio connection, so you must use a separate cable for audio. S-Video uses a mini-DIN connection, shown next. Chances are that DIN makes you think of "noise," but in fact DIN is an acronym for Deutsche Institüt für Normung, or German Institute for Standardization.

- **RCA connectors** RCA connectors are analog electrical connectors widely used for carrying audio signals, video signals, or both. For example, if you have a stereo receiver, chances are that it uses RCA connectors for connecting audio sources. RCA connectors are typically color-coded to help you plug them in correctly: A standard RCA audio cable has red plugs at the ends of the cable that carries the right audio channel, and white or black plugs at the ends of the cable that carries the left audio channel. An RCA audio/video cable adds to these cables a third cable with yellow plugs, which carries a composite video signal. You can also use a separate cable for the video; the plugs don't have to be yellow, as long as you put the correct plug in each socket. The next illustration shows cables with RCA connectors.

- **SCART** Widely used in Europe (it's also called Euroconnector or Péritel) but almost ignored in North America, SCART is a comparatively large, almost rectangular connector that contains 21 flat pins. The connector isn't quite rectangular, as one end is angled so that it fits in the socket only one way and cannot be inserted wrongly without the use of absurd force. SCART is the pleasantly compact acronym for Syndicat des Constructeurs d'Appareils Radiorécepteurs et Téléviseurs, or Syndicate of Radio and TV Constructors. SCART is easy to use but doesn't support component video (analog video transmitted as two separate signals rather than one signal).

- **RF connection** A radio-frequency (RF) connection is a basic type of connection used between video sources and televisions. You'll find RF connectors on various PC graphics cards and on many TVs, but you should always use one of the other types of connection discussed in this list rather than RF if you have the option. RF connectors come in different types, but many of those used for audio/video transfer have a central pin or wire in a circular housing. Here are examples of some RF connectors:

Start by checking the type or types of connection that your computer offers, and choose the most promising item on the above list. (Check your computer's documentation if you're not sure what the jacks are.) For example, if you have a choice between DVI and S-Video, you should use DVI unless you have a compelling reason to prefer S-Video.

Next, look at the TV and its documentation to see which connection types it supports and which of them should give you the best picture. As you might imagine, the higher the TV's price, the more and better connection options it usually offers. But even a modest TV should offer a fair-quality connection option, such as S-Video or three RCA connectors. Avoid an RF connection unless you have no alternative.

Now find a cable to connect the ports you've chosen. A straightforward cable that uses the same type of connection at each end is usually easiest to find—for example, S-Video at each end—but you can also find cables to connect many combinations of different ports (for example, S-Video to three RCA jacks). Some cables convert the video from one format to another, which degrades the quality somewhat. Avoid such conversions whenever possible.

Connect your computer to your TV. Configure the computer to pass a video signal through the port you're using, and set the TV to accept input through the appropriate port. Start the music and the visualizations, and enjoy the spectacle.

Connect Your Computer to a Projector

Using a large-screen TV can give you a great picture, but even the biggest TV can't compare with the size of picture a projector can give you, especially if you forego the confines of a traditional screen and simply project the visualizations onto a light-colored wall. Because the visualizations are rapidly moving fractal images, you don't need as perfect a surface as if you were projecting images that would suffer more from distortion, such as a movie or a TV show. So any light-colored wall that's roughly flat will do—or, if you don't have a suitable wall, stretch a white bed sheet across a wall or part of a room.

Most projectors connect via your computer's video port. Making the connection usually involves only connecting the projector's cable to your computer's video port, but here are three points to bear in mind:

● If your computer is a laptop, you may need to enable the external graphics port. Consult the computer's documentation if you don't know how to do this.

- To connect a projector to a DVI port, you may need a DVI to D-Sub cable or connector. You can get one of these from any computer store worth visiting.

- If your computer has two video ports, you may be able to run a projector in tandem with the computer's screen or monitor. Having both screens going can be helpful for keeping the music running while the visualizations play.

By now, you should be handling iTunes like a pro. It's time to turn your attention back to your iPod, and learn how to load it from multiple computers.

Load Your iPod from Multiple Computers (PCs, Macs, or Both)

What You'll Need:

- **iPod Required: Any iPod**
- **Cost: Free**

A good part of the iPod's appeal lies in how easy Apple has made synchronizing the iPod with your computer: just connect the iPod to the computer designated as its "home" computer, and iTunes springs into action, automatically synchronizing either all the contents of your music library or all the songs on the playlists you've designated. A few minutes (or even seconds) later, you're ready to hit the road with either your full music library or the parts of it you've chosen to carry.

That's great—assuming your entire music library fits on one computer. But what if your songs are spread across two or more computers? You might have some songs on your home computer and some on your work computer, or you might keep your songs on different computers scattered around the house. (If you keep your songs on different computers simply because no one computer can hold your entire music library, have a look at Project 21, which explains how to create a central music library or a music server.)

Having your songs split between two or more computers means that automatic synchronization is out, because your iPod can't synchronize with both or all the computers. Say you have two computers, A and B. When you synchronize your iPod with Computer B, iTunes removes all the songs from the iPod that are on Computer A unless they're on Computer B as well, so the iPod ends up containing only the songs on Computer B. When you synchronize with Computer A again, your iPod receives the Computer A songs and loses those from Computer B.

But if you use manual synchronization, you can load your iPod with songs from as many computers as you like. This project shows you how to do so.

Override Automatic Synchronization

Normally, as soon as you connect your iPod to your computer, the operating system (Windows or Mac OS X) activates iTunes, which checks the iPod to see whether it is set to synchronize automatically. If it is, iTunes starts the synchronization without prompting you for confirmation and finishes the synchronization as fast as possible—just what you want as long as the songs in the music library are available.

However, if some or all of the songs in the music library aren't available, you run into problems. For example, say you don't have enough space on your Windows laptop or your MacBook for your entire music library, so you keep it on an external drive. You set your iPod for automatic synchronization, because you use your computer at your desk most of the time, and synchronization works fine. But if you take your computer on the road and try to synchronize the iPod when the external drive containing the songs isn't connected, synchronization deletes all the songs from the iPod so that it has the same contents as your iTunes music library: no songs.

Usually, you don't want this to happen—and when you see the songs start to disappear from your iPod, you'll realize the problem and stop the synchronization by clicking the × button on the right of the "Updating" readout. But because iTunes can delete the songs from your iPod much faster than it can load them on to it, you can lose a good chunk of your songs this way—or even all of them—leaving you without music while you're on the road.

To avoid this happening, turn off automatic synchronization before you go on the road. While your computer still has all the songs available, connect the iPod and synchronize it. When synchronization is complete, click the iPod's entry in the Source pane, click the Summary tab, and then select the Manually Manage Music And Video check box or the Manually Manage Music check box (depending on the model of iPod), click the Yes button in the confirmation dialog box that warns you you'll need to eject the iPod manually, and then click the Apply button.

If you forget to turn off automatic synchronization like this before you move your computer away from the drive containing its songs, all is not lost. You can override automatic synchronization temporarily by holding down CTRL-ALT (Windows) or ⌘-OPTION (Mac) while you connect your iPod to the computer. Keep holding down these keys until iTunes has recognized the iPod and displayed an entry for it in the Source pane. You're then safe to change the synchronization settings as described in the previous paragraph.

Step 1: Decide Whether You'll Use Windows, Mac OS X, or Both

When loading your iPod from multiple computers, your first decision is whether you'll use Windows computers, Macs, or both. This decision should be easy, but it controls whether you need to restore your iPod to change the file system.

The reason this is important is that iPods use a different file system with Mac OS X than with Windows:

- With Mac OS X, iPods use the Mac OS Extended file system. This is the same file system used by most Mac hard disks. Windows computers can't read the Mac OS Extended file system unless you install special software.

- With Windows, iPods use the FAT32 file system. FAT32 can be read by almost all modern operating systems. FAT32 is widely used by older versions of Windows (such as Windows 98 and Windows Me) and by external disks, although computers running Windows XP usually use the NTFS file system, which is more stable, efficient, and resilient than FAT32. FAT32 is marginally less efficient than Mac OS Extended, but not enough to worry about. Macs can read the FAT32 file system just fine.

note *This discussion about file systems applies to the regular iPod and the iPod nano only, not the iPod shuffle. The iPod shuffle uses the FAT32 file system no matter which computer you connect it to. So if you're using an iPod shuffle, you can skip this step and the next step.*

No big deal. But what this means is that if your iPod is formatted using the FAT32 file system, you can use PCs, Macs, or both to load files onto your iPod. If your iPod is formatted using the Mac OS Extended file system, you can use only Macs; if you want to use a PC, you'll need to reformat your iPod's hard disk.

Step 2: Find Out Which File System Your iPod Is Using

The second step is to find out which file system your iPod is currently using. Have a look at the flowchart in Figure 11-1, which steps you through the process of establishing the file system. Here's the text version:

- If you've got an iPod shuffle, you don't need to worry. The iPod shuffle always uses FAT32, so you need neither check it nor change it.

- If you're using your iPod with Windows already, you don't need to change anything. The iPod is using FAT32, which works with both Windows and the Mac.

- If you're using your iPod with a Mac, the iPod will probably be using Mac OS Extended (which is how iPods all ship) or FAT32 (if the iPod has been connected to a Windows PC). If you just want to use your iPod with several Macs but not with Windows, you don't even need to find out which file system the iPod is using: Whichever file system it is, the iPod will work with

Figure 11-1

Follow this flowchart to find out whether you need to restore your iPod to reformat its hard disk or flash memory.

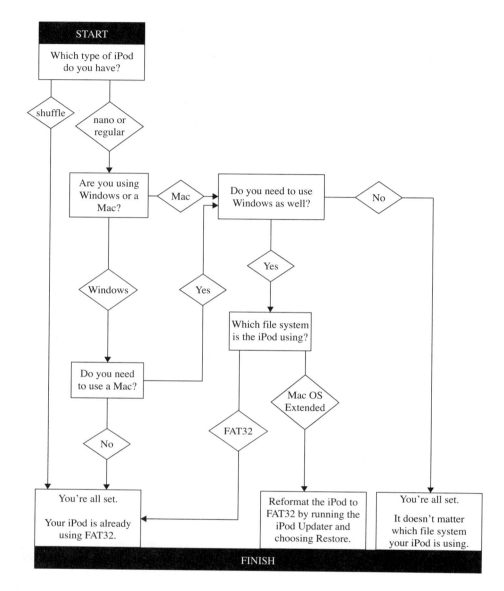

several Macs just as well as one. But if you want to use your iPod with one or more Windows computers as well as with a Mac, you need to find out which file system it's using.

To find out which file system an iPod is using with the Mac, follow these steps:

1. Connect the iPod to your Mac. If the iPod is set to synchronize automatically, allow synchronization to take place.

2. In the Source pane, click the iPod's entry, and then click the Summary tab.

3. Look at the Format readout in the iPod area. If it says "Windows," the iPod is formatted with FAT32, so you don't need to change it. If it says "Macintosh," you will need to change it.

Step 3: Restore Your iPod If Necessary

If you established in Step 2 that you need to restore your iPod because it uses the Mac OS Extended file system, follow these steps to reformat it using FAT32. You must use a Windows PC for the restore operation, because restoring the iPod on the Mac restores the iPod using the Mac OS Extended file system, which won't have the effect you want.

caution *Restoring your iPod deletes all the files from it and reformats the hard disk or flash memory. Before you restore your iPod, copy any valuable files from it to your computer so that you won't lose them. (See Project 13 for details on using your iPod as a disk.) If your iPod contains only songs and data synchronized from your computer, you shouldn't need to worry about copying files from the iPod, as the next synchronization with your computer after the restore operation will put the songs and data back on the iPod.*

To restore your iPod, follow these steps:

1. Connect the iPod to a Windows PC that has iTunes installed. Windows should display the iTunes dialog box shown here, telling you that the iPod is Macintosh-formatted:

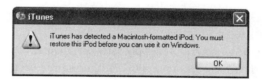

2. Click the OK button. iTunes selects the iPod in the Source pane and displays the Summary tab of information for it. (None of the other tabs of information is available because the iPod is Macintosh-formatted.)

3. Click the Restore button to start the restoration.

4. iTunes checks the iPod Updater site for the latest version of the iPod Updater software. If there's a newer version, iTunes downloads it. (If you have a dial-up connection, or no connection, and you want to skip this update, choose Edit | Preferences, clear the Check For Updates Automatically check box on the General tab of the iTunes dialog box, and then click the OK button.)

5. iTunes confirms that you want to restore the iPod, warning you that all your songs and data will be erased, as shown here:

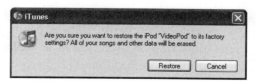

6. Click the Restore button if you're sure you can dispose of whatever is stored on the iPod.

7. Wait while iTunes completes the restore process. When it has finished, iTunes displays the dialog box shown here.

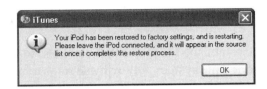

8. Click the OK button., iTunes displays the iPod Setup Assistant.

9. In the iPod Setup Assistant, type the name you want to give your iPod, and choose whether to use automatic updating:

- If you want to set the iPod up with manual updating from the start, so that you can load songs manually from this computer's music library, clear the Automatically Update Songs On My iPod check box.

- If you want to use automatic updating to synchronize all of this computer's music library on the iPod before you switch to manual updating, leave the Automatically Update Songs On My iPod check box selected (as it is by default).

10. If you chose automatic updating, allow iTunes to synchronize your music library with your iPod. Otherwise, you're ready to load it manually. Go to the next step.

note *You must use a Windows PC to apply software updates to a FAT32-formatted iPod. The iPod Updater for the Mac works only with iPods formatted using the Mac OS Extended file system.*

Step 4: Configure Your iPod for Manual Updating

Now you're all set to set your iPod to use manual updating. Take this step on your iPod's home computer (the one with which you've been synchronizing it). iTunes stores the synchronization setting on the iPod, so when you connect the iPod to a computer, the iPod can tell iTunes whether to use automatic synchronization or manual synchronization.

To configure your iPod for manual updating, follow these steps:

1. Connect your iPod to your Mac or PC. Allow synchronization to take place.

2. Click the iPod in the Source pane. iTunes displays the iPod information.

3. On the Summary tab, select the Manually Manage Music And Video check box or the Manually Manage Music check box (depending on the iPod model). iTunes displays the warning dialog box telling you that you'll need to un-mount your iPod manually before disconnecting it.

4. Click the OK button to dismiss the warning dialog box. iTunes selects the En-able Disk Use check box (if it wasn't already selected) and makes it unavail-able so that you can't clear it manually.

5. Click the Apply button to apply the changes to the iPod.

Step 5: Load Files onto Your iPod Manually

After you've configured your iPod for manual updating, you can load files onto it manually by following these general steps:

1. Connect your iPod to the computer that contains the files you want to load. Your iPod appears in the Source pane in iTunes.

2. Drag songs (or playlists, artists, or albums) from your iTunes library to your iPod or one of its playlists.

> **tip**   *Instead of dragging songs from your iTunes library, you can drag song files from a Windows Explorer window (Windows) or a Finder window (Mac). This trick is useful for adding to the iPod songs that you haven't put in your music library.*

3. After loading all the songs you want from this computer, unmount your iPod by issuing an Eject command before you disconnect it. For example, right-click or CTRL-click (Mac) the iPod's entry in the Source pane and choose Eject.

You can then disconnect your iPod from this computer, move it to the next computer, and then add more song files by using the same technique.

> **note**   *From this point on, to add further song files to your iPod from its home computer, you must add them manually. Don't synchronize your iPod with your home computer, because synchronization will delete from the iPod all the song files your music library doesn't contain.*

Step 6: Install iTunes on Any of the Computers That Don't Have It

At this point, you're all set to add songs to your iPod from any of your computers—provided that they have iTunes and the iPod software installed on them. If not, you'll need to install these programs so that the computers can recognize the iPod and deal with it.

What you may want to do is configure your iPod for disk use (see Project 13), put the latest distribution files for iTunes (which you can get from www.apple.com/itunes/download/) and the iPod Software (www.apple.com/ipod/download/) on your iPod, and take them with you wherever you go. The problem with this approach is that Windows PCs usually won't mount a regular iPod or an iPod nano as a drive until you've installed the iPod software—so if you're hoping to install the software from the iPod and then be able to use the iPod, you're likely to be out of luck. Taking the distribution files with you on an iPod shuffle (which should always be accessible as a USB drive once connected), a non-iPod USB drive, or a CD is a better bet.

Play Your
Music Across
the Internet
from a Remote
Computer

What You'll Need:

- **iPods Covered: Any iPod**
- **Windows Software Required: Oboe Sync, Oboe Plug-in for iTunes**
- **Mac Software Required: Oboe Suite, Oboe Plug-in for iTunes**
- **Cost: $50 U.S. or less**

When Apple first added song-sharing to iTunes in iTunes 4, sharing was free and easy. You could access the songs shared by any computer by entering its IP address into a particular dialog box. This means of connection meant that you could easily connect to any computer across the Internet provided that it had its own IP address (and you knew that address).

This sharing capability was briefly very popular with iTunes users, many of whom used it to connect to their home music library from other computers (for example, at work or at school). But the capability provoked such excitement within the recording industry that Apple quickly issued an updated version of iTunes that limited sharing to the same subnet, or subdivision, of the network to which the computer was attached, thus preventing sharing across the Internet. This sharing works well enough (see Project 21) but is far more limited than many people would like.

No matter what the recording industry wants, many people want to be able to access their music from anywhere, no matter which computer they're using. The good news is that there's a service that lets you do so: MP3tunes.com's Oboe Locker service. The bad news is that you have to pay a yearly subscription if you want good-quality music and all the features—but the good news is that those features are pretty impressive.

Step 1: Understand How Oboe Locker Works

Oboe Locker provides storage space for you to store your songs online. MP3tunes.com offers two types of Oboe Locker accounts:

● **Oboe Free Locker**   An Oboe Free Locker lets you add songs to your locker from online sites but not from your own music collection. You can stream the songs back to any computer at up to 56Kbps. This quality is roughly comparable to AM radio, and most people find it too low for listening to music enjoyably. A Free Locker is a good way of testing the Oboe service to see if you want to pay for a Premium Locker.

● **Oboe Premium Locker**   An Oboe Premium Locker costs $39.99 per year and provides unlimited space for music. You can put your own songs (for example, those in your iTunes music library) in your locker using the Oboe Sync software. You can also add songs to your locker from online sites. You can synchronize your music with computers or other devices (such as some handheld tablet computers), and you can stream the songs back to any computer at 192 Kbps—high enough quality for anyone but serious audiophiles to enjoy.

You can put files in most widely used compressed-audio formats in an Oboe Locker, including AAC (iTunes' default format), MP3 (perhaps the most widely used format worldwide), WMA (Windows Media Audio—Windows Media Player's default format), and Ogg Vorbis (a free, open-source format). If a song is protected by digital rights management (DRM), you probably won't be able to use it with Oboe Locker.

You can load songs into your Oboe Locker by using three different methods:

● **Webload**   You tell Oboe Locker where to find the song on the Web by providing a URL.

● **Sideload**   You add songs from websites partnered with MP3tunes.com.

● **Oboe Sync**   You upload songs from your computer to your Oboe Premium Locker and can then keep the locker synchronized with one or more computers. Oboe Sync doesn't work with Oboe Free Lockers.

Step 2: Sign Up for Oboe Locker

To sign up for an Oboe Locker, go to the MP3tunes.com website (www.mp3tunes.com), click the Create Locker link, and then follow through the process for creating a locker.

To create a Free Locker, you need to provide a verifiable e-mail address. To create a Premium Locker, you need a credit card to pay the yearly fee upfront.

Step 3: Download and Install the Oboe Software

If you created an Oboe Premium Locker, once you've completed the signup process, follow the links to download to the Oboe Sync software.

Install Oboe Sync on Windows XP

For Windows XP, download and run the OboeSync.exe program. You may get an Internet Explorer—Security Warning dialog box such as the one shown here when you run the program. As long as you've just downloaded it from the MP3tunes.com website, the program should be safe to run.

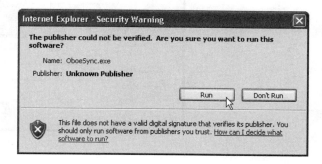

Follow through the installation routine. The default settings, to install Oboe Sync in a folder in your Program Files folder, work fine for most people. The installation routine automatically launches Oboe Sync for you unless you tell it not to do so.

Install Oboe Suite on Mac OS X

To install Oboe Suite on Mac OS X, follow these steps:

1. Download the Oboe Suite disk image file from the MP3tunes.com website.

2. If Mac OS X doesn't automatically mount the disk image for you, double-click the disk image file to mount it and open a Finder window showing its contents.

3. Drag the Oboe iTunes item and the Oboe item to your Applications folder.

4. Click the Close button (the × button) to close the Finder window, and then drag the Oboe Suite disk image to the Trash to eject it.

Step 4: Put Songs in Your Oboe Locker

You can put songs in your Oboe Locker in three ways:

- Synchronize songs from your computer into an Oboe Premium Locker.

- Webload songs from websites.

- Sideload songs from websites that support sideloading.

Synchronize Songs from Your Computer with Oboe (Premium Locker Only)

If you've installed Oboe Sync or Oboe Suite, you can use it to synchronize songs between your computer and your Oboe Premium Locker.

To do so, launch Oboe from the Start menu (Windows) or from your Applications folder (Mac). The first time you launch Oboe, read the license agreement and then click the I Accept button if you want to proceed. The Oboe dialog box appears (the Windows version is shown here).

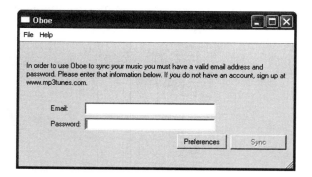

Set Oboe Synchronization Preferences

The first time you use Oboe, you need to set preferences to tell Oboe what to synchronize and how to synchronize it. Subsequent times you use Oboe, you may need to adjust these preferences—for example, if you decide to synchronize only part of your music library rather than all of it.

To set or change your preferences, follow these steps:

1. In the Oboe dialog box, click the Preferences button to display the Oboe Preferences dialog box. Figure 12-1 shows the Oboe Preferences dialog box for Windows. The Oboe Preferences dialog box for the Mac has the same controls except that it doesn't offer a Windows Media Player option button (even if you have installed the Mac version of Windows Media Player).

2. Decide whether you want to restrict Oboe to synchronizing songs in only a particular folder:

   ● You might want to start with a test folder to see how the service performs with your Internet connection.

   ● If you do want to use only a particular folder (and its subfolders), select the Only Search For My Music In A Specific Location check box, and then enter the folder in the Please Provide A Location To Search For Your Media Below text box.

   ● The best way to enter the folder name is to click the Browse button, use the resulting Browse For Folder dialog box (Windows) or Open sheet (Mac) to select the folder, and then click the OK button or the Choose button.

Figure 12-1

The Oboe Preferences dialog box.

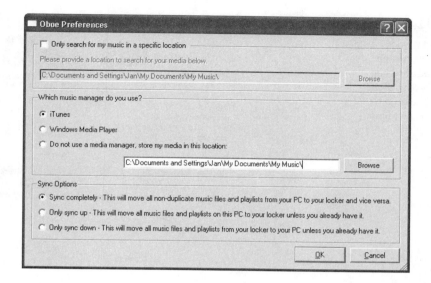

3. In the Which Music Manager Do You Use? group box, select the iTunes option button if you want to synchronize your iTunes music library. Oboe Sync also lets you synchronize Windows Media Player on Windows. You can also choose to synchronize just the files in a particular folder (and its subfolders) if you prefer: select the Do Not Use A Media Manager, Store My Media In This Location option button, and then specify the location in the text box. (Again, the easiest way to specify the location is to click the Browse button and use the resulting dialog box or sheet.)

4. In the Sync Options group box, choose what kind of synchronization to use:

   ● **Sync Completely** Synchronizes all your songs and playlists in the library or folder with your locker, so that the library (or folder) and the locker contain the same songs and playlists. Oboe ignores duplicate songs.

   ● **Only Sync Up** Copies all your songs and playlists in the library or folder to your locker.

   ● **Only Sync Down** Copies all your songs from your locker to the library or folder on your computer.

5. Click the OK button to close the Oboe Preferences dialog box. Oboe returns you to the Oboe dialog box for entering your e-mail address and password.

Perform the Synchronization

Once you've set synchronization preferences, you're ready to synchronize songs. Follow these steps:

1. Enter your Oboe e-mail address and password in the Oboe dialog.

2. Click the Sync button. Oboe connects to the server and synchronizes your songs and playlists. Figure 12-2 shows an example of synchronization on the Mac.

Figure 12-2

Synchronizing your Oboe Locker takes a while, especially when you're uploading all the songs from your computer for the first time.

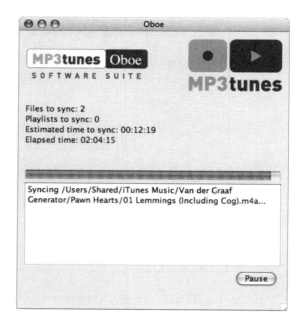

3. When Oboe has finished synchronizing files, it displays a message box telling you how many songs it has synchronized.

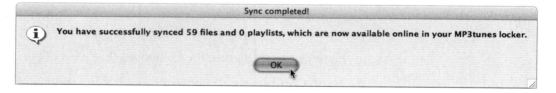

4. Click the OK button to chose the message box, and then choose File | Exit (Windows) or Oboe | Quit Oboe (Mac) to close Oboe.

Webload Files into Your Locker

When you find songs you like on the Web, you can webload them into your Oboe Locker. To webload a song, follow these steps:

1. Find a song you like on the Web. For example, you might find a song at your favorite artist's site.

2. Select the address in the Address Bar, and then copy it.

3. Open a new browser window, go to the MP3tunes.com website, and log in to your Oboe Locker.

4. Click the Webload link near the top of the page. The Webload page appears (see Figure 12-3).

Figure 12-3

Use the Webload page of the MP3tunes.com website to load a song from the Web into your Oboe Locker.

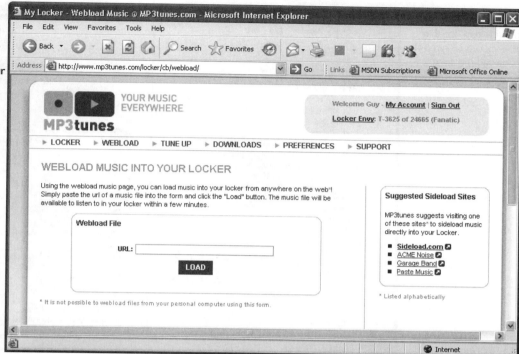

5. Paste the URL of the song into the URL box in the Webload File box, and then click the Load button. MP3tunes.com adds the file to your Oboe Locker, and then displays a window to confirm that it has done so.

Sideload Files into Your Locker

As you saw in the previous section, adding a song to your Oboe Locker via webloading is easy—but there's an even easier way. *Sideloading* means loading from a site affiliated with MP3tunes.com, such as Sideload.com (www.sideload.com).

Sideload-capable sites display an SL symbol next to a song, as in Figure 12-4. To sideload the song, simply click the SL symbol. If you're not currently logged in to your Oboe Locker, you'll be prompted to log in.

> **tip**   *If you use Internet Explorer or Firefox, you can use sideloading for sites other than those that directly support it. Go to the MP3tunes.com website, click the Download link, and then download and install the Oboe Sideload plug-in for your browser. These plug-ins make the browser display the SL sideload symbol next to links to song files, so that you can sideload them with a single click.*

Figure 12-4

On a sideload-capable site, click the SL symbol to sideload the song into your locker.

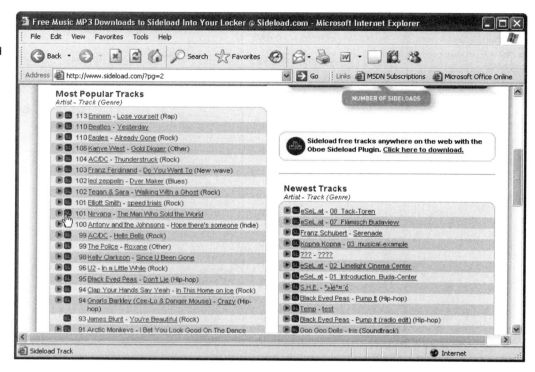

Step 5: Stream Files from Your Locker to a Web Browser

Once you've placed songs in your Oboe Locker, you can play them from any browser. To play songs from your Locker, follow these steps:

1. Launch your browser and steer it to www.mp3tunes.com.

2. Sign into your Oboe Locker. (If you're using a computer with which you've signed in to your Oboe Locker before, your browser may sign you in automatically.)

3. Click the Locker link to display the contents of your Oboe Locker.

4. Use the Artists list, Albums list, or Playlists list to find the song you want, and then click the song to start it playing (see Figure 12-5).

Step 6: Play Songs from Your Oboe Locker Using iTunes

Playing songs from your Oboe Locker via a web browser is easy, but if you're used to controlling your music with iTunes, you might prefer to use iTunes instead. To use iTunes, follow these steps:

Figure 12-5

The Oboe Locker interface lets you browse and play music using easy-to-grasp controls.

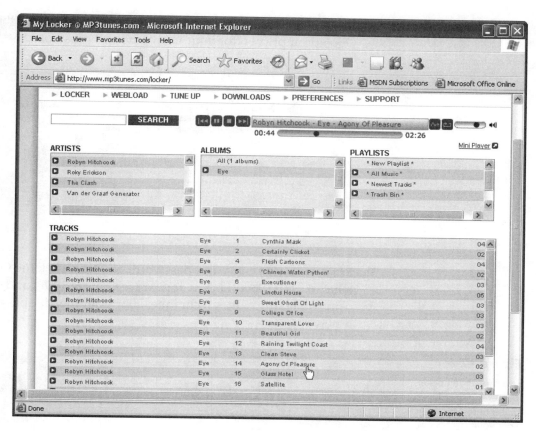

1. If you haven't installed Oboe Sync or Oboe Suite on this computer, download and install the iTunes Plug-ins to make iTunes aware of Oboe Locker:

   ● Open your browser, and then go to the MP3tunes.com website.

   ● Click the Download link, and then download and install the iTunes Plug-in for PC or the iTunes Plug-in for Mac.

2. Open iTunes.

3. If iTunes isn't set to look for shared music, set it up now:

   ● In Windows, choose Edit | Preferences or press CTRL-COMMA or CTRL-Y to display the iTunes dialog box. On the Mac, choose iTunes | Preferences or press either ⌘-COMMA or ⌘-Y to display the Preferences dialog box.

   ● Click the Sharing tab to display it.

   ● Select the Look For Shared Music check box.

   ● Click the OK button to close the dialog box.

4. In the Source pane, click the Oboe Locker item under the Shared category. Oboe prompts you for your username and password, as shown here:

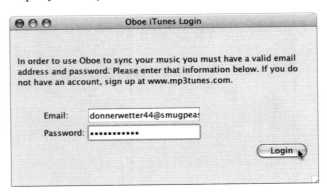

5. Enter your username and password, and then click the OK button. The contents of your Oboe Locker appear (see Figure 12-6), and you can play them using standard iTunes techniques. For example, double-click a song to start it playing.

Figure 12-6

Use the Oboe Locker item under the Shared category to play songs from your Oboe Locker through iTunes.

Use Your iPod as a Portable External Disk

What You'll Need:

- iPods Covered: Any iPod
- Cost: Free

Whichever model you have, your iPod packs an impressive amount of storage into a small and easy-to-carry form. Depending on the iPod model, you can carry plenty of music, thousands of photos, and even enough video to keep you cross-eyed for days. But you can also use your iPod to take with you any other kinds of files you need—even huge files. This project shows you how to make the most of your iPod's capability to act as an external disk.

note *If you use a Mac, you may also be able to boot your Mac from a hard drive–based iPod such as the iPod with video. See Project 22 for details. Whichever type of computer you use, you may need to recover your music library from your iPod if your computer gets damaged. Project 15 shows you how to do so.*

Step 1: Understand the Limitations of Your iPod as a Disk

Before you start using your iPod as a disk, it's a good idea to understand the iPod's limitations. Table 13-1 lists the current iPod models, the storage types they use, what they're suitable for, and considerations for using them as disks.

Even when connected via a USB 2 connection, the iPod with video gives relatively slow performance because its hard disk is slower than those in current desktops and laptops. The hard disk has a low rotational speed (4200 revolutions per minute) that's more than adequate for playing back video or audio and that helps economize on battery use, but it means that you should look to your iPod for portability rather than performance as a hard disk.

iPod model	Storage type	Suitable for	Considerations
iPod with video	Hard disk	Carrying large files or applications Backing up your hard disk Booting a Mac (see Project 22); Apple doesn't support this usage.	Make sure the USB connection is powering the iPod; if it's not, using the iPod as a disk will drain the battery quickly.
iPod nano	Flash memory	Carrying medium-size files or applications	Flash memory delivers good performance at small battery cost, but the iPod nano's smaller capacity prevents you from carrying large amounts of files.
iPod shuffle	Flash memory	Carrying essential files	The iPod shuffle lets you set aside an area of the memory for files.

Table 13-1   iPod Models, Storage Types, and Suitable Uses

note *If you're using your iPod with a Mac, and the iPod is formatted with the Mac OS Extended file system, you can put any size of file on the iPod providing that there's enough free space. Even if you have an iPod with video (or another hard disk–based iPod model) that has many gigabytes of hard disk space free, the biggest single file that you can put on it from a PC is 4 GB. This limitation is because the iPod uses the FAT32 file system, which can't handle files larger than 4 GB. But needs must when the devil drives, and there's a workaround for this problem, as you'll see in step 5.*

Step 2: Enable Disk Mode

To use your iPod as an external drive, you must first enable disk mode. "Disk mode" simply means telling your computer to use your iPod as an external disk rather than as a special iPod-like disk. Once you've turned on disk mode, you can copy to your iPod any files and folders that will fit on it.

note *You can copy song files, video files, and playlists to your iPod in disk mode, but you won't be able to play them on the iPod. When you use iTunes (or another media-management application, such as EphPod) to copy media files to your iPod, it adds them to the iPod's database, so you can play the files on the iPod. But when you add files to the iPod manually, the iPod's database doesn't know the files are there, and you can't play them.*

To enable disk mode on your iPod, follow these steps:

1. Connect your iPod to your computer as usual.

2. Launch iTunes if it doesn't launch automatically.

3. In the Source pane, click the icon for your iPod.

4. Click the Summary tab if it isn't already displayed.

5. Select the Enable Disk Use check box. iTunes displays the following warning dialog box, telling you that using disk mode requires you to manually unmount the iPod before each disconnect, even when you're automatically updating music:

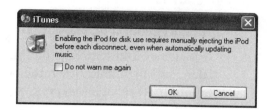

6. Select the Do Not Warn Me Again check box and then click the OK button.

7. For an iPod shuffle, drag the slider along the More Songs—More Data continuum to specify how much space you want to devote to data and how much to songs.

8. Click the Apply button. iTunes applies the change to the iPod.

Once you've enabled disk mode, your iPod appears to Windows Explorer as a removable drive. Windows Explorer automatically assigns a drive letter to the drive, so you can access it as you would any other drive connected to your computer. On the Mac, your iPod appears on the Desktop and in Finder windows.

To eject your iPod, take any of the following actions:

- In the Source pane in iTunes, click the Eject icon next to your iPod's name. (This is by far the easiest means of ejection.)

- In the Source pane in iTunes, right-click or CTRL-click (Mac) the icon for your iPod and then choose Eject.

- In the Source pane in iTunes, select the icon for your iPod and then click the Eject iPod button in the lower-right corner of the iTunes window.

- On Windows, choose Start | My Computer to open a Windows Explorer window to My Computer view, right-click the icon for your iPod, and choose Eject from the shortcut menu to eject it.

- On the Mac, drag the desktop icon for your iPod to the Trash.

When your iPod displays the "OK to disconnect" message or its regular menus on its screen, you can safely disconnect it.

Step 3: Transfer Files to and from Your iPod

When your iPod is in disk mode, you can transfer files to it by using Windows Explorer (Windows), the Finder (Mac), or another file-management application of your choice. (You can transfer files by using the command prompt, if you so choose.)

Force Disk Mode

If your USB port is underpowered, you may need to force your iPod to enter disk mode. To do so, follow these steps:

1. Connect your iPod via USB as usual.

2. Move the Hold switch to the On position and then back to the Off position, and then hold down the Select button and the Menu button for about five seconds to reboot your iPod.

3. When your iPod displays the Apple logo, hold down the Select button and the Play button. Your iPod sends the computer an electronic prod that forces the computer to recognize it.

caution *If your iPod appears in the My Computer window as a drive named Removable Drive, and Windows Explorer claims the disk isn't formatted, chances are you've connected a Mac-formatted iPod to your PC. Windows Explorer can't read the HFS Plus disk format that Mac iPods use, so the iPod appears to be unformatted. (HFS Plus is one of the disk formats Mac OS X can use and is also called the Mac OS Extended format.)*

You can create and delete folders on your iPod as you would any other drive. But be sure you don't mess with the iPod's system folders, such as the Calendars folder, the Contacts folder, the Notes folder, the Photos folder, and the iPod_Control folder.

Step 4: Connect Your iPod to Another Computer to Transfer Files

Keeping files on your iPod as backups or for security is handy, but what you'll often need to do is use your iPod to transfer files from one computer to another.

When you connect your iPod to another computer, iTunes may point out that the iPod is linked to another music library and prompt you to change the link to the music library on this computer, as shown here. Click the No button to prevent iTunes from replacing all the music on your iPod.

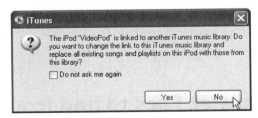

You should be able to suppress this prompt by holding down CTRL+ALT (Windows) or ⌘+OPTION (Mac) from when you connect your iPod to the computer until when the iPod appears in the Source pane in iTunes, but sometimes iTunes seems to miss your pressing these keys.

Step 5: Use Your iPod to Transfer Huge Files

If you're using a Mac and you have a Mac-formatted iPod, you can load any size file onto it up to the iPod's capacity. For example, if you have a 60 GB iPod with 40 GB free, you can load a 39 GB file onto it. But if you're using your iPod with Windows, you can't put any file larger than 4 GB on your iPod because the iPod uses the FAT32 file system. Four gigabytes is a pretty hefty file, but if you create large files (for example, videos), you may need to be able to transfer files larger than this—and perhaps larger than can fit on a recordable DVD.

This section shows you how to circumvent this limitation on a Windows PC. The procedure is ugly, as it involves the following:

- Reformatting your iPod with the NTFS file system. Reformatting wipes all the files off the iPod, so before you start, you'll need to back up any file you want to keep.

- Using the iPod to transfer the files. You won't be able to use the iPod for music, videos, or photos at this stage.

- Restoring the iPod to the FAT32 file system using iTunes. Restoring the iPod wipes its file system again. After you've restored the iPod, you can use it for songs, videos, and photos as normal—but you'll be stuck with the 4 GB restriction again.

If you've only ever used your iPod with a Mac, your iPod is Mac formatted—that is, its hard disk or flash memory is formatted using the Mac OS Extended file system. If you've used your iPod with a PC and then moved it back to the Mac without restoring it, the iPod may still be formatted with the FAT32 file system. If in doubt, see the nearby sidebar for details on how to check which file system your iPod is using.

note *If you've read the small print on the iPod's box, you'll know that Apple measures the iPod's capacity in "marketing" gigabytes (1GB = 1 billion bytes) rather than real gigabytes (1GB = 1024 × 1024 × 1024 bytes, or 1,073,741,824 bytes). This deliberate confusion is why a 60 GB iPod has less than 56 GB of free space (the iPod's operating system also takes up some space). The amount of free space shown at the bottom of the iTunes window when you select the iPod in the Source pane is measured in real gigabytes.*

Reformat a Windows iPod with the NTFS File System

To reformat an iPod so that you can use it to transfer large files between Windows computers, take a steadying breath, and then follow these steps:

1. If disk mode isn't already turned on, turn it on now. (See "Enable Disk Mode," earlier in this chapter, for instructions.)

2. Choose File | Exit or click the Close button (the × button) to quit iTunes.

3. Choose Start | My Computer to open a My Computer window.

Check Whether Your iPod Is Formatted with the Mac OS Extended File System

If you're not sure whether your iPod uses the Mac OS Extended file system or FAT32, you can find out in either of these ways:

- **On the iPod**   Go to the Settings menu, select the About item, and then scroll down to the bottom. If there's a Format line that says "Windows," the iPod is using FAT32. If there's no Format line, the iPod is using Mac OS Extended.

- **In iTunes**   In the Source pane, click the iPod's entry, and then look at the Format readout on the Summary tab. This readout says "Macintosh" for Mac OS Extended or "Windows" for FAT32.

4. In the list of drives, right-click the iPod's icon and choose Properties from the shortcut menu to display the Properties dialog box for the iPod.

5. Click the Hardware tab to display its contents (see Figure 13-1).

6. In the All Disk Drives list box, click the Apple iPod USB Device entry, and then click the Properties button to display the Apple iPod USB Device Properties dialog box.

7. Click the Policies tab to display its contents (see Figure 13-2).

8. Select the Optimize For Performance option button instead of the Optimize For Quick Removal option button (which is selected by default). Selecting Optimize For Performance persuades Windows to allow you to format the drive with NTFS rather than FAT32.

Figure 13-1

On the Hardware tab of the iPod's Properties dialog box, select the Apple iPod USB Device entry, and then click the Properties button.

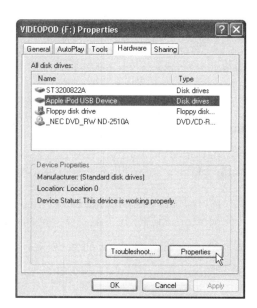

Figure 13-2

Before you can format the iPod with the NTFS file system, you must change the iPod's policy from Optimize For Quick Removal to Optimize For Performance.

9. Select the Enable Write Caching On The Disk check box if you want to get the best performance when copying files to and from the iPod. Enabling write caching puts you at slight risk of data loss if your computer or iPod crashes, but if you're copying files to and from the iPod rather than creating original files on the iPod, the risk is minimal.

10. Click the OK button to close the Apple iPod USB Device Properties dialog box, and then click the OK button to close the iPod's Properties dialog box.

11. Back in the Windows Explorer window, right-click the iPod's icon and choose Format from the shortcut menu to display the Format dialog box (see Figure 13-3).

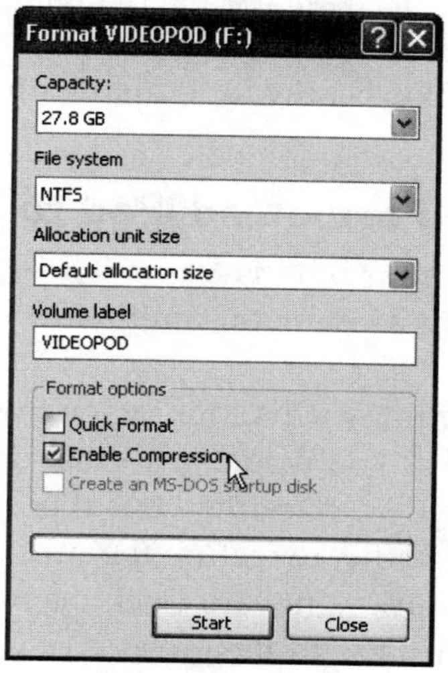

Figure 13-3

Use the Format dialog box to format the iPod's hard drive or flash memory with the NTFS file system.

12. In the File System drop-down list, choose NTFS.

13. In the Allocation Unit Size drop-down list, select the Default Allocation Size item.

14. Select the Enable Compression check box if you want to be able to shoehorn as much data onto your iPod as possible. Enabling compression reduces disk performance a bit, but it helps you fit more data on the disk provided that the data is compressible. (If the data is already fully compressed, NTFS can't compress it any more.)

15. Select the Quick Format check box if you want to perform a quick format rather than a full format. A quick format saves time, but it's a better idea to perform a full format to make sure the iPod is in good shape.

16. Click the Start button. Windows displays a warning dialog box to make sure you understand you're about to erase all the data on the disk, as shown here.

17. Click the OK button. Windows formats the iPod and then displays the Format Complete message box, as shown here.

18. Click the OK button to close the message box, and then click the Close button to close the Format dialog box.

Your iPod is now formatted with NTFS.

Use Your NTFS-Formatted iPod to Transfer Large Files

Now that your iPod is formatted with NTFS, you can copy files larger than 4 GB to it and from it—but you can't use it with iTunes, play music or videos on it, or view photos.

Use Windows Explorer or another file-management tool to copy files to and from your iPod as you would any other drive.

Before disconnecting your iPod, you must dismount your iPod using the Safely Remove Hardware feature (because you optimized the iPod for performance rather than for quick removal). Click the Safely Remove Hardware icon on the notification area (the icon with the green arrow pointing to the left, and then choose the Safely

Remove USB Mass Storage Device item from the menu that appears, as shown here. (If you have two or more USB drives connected to your computer, make sure you get the right one.)

Restore Your iPod to FAT32 and Full Functionality

When you've finished transferring large files from point A to point B with your iPod, you'll need to restore it to FAT32 to regain its full functionality. To restore your iPod, follow these steps:

1. Plug the iPod into your computer.

2. Choose Start | My Computer to open a My Computer window.

3. In the list of drives, right-click the iPod's icon and choose Properties from the shortcut menu to display the Properties dialog box for the iPod.

4. Click the Hardware tab to display its contents.

5. In the All Disk Drives list box, click the Apple iPod USB Device entry, and then click the Properties button to display the Apple iPod USB Device Properties dialog box.

6. Click the Policies tab to display its contents.

7. Select the Optimize For Quick Removal option button. (You're doing this so that you don't need to use the Safely Remove Hardware icon each time you disconnect your iPod.)

8. Click the OK button to close the Apple iPod USB Device Properties dialog box, and then click the OK button to close the iPod's Properties dialog box.

9. iTunes may launch automatically; if not, launch it manually. iTunes displays a dialog box saying that it has detected an iPod in recovery mode, as shown here:

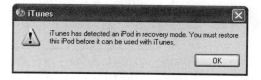

10. Click the OK button. iTunes selects the iPod in the Source pane and displays the Summary tab.

11. Click the Restore button. iTunes checks the iPod Updater site for the latest version of the iPod Updater software. If there's a newer version, iTunes downloads it.

12. iTunes confirms that you want to restore the iPod, warning you that all your songs and data will be erased, as shown here:

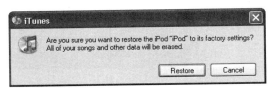

13. Click the Restore button if you're sure you can dispose of whatever is stored on the iPod.

14. Wait while iTunes completes the restore process. When it has finished, iTunes displays the dialog box shown here.

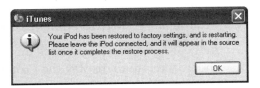

15. Click the OK button. iTunes displays the iPod Setup Assistant so that you can assign your iPod a name and choose whether to load items onto it automatically.

16. Type the name for the iPod, choose options, and then click the OK button.

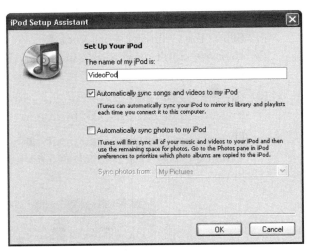

By now, chances are that your iPod contains some important files. If you don't have copies of those files elsewhere (for example, on your computer), you should back them up. See Project 15 for instructions on backing up your iPod.

cnet See a CNET video on using your iPod as a hard disk drive at http://diyipod.cnet.com

Make Your iPod an Invaluable Companion for Your Digital Camera

What You'll Need:

- iPods Covered: iPod with video, fourth-generation iPod with color screen, third or fourth-generation iPod without color screen
- Hardware Required: Camera, cable or camera connector, card reader
- Cost: $30–$75 U.S.

These days, it seems that every time you look at an ad for digital cameras, the manufacturers have bumped up the resolution by a megapixel or two. These constant increases are great for capturing more detail in your photos (assuming the camera's sensor is up to the job), but they mean that the photo files keep getting bigger. Given the modest amount of storage in many digital cameras, and given the expense of buying a larger memory card, you're likely to find that you need to keep offloading photos so that you can take more. If you have your computer to hand, that's tedious but not much of a problem—but if you're away from your computer, it can quickly become a problem.

But in your pocket is your iPod—with plenty of space on its hard disk. Why not offload the photos onto that for the time being so that you can take more?

Step 1: Get the Hardware

To transfer photos from your digital camera to your iPod, you need the following items:

- **Digital camera** Some digital cameras directly support the Apple iPod Camera Connector (see www.apple.com/ipod/compatibility/cameracon-nector.html for the latest list). That means you plug one end of a USB cable into your camera and the other into the iPod Camera Connector, and you're away. If your camera doesn't appear on the list, you should be fine as long as the camera uses a removable memory card that you can put in a card reader. You then attach the card reader to the iPod Camera Connector.

- **Apple iPod Camera Connector** The iPod Camera Connector ($29 U.S.; http://store.apple.com) is one of the smallest iPod accessories around—a flat little barrel with a dock connector at the top and a USB socket at the bottom. Figure 14-1 shows the iPod Camera Connector.

- **USB cable or memory card reader**   If your camera supports USB data transfer, it probably came with a USB cable—most likely one with a mini-USB plug for the camera's end and a full-size USB plug for the computer's end. If your camera doesn't support USB data transfer or doesn't work directly

Figure 14-1

The iPod Camera Connector is small enough to fit in any pocket or even in your camera's case.

with the iPod Camera Connector, you'll need a USB memory card reader that fits the type of memory card your camera uses (for example, CompactFlash, Memory Stick, or SD card).

Step 2: Transfer Photos to Your iPod

To transfer photos to your iPod, follow these steps:

1. Connect your camera or the memory card reader to the iPod Camera Connector.

2. Connect the iPod Camera Connector to your iPod via the dock connector port. Your iPod displays the Import screen, which shows the number of photos

Transfer Photos to a Third-Generation or Fourth-Generation iPod without Color Screen

If you have a third-generation iPod or a fourth-generation iPod that *doesn't* have a color screen (a rarity; Apple made them for only a short time), the Apple iPod Camera Connector won't work—but you can get a different accessory that will let you read memory cards.

You'll need to find the Belkin Media Reader for iPod, an older device that performs a similar function and works with third-generation iPods. At this writing, you can find the Media Reader for iPod through Amazon.com, eBay, and similar sites.

The Media Reader for iPod (shown in the next illustration) is a bit larger than a third-generation iPod and runs off four AAA batteries, so it's not as handy as the iPod Camera Connector—but it's effective, and it works with Type 1 and Type 2 CompactFlash cards, SmartMedia cards, Secure Digital (SD) cards, Memory Stick cards, and MultiMedia Card (MMC) cards.

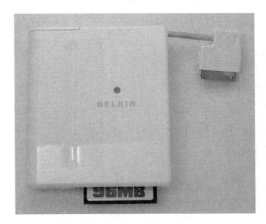

To use the Media Reader, insert the media card you want to read in the appropriate slot on the Media Reader, and then plug the dock connector on the Media Reader into the iPod.

The Media Reader's user interface consists of a single LED on the top of the unit:

- A solid green light indicates that the Media Reader is on and the battery has plenty of power.

- A flashing green light indicates that the Media Reader is transferring data.

- A solid amber light indicates that the battery is low.

The Media Reader works almost exactly in the same way as the iPod Camera Connector.

the camera or card contains and the amount of space they take up, as shown here.

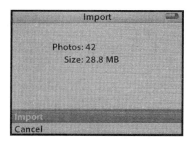

note *If your iPod doesn't display the Import screen, choose Photos | Photo Import | Import Photos to display the Import screen manually.*

3. Make sure the Import Photos item is selected (scroll if necessary), and then press the Select button to start the import process. Your iPod displays the Photo Import screen to show you the progress, as shown here.

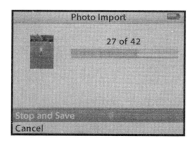

4. When the import is finished, your iPod displays the Import Done screen, as shown here.

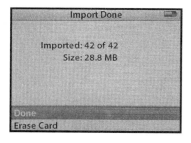

note *Most digital cameras save their images as JPEG files by default, but many can also create RAW (uncompressed) image files. Many digital cameras also have a movie mode that takes a series of lower-resolution images in sequence and saves them in a format such as Audio Video Interleave (AVI). If your digital camera uses standard formats, you can transfer both RAW files and movie files to your iPod.*

Step 3: Delete the Photos from the Memory Card

Once you've transferred the photos to the iPod, you'll probably want to delete them from the memory card so that you can put it back in your camera and take more photos. You can delete them directly from the iPod, but you may prefer to check the photos on the iPod, and then delete the photos by using your camera's features. (For example, many cameras have a Format Card feature or a Delete All feature).

To delete all the photos from the memory card, follow these steps:

1. On the Import Done screen, scroll down to the Erase Card item, and then press the Select button. Your iPod displays the Erase Card screen (shown here).

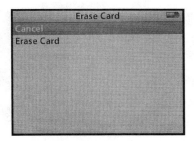

2. Scroll down to the Erase Card item, and then press the Select button to erase the contents of the memory card.

After erasing the card, or after you select the Done item on the Import Done screen, your iPod displays the Photos screen, from which you can check the details of the rolls you've imported.

Step 4: View the Photos on Your iPod

Once you've copied the photos to your iPod, it's a good idea to view them quickly to make sure they've transferred properly before you delete them from the camera's memory card. Of course, they should have transferred fine—but better safe than sorry.

 You can view JPEG photos on your iPod, but you can't view RAW files. Each RAW file appears as a symbol with the word RAW inside it.

To view the photos on your iPod, follow these steps:

1. From the Photo Import screen, scroll down to select the roll, and then press the Select button to display its screen, as shown here.

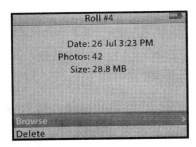

2. Select the Browse item (it should be selected already), and then press the Select button to display thumbnails of the photos, as shown here.

3. Scroll to select the photo you want to view, and then press the Select button to display it full screen. You can then press the Next button to display the next photo, press the Previous button to display the previous photo, or scroll rapidly through photos using the Click wheel.

4. Press the Menu button to return to the thumbnails, and then press it again to return to the roll's screen.

Step 5: Delete a Roll of Photos from the iPod

Normally, you'll just add photos to your iPod while away from your computer—but if you find that a roll isn't worth keeping, you can delete its contents. To do so, follow these steps:

1. From the Photo Import screen, scroll down to select the roll, and then press the Select button to display its screen.

2. Check the roll's date and the number of photos on it to make sure you're deleting the right roll.

3. Scroll up to the Delete Roll item, and then press the Select button. Your iPod displays the Delete Roll screen, as shown here.

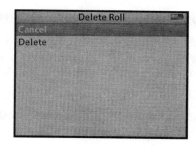

4. Scroll down to the Delete item and press the Select button.

Step 6: Transfer Photos from Your iPod to Your Computer

When you return to your computer, transfer the photos from your iPod to your computer so that you can work with them. You'll find the photos in your iPod's DCIM folder. (DCIM is the industry standard abbreviation for digital camera images).

Inside the DCIM folder, you'll find a folder for each roll of photos you stored on the iPod. The folders are numbered sequentially with a three-digit number and APPLE, starting with 100APPLE, 101APPLE, and so on.

Transfer Photos from Your iPod to Your PC

To transfer photos from your iPod to your PC, follow these steps:

1. Connect your iPod to your PC. If your iPod is set to synchronize with iTunes, allow it to do so.

2. Choose Start | My Computer to open a My Computer window.

3. Enable disk mode on your iPod (see "Enable Disk Mode" in Project 13) if it's not already enabled.

4. Double-click the drive allocated to your iPod to display its contents in a window.

5. Double-click the DCIM folder to open it. You'll see a folder for each roll of photos.

6. Copy or move the folders to your hard disk by using standard Windows Explorer techniques.

7. After importing or copying all the photos to your PC, delete the photos from your iPod if appropriate. (You might also choose to keep the photos on your iPod as a backup).

Transfer Photos from Your iPod to Your Mac

To transfer photos from your iPod to your Mac, follow these steps:

1. Connect your iPod to your Mac. If your iPod is set to synchronize with iTunes, allow it to do so.

2. Enable disk mode on your iPod (see "Enable Disk Mode" in Project 13) if it's not already enabled.

3. Double-click your iPod's icon on the desktop to open a Finder window to its contents.

4. Double-click the DCIM folder to open it. You'll see a folder for each roll of photos.

5. To load your photos into iPhoto, drag each folder in turn into the iPhoto window and drop it there:

   - To add the photos to your Photo Library, select your Photo Library in the Source pane, and then drop the photos in the viewing area.

   - To add the photos to an existing album, select the album in the Source pane, and then drop the photos in the viewing area.

   - To create a new album and put the pictures of a folder into it, drag the folder to the Source pane in iPhoto and drop it in open space. iPhoto creates a new album with the name of the folder.

6. To copy the photos to a folder on your hard disk, use normal Finder techniques.

7. After importing or copying all the photos to your Mac, delete the photos from your iPod if appropriate. (You might also choose to keep the photos on your iPod as a backup).

That's all you need to know. You're ready to pack your camera bag and head out the door for an extended shooting session.

Back Up Your Music Library or Recover It from Your iPod

What You'll Need:

- iPod Covered: **Any iPod**
- Hardware Required: **An external hard disk**
- Windows Software Required: **EphPod**
- Mac Software Required: **PodWorks**
- Cost: **$75–$150 U.S.**

By the time you've ripped all your CDs, and perhaps ripped songs from analog sources such as your LPs and cassettes, you'll have invested a serious amount of time in your music library. If you've bought songs from the iTunes Music Store or other online stores, you'll have a direct financial investment as well.

All your investment of time and money can go in the zap of a lightning bolt into nearby electric lines, the slosh of a cup of coffee over your laptop, or the grinding to death of your computer's hard drive. Before any of these or similar mishaps happen, back up your music library to either to a hard drive or to an online service such as Oboe—or both—so that you can recover your songs. This project shows you how to do that.

If your iPod contains all (or even a good part) of your music library, you can also recover the songs from it using special software. This project also shows you how to recover songs from your iPod.

Step 1: Back Up Your Music Library

To protect your music library against loss, you need to back it up. If possible, the best strategy is to have a copy of your music library on an external hard disk and another copy stored online. Copying to an external hard disk is fast, but there's always the risk that it will suffer the same fate as your computer (for example, a fire or flood). Copying to an online drive is far slower, even with a high-speed Internet connection, but it ensures your data is safe from local devastation.

You may also want to back up your music library to DVDs.

Back Up Your Music Library to an External Hard Disk

The easiest way to back up your music library is to use an external hard disk connected via USB 2 or FireWire:

- **USB 2**   USB 2 can transfer data at up to 480 megabits per second (Mbps). All recent Windows PCs include USB 2, making USB 2 the best choice for an external hard disk for a Windows PC.

caution   *USB 1.0 and 1.1 are far slower than USB 2.0, managing only 12Mbps at most. This speed (if that's the word) is far too slow for using external drives satisfactorily.*

- **FireWire**   FireWire comes in two varieties, FireWire 400 (400 Mbps) and FireWire 800 (800 Mbps). Both speeds are plenty fast enough for external drives. All recent Macs have both FireWire 400 and USB 2 built in. Some higher-end Macs also include FireWire 800. If your Mac has FireWire 800, a FireWire 800 drive will give you the best performance. Otherwise, FireWire 400 and USB 2 are pretty evenly matched.

tip   *An old iPod that has been displaced from your affections by a newer model can be a great backup device.*

Once you've connected your external hard disk to your PC or Mac, you can back up your songs by copying your music folder to the hard disk:

- **Windows**   By default, iTunes stores your songs in the My Music\iTunes\ iTunes Music folder. By copying the iTunes folder, you can back up the iTunes Library.itl file and the iTunes Music Library.xml file, which contain the metadata about your music library, as well as the iTunes Music folder.

note   *If you've stored your music in a different folder, you'll need to back that folder up instead. If you're not sure where the songs are, choose Edit | Preferences (Windows) or iTunes | Preferences (Mac), click the Advanced tab, and look at the iTunes Music Folder Location readout on the General subtab. Be sure to back up the iTunes Library.itl file (Windows) or iTunes Library file (Mac) and the iTunes Music Library.xml file from your iTunes Music folder to get the metadata.*

- **Mac**   By default, iTunes stores your songs in the iTunes/iTunes Music folder inside your ~/Music folder (the Music folder in your home folder). By copying the iTunes folder, you can back up the iTunes Library file and the iTunes Music Library.xml file, which contain the metadata about your music library, as well as the iTunes Music folder.

> **note** As you almost certainly know, you should back up your other valuable files as well. Rather than back up just your songs, you should develop a comprehensive backup strategy that includes your songs together with all your other files.

Back Up Your Music Library to DVDs

If you have a DVD burner, another possibility is to back up your music library to DVDs from iTunes. The problem is that your music library likely will require several DVDs to contain it all, which makes the process cumbersome. If you choose to use this backup method, follow these steps:

1. In iTunes, choose File | New Playlist. iTunes creates a new playlist and displays an edit box around its name in the Source pane.

2. Type a name for the playlist (for example, **Backup of All Songs**) and then press ENTER (Windows) or RETURN (Mac).

3. Drag the Library item from the top of the Source pane to the new playlist to add all the songs in the library to the playlist.

4. Click the new playlist to select it.

5. Click the Burn Data Disc button in the lower-right corner of the iTunes window.

6. Insert a blank recordable DVD in your computer's DVD drive.

7. If iTunes warns you that the songs in the playlist won't fit on one disc, as shown here, click the Data Discs button to start the burn with multiple DVDs.

8. When iTunes prompts you to insert another disc, insert the DVD, and let iTunes proceed with the burn.

9. Label the DVDs and store them safely so that you will be able to find and identify them when you need them.

To make sure you can restore your entire music library, you should repeat the backup process frequently. If it involves many DVDs, you may feel unwilling to devote that much time and effort. One shortcut is to note the date at which you backed up the music library, and then use that date as the cutoff point for backing up new additions to the music library. Sort your music library by date in descending order so that the newest songs appear at the top of the list. Working by date, select the songs that you've added since the last backup, add them to a playlist, and then burn that playlist to DVD (or CD, if they'll fit).

The disadvantage to this shortcut is that you lose the details of any songs that you've deleted from your music library and songs whose rating or information (for example, tags) you've changed. You may feel that this small loss is a price worth paying for not having to perform a multi-DVD backup each time.

Use Oboe to Back Up Your Music Library Online

One of the best ways to back up your music is to store it on servers online. That way, even if your computer goes south, your external drive buys the farm, and your DVDs turn out to have become corrupted, you can still recover your music.

At this writing, the best option for backing up your iTunes music library is Oboe Locker, a service offered by MP3tunes.com (www.mp3tunes.com). See Project 12 for instructions on signing up for, installing, and using Oboe Locker. You'll need the Oboe Premium Locker service, which costs $39.99 U.S. a year at this writing, rather than the Oboe Free Locker, but it's a pretty good deal. Apart from protecting your songs, Oboe Locker also lets you play your music on any computer connected to the Internet at a 192Kbps bitrate—plenty good enough for enjoyable listening.

Step 2: Recover Your Music Library from Your iPod

If you have synchronized your full music library onto your iPod, your iPod effectively contains a backup of the music library. If your music library suffers a disaster, you can recover all the songs from your iPod—but not by using iTunes, which Apple has restricted (for copyright reasons) to copying songs to but not from an iPod. Instead, you need to use special software that isn't bound by iTunes' limitations.

This section shows you how to use the freeware EphPod to recover your music library from your iPod on Windows and the inexpensive PodWorks to recover your music library on Mac OS X.

Recover Your Music Library with EphPod on Windows

EphPod (pronounced *eef*pod rather than *eff*pod, and downloadable from www.ephpod .com and other sites) is a free and very full-featured application for managing iPods on Windows. Technically, EphPod is donationware rather than freeware—the author invites you to contribute to his beer fund and even allows you to request that a donation be spent on something better than beer.

Get and Install EphPod

Download the latest stable version of EphPod from the EphPod website (www.ephpod .com), and then double-click the file to install it. Follow through the installation procedure, which is straightforward, and then launch EphPod from the Start menu.

Figure 15-1

Identify your iPod to EphPod.

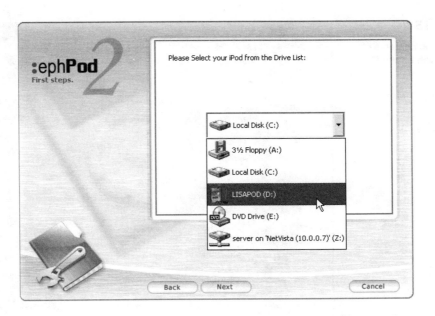

> **note**   *If you're using Windows XP with Service Pack 2 or later, when you double-click the EphPod distribution file, you may see an Open File—Security Warning dialog box warning you that the publisher cannot be verified. This is because EphPod is not signed with a digital signature. But if you've just downloaded the file from the EphPod website, it should be fine.*

The first time you run EphPod, it prompts you to select the drive that represents your iPod (see Figure 15-1).

View the Contents of Your iPod

Once you've identified your iPod, EphPod displays the contents of your iPod. You can view them by playlist, by artist, by album, by genre, by song, by comment (if you've added any), or by recent items. Figure 15-2 shows the song database with the Artists category selected.

Recover Song Files from Your iPod with EphPod

To recover song files, first configure downloading options:

1. Click the Configure EphPod button on the toolbar, or choose Extras | Configuration, to display the Configuration dialog box.

2. Click the Advanced Options tab to display its contents (see Figure 15-3).

3. Make sure the Preserve MP3 Filename In Copy check box is cleared.

4. Make sure the Use Internal Copy Routines option button is selected.

5. To improve performance, increase the size of the Internal Copying Buffer Size drop-down list from its default setting of 1024 KB to 4096 KB.

Figure 15-2

Viewing the contents of
an iPod with EphPod.

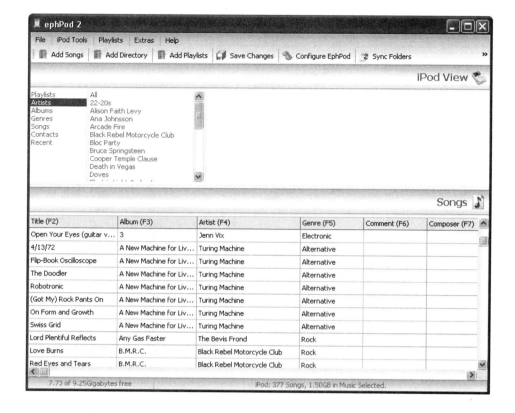

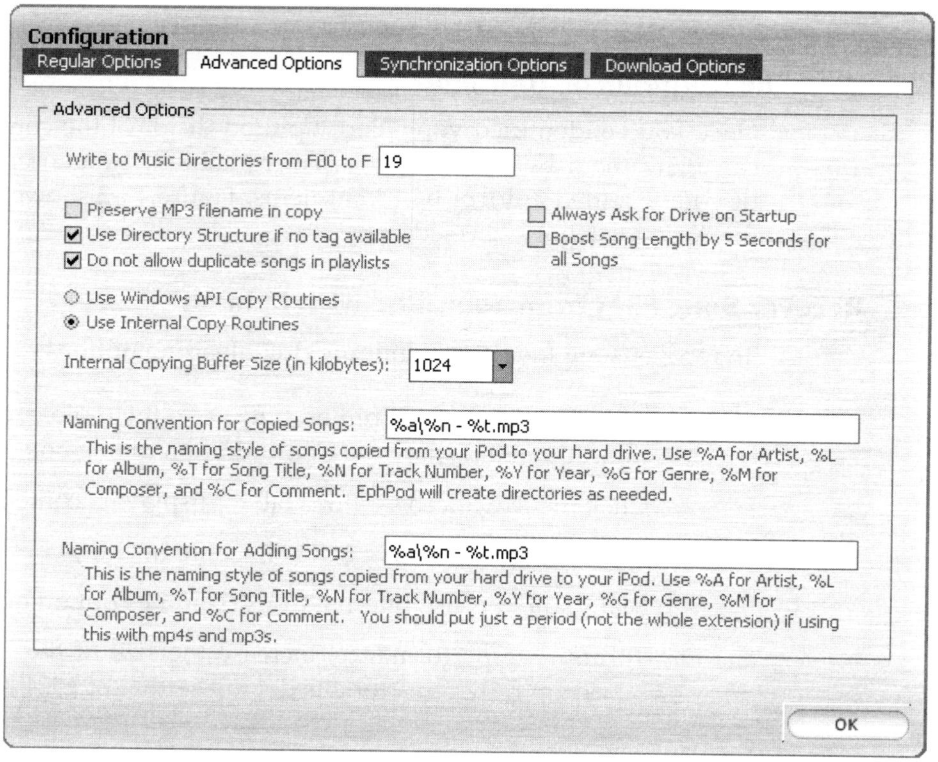

Figure 15-3

Before downloading
song files using EphPod,
make sure that the
naming convention suits
your needs.

6. In the Naming Convention For Copied Songs text box, enter the format EphPod should use for creating folders and naming the MP3 files it saves to your hard disk. You can use the variables shown in the following list to use information from the tags on the MP3 files. For example, you might use **%A\%L\%A—%T.mp3** to create folders and files such as Artist\Album\ Artist—Song Title.mp3. If you're copying files in formats other than MP3, put a period at the end but don't include the mp3 extension. These are the variables that you can use:

Variable	Explanation
%A	Artist name
%L	Album title
%T	Song title
%N	Track number
%Y	Year
%G	Genre
%C	Comment

7. Click the OK button to close the Configuration dialog box.

Once you've chosen the settings, export the song files by following these steps:

1. Navigate through the EphPod interface to the songs you want to export.

2. Select the songs and press CTRL-ALT-C, or right-click, and then choose Copy Songs To Directory from the shortcut menu (see Figure 15-4).

3. In the Browse For Folder dialog box, select the folder in which you want EphPod to create the folders and files.

4. Click the OK button. EphPod copies the files and folders and names them according to the convention you specified.

5. Choose File | Exit to close EphPod.

Recover Your Music Library with PodWorks on the Mac

PodWorks is a neat utility for transferring song and video files from your iPod to your Mac. You can download an evaluation version that limits you to 30 days, copying 250 items total, and copying one item at a time. These limitations allow you to make sure that PodWorks suits your needs before buying it but ensure that you need to pay in order to recover a whole iPod's worth of songs.

Figure 15-4

Recovering song files from an iPod to a computer with EphPod.

Get and Install PodWorks

To get and install PodWorks, follow these steps:

1. Open your browser, go to the Sci-Fi Hi-Fi web site (www.scifihifi.com/pod-works/), and then download the evaluation version of PodWorks.

2. If your browser doesn't automatically mount the disk image file for you and open a Finder window showing its contents, double-click the disk image file, and then double-click the disk image to open the Finder window.

3. Drag the PodWorks icon to your Applications folder.

Recover Songs with PodWorks

To recover songs with PodWorks, follow these steps:

1. In your Applications folder, double-click the PodWorks icon to start PodWorks.

2. Click the Preferences button on the Toolbar to display the PodWorks Preferences dialog box, and then click the Finder Copies tab (shown here) if it's not already displayed.

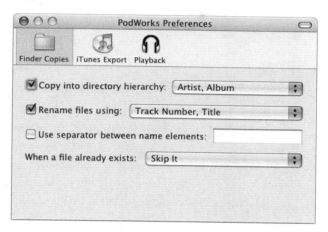

3. If you want to copy the songs into folders named by artist and then album (for example, Paris Hilton/Stars Are Blind), select the Copy Into Directory Hierarchy check box, and then choose Artist, Album in the drop-down list. This drop-down list also offers an Artist choice and an Album choice.

4. If you want to ensure consistent naming of songs, select the Rename Files Using check box, and then choose the naming convention you want in the drop-down list. The choices are: Track Number, Title; Disc Number, Track Number, Title; and simply Title.

5. If you want to use a separator character between name elements, select the Use Separator Between Name Elements check box, and then type the character in the text box. For example, you might use a hyphen.

6. In the When A File Already Exists drop-down list, choose what you want PodWorks to do: Skip It, Overwrite It, or Rename it.

7. If you have multiple iPods connected to your Mac, use the Connected iPods drop-down list to specify which iPod contains the songs. PodWorks shows the songs on the iPod (see Figure 15-5).

8. In the list box, choose which song or songs to recover, and then click the Copy Selected button or the Copy All button. If you're trying the evaluation version of PodWorks, you can use only the Copy Selected button to copy a single song at a time. If you have the full version of PodWorks, you'll probably want to use the Copy All button to recover all the songs from your iPod at once.

Figure 15-5

PodWorks can quickly recover one or all songs from your iPod.

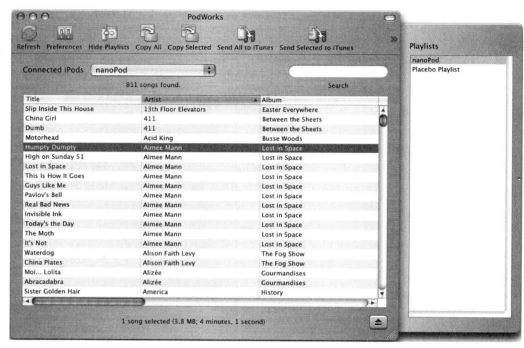

Looking at Figure 15-5, you'll see that PodWorks also offers a Send All To iTunes button and a Send Selected To iTunes button. These buttons are useful when you need to integrate the contents of your multiple iPods into a single music library.

DJ Using Your iPods or Your Computer— or Both

What You'll Need:

- iPods Covered: iPod with video, iPod nano, iPod mini, third- and fourth-generation iPod
- Hardware Required: Mixing deck, cables
- Windows Software Required: Traktor DJ Studio
- Mac Software Required: Traktor DJ Studio
- Cost: $25–800 U.S.

Many a trendy club lets its patrons patch their iPods into the mixing deck and give their fellow clubbers a taste of their music. But if you like serving up great music for other people to dance to, you'll probably want to set up as a DJ on your own. With an iPod and up to 15,000 songs in your pocket, you can be a DJ pretty much wherever you go.

This project explains how to DJ with your iPod in three ways: by connecting your iPod (or iPods) to a standard mixing deck; by connecting it (or them) to a mixing deck specially designed for iPods; and by running software on your PC or Mac that lets you DJ using either songs on the computer or on one or more iPods connected to it. The project also tells you how to get the most out of iTunes for playing party music—lightweight DJing without a mike.

Step 1: Connect Your iPods to a Mixing Console

The first approach is to connect your iPods to a standard mixing deck—one that's not specifically designed for use with iPods. Instead of plugging a record deck into each of the console's phono inputs, connect an iPod or two to the line-level inputs.

When connecting your iPod, make sure you use a line input rather than a phono input. Phono inputs are extra sensitive because record decks produce only a low volume. Unless you're extremely careful to keep the iPod's volume low, chances are that you'll either get grotesque distortion or blow the phono input.

To connect the iPod, you'll need a cable that has a 3.5 mm stereo connector at one end (for the iPod) and two RCA connectors at the other end (for the mixing deck). The easy option is to use the iPod's headphone socket, but you'll get better audio quality by using the line-out socket on the iPod's dock. (If you don't yet have a dock for your iPod, now is the time to get one. A dock that supports the iPod Universal Dock standard will work with all current models of iPod as long as you get the right plastic inserts.)

If you use the headphone socket, turn down the volume all the way on the iPod. Plug the 3.5 mm plug into the iPod's headphone socket, and then plug the RCA connectors into the mixing deck. Set a song playing on the iPod, and turn the volume up gradually until you're getting suitable volume without distortion.

If you use the line-out socket, you don't need to worry about the iPod's volume, as the line-out socket supplies a standard volume.

Step 2: Connect One or Two iPods to a iPod-specific Mixing Console

If you're committed to iPods and to DJing, what you'll probably want is a mixing deck that makes it easy to use your iPod or iPods as music sources. At this writing, the leading products in this area are the iDJ mixing decks from Numark.

Numark's initial iPod mixing deck, the iDJ, is a twin-iPod console that's easy to use but short on features. You can cue songs from each of the iPods and add input from microphones, but you can't change the pitch, which most DJs find essential to segueing one song into another. Figure 16-1 shows the iDJ, which costs $249.99 U.S. and is available from the Apple Store (http://store.apple.com) and other retailers.

Figure 16-1

The iDJ is a two-iPod mixing deck that makes it easy to cue up songs but doesn't allow you to change the pitch.

Figure 16-2

The iDJ2 mixing deck lets you dock only one iPod—but it can play two songs from that iPod at the same time.

The iDJ is a great way to do some lightweight DJing with your iPod, but its lack of pitch control is a bind. If you're serious about DJing, you'll almost certainly want a more capable mixing deck than the iDJ. You may find the iDJ2 (see Figure 16-2) more to your liking. Not only does the iDJ2 offer pitch control and scratching (via the two jog wheels), but it also lets you record your mixes to an iPod, which is a great capability. The downside is the price—$899 list, but you should be able to find it for $599 and up if you look hard.

tip *With the iDJ2, you can also attach further iPods through USB connections—or use the connections to attach USB hard drives, memory keys, or keyboards.*

Step 3: DJ Using Your Computer (and Maybe Your iPods)

Hardware designed for use with iPods can be expensive—and that applies to mixing decks, as you saw in the previous section. If your computer is portable or will be at the scene of the party anyway, you can use it as a virtual DJ.

At this writing, one of the best DJ programs is Traktor DJ Studio from Native Instruments, Inc. ($119 U.S.; www.nativeinstruments.de/index.php?id=traktor3_us). Traktor (see Figure 16-3), which runs on both Windows and Mac OS X, lets you pull in songs from your iTunes music library and a variety of other sources, including iPods connected to your computer.

Figure 16-3

Traktor DJ Studio lets
you DJ using your PC
or Mac.

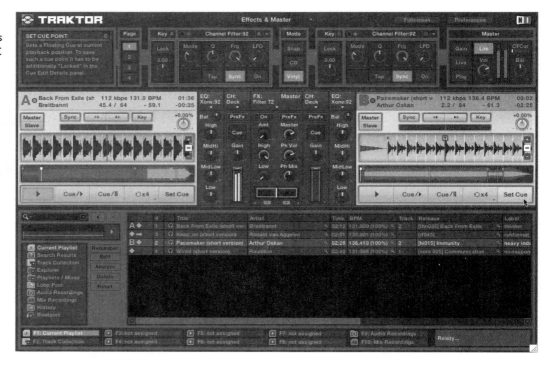

Traktor provides a full range of controls for controlling the music. For example, you can:

- Adjust the pitch of songs to make beats match (for smooth transitions from one song to the next).

- Cross-fade one song into another by dragging the cross-fader slider.

- Apply cue marks to songs so they start exactly where you want them to.

- Scratch by clicking and dragging.

- Apply separate equalization to songs on different playback decks.

Native Instruments offers a demo version of Traktor that lets you get a feel for the program before buying it.

Cross-Fade a Carefully Constructed Playlist

If you need to DJ only in the sense of providing nonstop music without gaps between songs, you can use iTunes itself in a pinch. Follow these steps:

1. Create one or more playlists of suitable music:

   - For example, you might create one playlist of fast dance music, another of medium-pace dance songs, and another of slow songs or ballads.

   - If any of the songs has a long intro or outro that will drop the tempo or spoil the mood, right-click or CTRL-click (Mac) it, choose Get Info, click the Options tab, and use the Start Time option or the Stop Time option to cut off the offending portion. Allow for the amount of cross-fading you'll set in the next step.

   - You might create a Smart Playlist (see Project 10) that uses the Genre and BPM (beats per minute) tags to select suitable songs.

2. Turn on cross-fading in iTunes:

   - Choose Edit | Preferences to display the iTunes dialog box on Windows, or choose iTunes | Preferences to display the Preferences dialog box on the Mac.

   - Click the Playback tab to display its contents.

   - Select the Crossfade Playback check box, and then drag the slider to a suitable number of seconds—all the way up to 12 if the songs have longer fadeouts, less if the fadeouts are shorter.

   - Click the OK button to close the dialog box.

3. Test the playlist, and adjust the cross-fading or song intros and outros as needed so that the music keeps going at the tempo you're shooting for.

Part III

Advanced

Troubleshoot Your iPod and Diagnose Its Problems

What You'll Need:

- iPods Covered: iPod with video, iPod nano, iPod shuffle
- Cost: Free

No computer hardware or software is entirely free from errors, and you may find that sometimes your iPod gets confused, that iTunes or your computer won't recognize your iPod, or that some other frustrating error has occurred. This project shows you how to blast your way through common iPod/iTunes/computer problems by using Apple's "Five Rs" troubleshooting approach, how to use the diagnostics to test components of the iPod with video and the iPod nano, and how to interpret the iPod shuffle's blinking lights.

Along the way, you'll learn how to update your iPod's operating system—and how to restore it if it gets confused enough to be intransigent.

Step 1: Fix Various Problems with Apple's "Five Rs" Troubleshooting Mantra

Apple recommends a "Five Rs" troubleshooting approach to iPods for a wide range of problems ranging from the iPod not responding to its controls all the way to iTunes and the computer not recognizing the iPod or being able to work with it.

These are the Five Rs:

- Reset the iPod
- Retry using a different USB port
- Restart your PC or Mac, and then install any updates

- Remove and reinstall iTunes

- Restore the iPod

This section walks you through these steps. Stop the troubleshooting when your iPod starts working—you don't normally need to continue to the end.

Reset Your iPod

The most basic troubleshooting maneuver is to reset your iPod. Reset it when the iPod doesn't respond to the controls at all or starts giving erratic responses to them.

To reset an iPod with video or an iPod nano, follow these steps:

1. Connect it to a power source—either a computer that's not sleeping or the iPod Power Adapter plugged into an electrical socket.

2. Move the Hold switch to the On position, and then move it back to the Off position.

3. Hold down the Menu button and the Select button for about six seconds, until the iPod displays the Apple logo.

4. After you release the buttons, give your iPod a few seconds to finish booting.

If your iPod freezes when you don't have a power source available, try resetting it by using the preceding technique without the power source. Sometimes it works; other times it doesn't. But you've nothing to lose by trying.

note   *To reset an iPod shuffle, switch it off and then on again.*

Retry Using a Different USB Port

If resetting your iPod didn't solve the problem, plug the iPod into a different USB port. Usually the problem is that the USB port you were trying to use doesn't have enough power for the iPod—for example, the USB port is a low-power one on a keyboard rather than a full-power port.

Restart Your PC or Mac, and Then Install Any Updates

If trying a different USB port didn't help, close all applications, and then restart your PC or Mac. Restarting can help to clear any confusion between the operating system and the USB hardware—so when Windows or Mac OS X restarts, your computer may recognize your iPod and start working normally.

If that doesn't happen, go to the second part of the step and install any updates to iTunes.

Install Updates to iTunes on Windows

iTunes for Windows comes set to check automatically for updates, but you can also check manually. To do so, follow these steps:

1. Start iTunes, and then choose Help | Check For iTunes Updates.

2. If you see a message box saying that a new version of iTunes is available, click the Yes button, and then follow through the rest of these instructions. Otherwise, if you see a message box telling you that your version is current, click the OK button, and then restart Windows manually.

3. iTunes opens a browser window to the page on the Apple website from which you can download the latest version of iTunes.

4. When the download finishes, click the Run button to run the setup routine, and then follow through its prompts to complete the installation.

5. When the setup routine tells you that you need to restart Windows, select the Yes, Restart My Computer Now option button, and then click the Finish button.

Install Updates to iTunes on the Mac

On the Mac, to install any updates to iTunes, follow these steps:

1. Choose Apple | Software Update to run Software Update. Software Update checks for iTunes updates along with all other updates, and then presents them to you in the Software Update dialog box.

2. Select the check box for each item you want to install.

3. Click the Install button. Mac OS X displays the Authenticate dialog box.

4. Enter an administrative password in the Authenticate dialog box to show the installer that you have authority to install the software.

5. Accept any license agreement. Mac OS X then downloads the updates and installs them.

Update Your iPod

To update your iPod, follow these steps:

1. Connect your iPod to your computer as usual.

2. In the Source pane, click your iPod. iTunes displays the iPod's information.

3. Click the Update button. iTunes checks online for the latest version of the updater software and then updates your iPod's software. On the Mac, you'll need to enter your password in the Authenticate dialog box to proceed. At the end of the update, iTunes displays any extra instructions for updating your iPod. Here's an example:

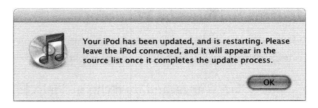

4. Follow the instructions, click the OK button, and then check whether your iPod now works with iTunes.

Remove and Reinstall iTunes and the iPod Software

If your iPod's still not working by this point, it's time to remove and reinstall iTunes and the iPod software. The process is different on Windows than on the Mac.

Remove and Reinstall iTunes on Windows

To remove and reinstall iTunes on Windows, follow these steps:

1. Close iTunes if it's running. Close any other applications, because you'll need to restart Windows.

2. Choose Start | Control Panel to open a Control Panel window.

3. In Category view, click the Add Or Remove Programs link to open the Add Or Remove Programs dialog box.

4. If the Change Or Remove Programs button in the left column isn't already selected, click it.

5. In the Currently Installed Programs And Updates list box, click the iTunes item.

6. Click the Change/Remove button to launch the InstallShield Wizard.

7. On the Welcome page (shown here), select the Remove option button, and then click the Next button.

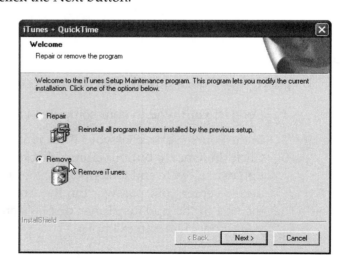

8. In the Confirm Uninstall message box that appears, click the OK button.

9. When the uninstall routine prompts you to restart your computer, select the Yes, I Want To Restart My Computer Now option button, and then click the Finish button.

After Windows restarts, follow these steps to reinstall iTunes:

1. Open your browser, go to www.apple.com/itunes, and then follow the link to download the latest version of iTunes.

2. When the download has finished, click the Run button to start the iTunes installer, and then follow through the installation routine.

3. When the installation routine prompts you to restart your computer, select the Yes, I Want To Restart My Computer Now option button, and then click the Finish button.

Remove and Reinstall iTunes on the Mac

To remove and reinstall iTunes on the Mac, follow these steps:

1. If iTunes is running, press ⌘-Q or choose iTunes | Quit iTunes to close iTunes.

2. Click the desktop to activate the Finder, and then choose Go | Applications to open the Applications folder.

3. Drag the iTunes icon to the Trash.

4. Restart your Mac.

5. Empty the Trash.

6. Open your browser, go to www.apple.com/itunes, and then follow the link to download the latest version of iTunes.

7. If Mac OS X doesn't automatically mount the disk image for you and open a Finder window showing its contents, double-click the disk image file, and then double-click the resulting disk image.

8. Double-click the iTunes.mpkg file to launch the iTunes installer, and then follow through the installation routine.

9. Drag the disk image to the Trash to eject it.

Restore the iPod

If your iPod still won't work with your computer even after you're uninstalled and reinstalled iTunes, you're down to the last resort in Apple's Five Rs: restoring the iPod's software. Restoring is the last resort because it involves wiping the iPod's hard disk or memory clean, and then reinstalling the iPod's software.

Normally, you'll need to restore an iPod only when you have (or a program has) deleted or corrupted vital files on the iPod so that it's no longer functional. However, if you move your iPod between a Mac and a PC, you may also need to restore it:

● When moving a Mac-formatted iPod or a brand-new iPod to a Windows computer, you always need to restore it. (Windows can't handle Mac-formatted iPods.)

● After moving a Windows-formatted iPod to the Mac, you can't update the iPod's software to the latest version unless you restore it.

 Restoring the iPod's software deletes all the files that you've placed on the iPod. If you can still access your iPod's contents, back up any files that exist only on the iPod (not on the computer).

To restore the iPod, follow these steps:

1. Install the latest version of iTunes. If you've just followed through the first four of the Five Rs, you've already installed the latest version. If not, download the latest version from www.apple.com/ipod/ipod.html, and then install it.

2. Connect your iPod to your PC via USB as usual.

3. Click the iPod in the Source pane. iTunes displays the iPod's information.

4. Click the Restore button on the Summary tab. iTunes warns you that you will lose all the data currently stored on the iPod:

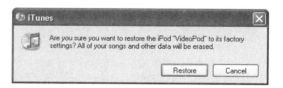

5. Click the Restore button. On the Mac, you need to enter your password in the Authenticate dialog box. iTunes then formats your iPod's hard disk or flash storage, and tells you when it has finished (as shown here).

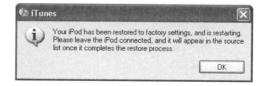

6. Click the OK button. The iPod Setup Assistant runs and walks you through the process of naming your iPod and deciding whether to load it automatically with songs from your music library.

7. After you disconnect your iPod, set the language it uses.

Step 2: Troubleshoot an iPod with Video or an iPod nano

The Five Rs discussed in Step 1 work well for many problems, but if you're sure the problem lies with your iPod, you may need to troubleshoot the iPod rather than iTunes and the iPod Software.

This section shows you how to troubleshoot problems that you may experience on an iPod with video or an iPod nano. Your first move is to access the iPod's diagnostic tools, which let you find out what's working and what may be broken.

Access Your iPod's Diagnostic Tools

To access your iPod's various diagnostic tools, enter diagnostic mode. Follow these steps:

1. Toggle the Hold switch on and off.

2. Hold down the Select button and the Menu button for about six seconds, until the Apple logo appears.

3. Hold down the Previous and Select buttons for a few seconds until the iPod displays a reversed Apple logo.

 The iPod nano sometimes fails to register your pressing the Previous and Select buttons. If this happens, restart the iPod and try again—and again if necessary.

4. In an iPod with video, you'll see the FA Diag Boot screen. Press the Menu button to access the main iPod diagnostics screen (see Figure 17-1). In an iPod nano, you get straight to the diagnostics screen.

Figure 17-1

The initial diagnostic screen for an iPod with video.

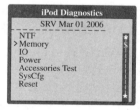

caution *Sometimes Apple changes the diagnostic tests in iPod firmware updates, so your iPod may show you different diagnostics than those listed here.*

To use the diagnostic tests, use the following keys:

● Press the Next and Previous buttons to navigate through the list of tests. On iPod with video, you can also scroll up and down.

● Press the Select button to run the highlighted test.

● Press the Menu button (on an iPod with video) or the Play button (on an iPod nano) to return from the results of a test to the diagnostic screen.

● To leave the diagnostic screen, either run the Reset test or reset your iPod again by holding down the Menu button and the Play/Pause button for a few seconds.

Because it has more extensive features, the iPod with video includes more diagnostic tests than the iPod nano. To make the tests more accessible, the iPod with video arranges the tests in a hierarchy of submenus rather than in a single menu. Figure 17-2 shows the hierarchy of menus for a fifth-generation iPod.

Figure 17-2

The hierarchy of diagnostic tests on the fifth-generation iPod.

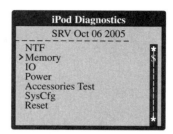

Test Whether the iPod's Buttons Are Working

If one of the buttons on your iPod seems to stop working, you'll probably be able to tell without diagnostics. But before you call for backup, you may want to check that your iPod agrees with you that there's a problem. To do so, run the Key Test on the Wheel menu of an iPod with video or the KeyTest on an iPod nano, and then press the iPod's buttons when prompted.

If the iPod doesn't register you pressing one of the listed buttons, it continues to wait until you reset it by holding down the Select button and the Menu button for a few seconds. (If one or both of these buttons aren't working, you're in trouble here.)

Check the USB Connection

To check a USB connection on an iPod with video, run the USBTest. If the test returns an ID number, such as ID=0x22FA05, the connection is working. If the test detects no connection, it displays No Cable Connection.

To check the USB connection on an iPod nano, run the Status test and check the USBPWR_Det readout. The value 1 indicates that power is detected; the value 0 indicates no power is detected.

Check the RAM

To check the RAM on an iPod with video, run the SDRAMFullTest test. If you see the message SDRAM OK, all is well.

On an iPod nano, run the FiveInOne test and look at the SDRAM line. If all is well, your iPod nano displays SDRAM OK.

Check the Click Wheel

To test the Click wheel on an iPod with video, run the WheelTest diagnostic on the Wheel menu. The iPod verifies the wheel's ID, displays WHEEL ID PASS if it's okay, and prompts you to press the Menu button to "exit." When you press the Menu button, the iPod displays a list of blocks that represent the touch sensing on the wheel. Scroll around the wheel until the iPod removes each of the block numbers and displays the WHEEL PASS message.

To test the Scroll wheel on an iPod nano, run the WheelTest diagnostic. The iPod prompts you to spin the wheel and displays the value of the current reading of your finger position as you spin it. If you want to see the register of Touchwheel values, run the TouchwheelID diagnostic.

Check How Your iPod Is Receiving Power

To check whether your iPod with video is receiving power across a USB cable or FireWire cable connected to an iPod Power Adapter, run the Accessories test. On the Accesorize Test (*sic*) screen, connect the FireWire adapter when prompted. If the iPod detects power, it changes the FWPWR: 0 readout to FWPWR:1 and prompts you to plug in the USB. After you plug in a USB cable connected to an iPod Power Adapter, the USBPWR:0 readout changes to USBPWR:1, the screen displays PASS, and the test ends.

caution   *If you don't have a FireWire cable connected to a FireWire iPod Power Adapter and a USB cable connected to a USB iPod Power adapter, you won't be able to complete the Accessories test. To escape from the test, hold down the Select button and the Menu button for several seconds to reset the iPod.*

To check whether your iPod nano is receiving a charge along a FireWire cable, run the Status test and look at the FW_PWR_GOOD line and the CHRG line, as shown next. A value of 0 for each of these indicates that the iPod nano is receiving power along a FireWire cable; a value of 1 indicates that the iPod nano is not receiving power.

```
LCD        :   01
SrNm:TM35418ZTK3
MOD#:MA107
HP         :   0
FW_PWR_GOOD    :   0
USBPWB_Det  :  0
CHRG       :   0
```

Run a Flash Scan (iPod nano Only)

To check that an iPod nano's flash memory is all present and correct, run the FlashScan test. Wait until the test completes, and then read the resulting screen. If you see the readout "Test OK," all is well.

Step 3: Troubleshoot the Original iPod shuffle

As the iPod shuffle has limited functionality and no screen, it doesn't have a suite of diagnostic tests that you can access. Instead, the iPod shuffle uses its green and orange lights in different combinations to indicate problems. This section explains what the lights mean and what actions you can take to sort out the problems.

Orange and Green Blinking Lights

Orange and green blinking lights mean that the iPod is confused. Turn it off, wait five seconds, and then turn it on again.

If that doesn't work, use iPod Updater to restore the iPod shuffle (see the section "Restore the iPod," earlier in this project). You'll lose all the files the iPod shuffle contains.

Orange Blinking Light

An orange blinking light means that the iPod shuffle's buttons are disabled. Hold down the Play/Pause button for three seconds or so until you see the status light blink green.

Green Blinking Light When You Press Play

A green blinking light when you press the Play button means that your iPod shuffle contains no songs (or no songs that it can play). Connect the iPod shuffle to your computer and load some songs.

iPod shuffle Doesn't Respond to Button Presses

If the iPod shuffle doesn't respond to button presses when the switch on the back isn't in the Off position and the battery has power, you may have moved the switch to between the Play In Order position and the Shuffle Songs position. Move the switch to the Off position, wait five seconds, and then move the switch to the Play In Order position or the Shuffle Songs position.

Project 18

Replace the Battery in an Original iPod Shuffle

What You'll Need:

- iPods Covered: iPod shuffle (original model)
- Hardware Required: iPod shuffle battery, craft knife, soldering iron, ballpoint pen or thin round stick, superglue, wire-cutter and stripper, adhesive tape
- Cost: $25–$50 U.S.

Amply protected by its plastic carapace, the original iPod shuffle is a tough little customer. Unlike the iPod nano, it has no screen that you can scratch; and unlike the iPod with video, there's no hard disk that can suffer damage. Drop an iPod shuffle, and its slight weight reduces the impact—if the headphones or the neck lanyard don't save it altogether.

Short of running your iPod shuffle over with a vehicle or taking it swimming, you're not likely to damage it. The iPod shuffle's key point of failure is its lithium-ion battery, which is rated for 500 charge cycles. With luck and daily use, you'll get a year and a half out of your iPod shuffle before the battery life really starts to taper off. If you're less lucky, your iPod shuffle will barely make it out of its one-year warranty period before you start to lose battery life.

You don't have to be especially cynical to reckon that Apple encourages customers to think of the iPod shuffle as a disposable item. But the iPod shuffle's plastic casing, insubstantial size, and lightweight belie the high-tech engineering it contains. If your iPod shuffle's battery dies, you can replace it.

Read on.

Step 1: Make Sure the iPod Is Out of Warranty

Before you take a craft knife to your iPod shuffle, make sure the little wonder's one-year warranty has expired. If the iPod shuffle fails before that time, or if its battery loses 50 percent or more of its charge time, you should be able to get Apple to fix it under warranty.

You should also check that the iPod shuffle isn't covered by an AppleCare Protection Plan for iPod. Chances are that it's not, because—not surprisingly—few people are willing to pay $59 U.S. for an extra year's cover on a player that costs something like $69 (for the 512 MB model) or $99 (for the 1 GB model). But if you've paid for the coverage, be certain to use it.

Right, that didn't take long. On we go.

Step 2: Get the Replacement Battery and the Tools

You've guessed the next step: to get the replacement battery and the tools you need:

- **iPod shuffle battery**   At this writing, the best place to get a replacement battery for the original iPod shuffle is eBay (www.ebay.com) because most of the main iPod battery sites (see the list in Project 20) do not currently carry iPod shuffle batteries. The situation may have changed by the time you read this. Put the search phrase **"iPod shuffle" replacement battery** into your favorite search engine and see what comes up. Use the double quotation marks around "iPod shuffle" to make the search engine treat it as a single term. You may get results for the second generation of iPod shuffle as well, but you'll be able to distinguish them easily enough.

- **Craft knife**   Find an Exacto knife or other very sharp knife with a slim blade and a strong point. A sharp kitchen knife *might* work, but you're likely to damage the iPod, the knife, and yourself. Your call.

- **Soldering iron**   Get a soldering iron with a fine point—and some solder (you don't need much) and lubricant.

- **Ballpoint pen or stick**   Dig out a pen that you don't care if you break. You'll use the point to push the iPod shuffle's guts out. You can also use a thin round stick (just narrower than the headphone-connector hole at the top of the iPod).

- **Wire-cutter and -stripper**   You'll need a delicate wire-cutter (or a pair of small, sharp scissors) and a wire-stripper (or great delicacy with that craft knife).

- **Superglue**   You may need a few drops of superglue to stick your iPod back together after you've reassembled it.

- **Adhesive tape**   Any kind of adhesive tape will do. You need less than an inch.

Step 3: Back Up Any Valuable Data from the iPod

Replacing the iPod shuffle's battery shouldn't affect what's stored in the iPod's flash memory—but if you give the memory an electrical shock when you're opening the iPod, you might need to restore the iPod's firmware.

So before you open the iPod, then, back up any valuable data from the iPod to your computer. You don't need to back up songs that are in your music library, because iTunes will put them back on the iPod at the next synchronization. But if you're using the iPod's disk mode to transport valuable files, copy them to your computer.

Step 4: Open the iPod Shuffle and Replace the Battery

To open your iPod shuffle, follow these steps:

1. Take the cap off the iPod shuffle, exposing the USB connector.

2. Use the craft knife to cut all the way round the join between the base and the main body, as shown here. You'll need to be patient as you work your way around several times. If there's a gap between the two pieces of plastic, you may be able to pry rather than cut: insert the blade a little, and twist it gently. Either way, proceed carefully. Dissection is the better part of vigor here.

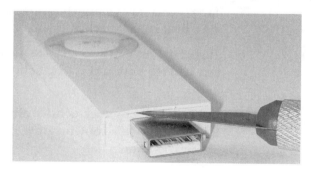

3. Once you've cut through the glue all the way around, you should be able to loosen the base. Grasp the USB connector with your fingers and rock it back and forth and from side to site to loosen any remaining glue. You should then be able to pop it loose, as shown here. The USB connector is secured by a ribbon, so don't pull it far.

note *Apart from being glued all the way around, the base is also secured to the iPod shuffle's body by a small plastic pressure clip at the middle of each of the short sides. You may be able to poke the knife blade in and pop the clip open, but it's tricky. Rocking the base is usually an easier way of opening the clips.*

4. Turn the iPod shuffle over so that you can see the Off/Play/Shuffle switch. With the switch in the Off position, poke the blade under the left side between the Off label and the Play symbol, and gently lift the switch up, as shown here. There will be a slight pop as it comes loose.

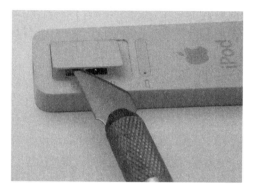

5. Tape the Battery Charge button in place—you don't need to remove this, and it's a brute to get back in if you do take it out.

6. Turn the iPod shuffle over so that the play controls are on the top and the Battery Charge button is on the bottom, where it can't fall out if the tape comes loose.

7. Insert the pen or stick gently into the headphone socket and use it to push the iPod shuffle's contents down the body, so that they start coming out of the end, as shown here.

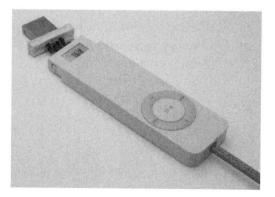

8. Grab the iPod shuffle's contents as they start coming out of the bottom of the body, and pull them the rest of the way. *Don't* pull the USB connector or its flimsy cable: Instead, push the contents far enough that the white plastic

box starts coming out. When the contents are free, lay the case aside, prefer-ably with the play controls up (so that the Battery Charge button can't fall out if it comes unstuck from the tape.) The next illustration shows the iPod's innards.

9. Working very gently, unstick the USB connector cable from the battery. Un-stick it all the way to where the cable runs along the side of the iPod, as shown here.

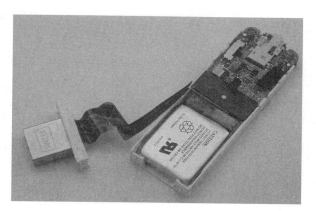

10. Put your finger underneath the battery holder so that you can push the bat-tery up through the hole in the holder's floor. Push the battery up gently until it comes free from the glue that sticks it down around the edges. Move the bat-tery outside the battery holder so that you can see the wires, as shown here.

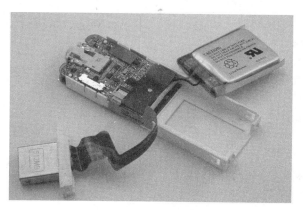

11. Unwrap the yellow plastic that covers the battery's connection, and then clip through each cable using a small pair of wire-cutters.

12. Prepare the replacement battery. Strip off any extra insulation on the ends of the wires and remove any unnecessary labels.

13. Heat up your soldering iron. Don't forget to lubricate the tip.

14. Strip the insulation off the end of each battery wire, and then carefully solder each wire to its connector. Some replacement batteries have connectors in different positions than on the iPod's original battery, but the positive (red wire) and negative (black wire) terminals should be clearly marked, as shown here.

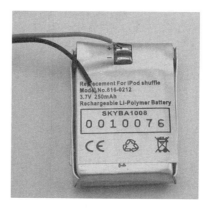

15. Place the battery in its holder. If there's not enough glue residue on the battery holder to stick the battery down, you might want to add a drop or two. The battery can't go far, but its cable might come loose.

16. Stick the USB connector cable across the battery so that it's routed to the end of the iPod.

17. Slide the iPod's body back into its case, making sure the USB connector cable.

18. Put the base back on. If the little clips at the sides survived your opening them, they should hold the base in place. You might want to reinforce them with a few drops of glue, especially if you want your iPod to be weather-resistant.

19. Replace the switch. Put the right side in first, align the two tiny hooks on the left side with the gaps they pass through, and then snap the switch into place.

20. Remove the tape you used to hold the Battery Charge button in place.

Now that the iPod is back together, charge the battery before trying to use it. The full charge takes between three and four hours. The battery will give best performance if you allow it a full charge the first time, so be prepared to wait.

Replace the Battery in an Original iPod nano

What You'll Need:

- iPods Covered: iPod nano (original model)
- Hardware Required: iPod nano battery, soldering iron, solder, spudger, small flat-blade screwdriver
- Cost: Around $25 U.S.

The first-generation iPod nano is probably the most delicate member of the iPod tribe, and many nanos suffer premature death through active or clumsy use. If you treat your nano gently, however, it can last for years—especially as it contains flash memory (which is tough) rather than a hard disk (which can fail much more easily).

Barring physical damage, the battery in your iPod nano is the most likely component to fail. If the battery fails, you can replace it as described in this project.

Step 1: Make Sure the iPod Is Out of Warranty

Before you open your iPod nano, make sure that its one-year warranty has expired. If the battery loses 50 percent or more of its charge time, you should be able to get Apple to fix it under warranty.

If you've bought an AppleCare Protection Plan for iPod ($59), your iPod has two years' coverage from the original date of purchase. In this case, you should let Apple do the work, even though it'll mean you being without your iPod for days or weeks.

note *Replacing the iPod nano's battery is a delicate operation. If you choose not to replace the battery yourself, you can have Apple replace it for you for $59 plus shipping. Other battery retailers may charge less. For example, PDASmart.com (www.pdasmart.com) charges $55 to replace an iPod nano's battery with a battery that provides up to 20 percent extra capacity.*

Step 2: Get the Replacement Battery and the Tools

Your next move is to buy a replacement battery and assemble the tools you need:

- **iPod nano battery**   At this writing, the best place to get a replacement battery for the iPod shuffle is eBay (www.ebay.com) because most of the main iPod battery sites (see the list in Project 20) do not currently carry iPod nano batteries. The situation may have changed by the time you read this. Put the search phrase **"iPod nano" replacement battery** into your favorite search engine and see what comes up. Use the double quotation marks around "iPod nano" to make the search engine treat it as a single term.

- **Spudger or similar tool**   A *spudger* (see Figure 19-1) is a prying tool made of plastic or similar material soft enough to avoid marking the iPod but strong enough to get it open. Many replacement battery kits include a spudger (or a pair of spudgers); if the kit you order doesn't include one, the store that sells you the battery will almost certainly be happy to sell you a spudger separately. You can also use an out-of-date credit card (don't use a current one—you may damage it), a guitar pick, or a similar object with a thin, strong, and nonscratching edge.

tip *Consider buying an extra spudger or pair of spudgers, as they're easy to damage—and they're inexpensive.*

- **Soldering iron**   Get a soldering iron with a fine point, some solder (you need only a little), and lubricant.

- **Small, flat-blade screwdriver**   You may need a standard electrical screwdriver for levering the front and back of the iPod apart.

Figure 19-1

Spudgers are tools for opening delicate hardware without damage.

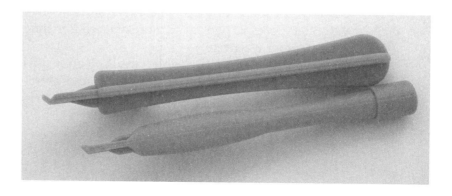

Step 3: Back Up Any Valuable Data from the iPod

Replacing the iPod nano's battery shouldn't affect what's stored in the iPod's flash memory—but if you give the memory a surprise when you're opening the iPod, you may need to restore the iPod's firmware.

So before you open the iPod, then, back up any valuable data from the iPod to your computer. You don't need to back up songs that are in your music library, because iTunes will put them back on the iPod at the next synchronization. But if you're using the iPod's disk mode to transport valuable files, copy them to your computer.

Step 4: Open the iPod nano and Replace the Battery

To open the iPod nano, follow these steps:

1. Lay the iPod nano on its back on a flat surface with the iPod's left side facing toward you. Use a soft surface such as a mouse pad, cloth, or pad of paper rather than a hard surface that might scratch the iPod.

2. At the point just below the bottom of the Click wheel, work the spudger's blade into the crack between the iPod nano's front plate (the white or black part) and the back plate (the chrome plate). Don't force the spudger's blade in; instead, slide it back and forth along the seam repeatedly, applying only gentle pressure, until the front plate and the back plate spring apart slightly (see Figure 19-2).

3. Once you've made a crack at the bottom corner, work the spudger along the crack to widen it.

4. Depending on your delicacy of touch, your iPod's fit and finish, and the strength of your spudger, you may now be able to pop open the iPod's side one clip at a time. More likely, you may need to insert a screwdriver carefully into the crack

Figure 19-2

Start by working the spudger into the crack between the front plate and the back plate.

Figure 19-3

You may need to use a screwdriver or other tool for extra torque to widen the crack and open the clips.

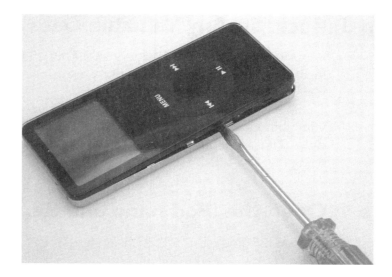

and twist the blade very gently to widen it (as shown in Figure 19-3). It's much easier to exert enough force with the screwdriver than with the spudger, but it's also easy to put nicks into the edges of your iPod's front plate. You could use a credit card or another piece of tough plastic to protect the iPod's front plate.

tip   *You may find it helpful to have a second spudger, or another nonscratching object such as a guitar pick or the corner of a credit card you no longer value, to wedge into one end of the crack to hold it open. Another pair of hands may also be useful at this stage.*

5. Apply gentle pressure to pop the first clip open.

6. Work around the iPod's top, using the spudger to loosen each of the clips in turn.

7. If you get stuck after going around the top of the iPod, try opening the other side from the bottom end (the dock connector end). You may find you make better progress by using a variety of tools, such as a guitar pick, as shown in Figure 19-4.

8. Once you've got the back plate loose, take it off gently and lay the iPod's front part (which has all the contents) face down. Figure 19-5 shows the iPod nano's insides.

9. Slide the spudger between the iPod's side and the battery, and then gently work the battery loose (see Figure 19-6). The battery is glued down lightly with glue strips, so work your way along its side patiently rather than applying brute force.

10. Free the battery cable from the two patches of tape that hold it down. The easiest way to do this is to lift the battery so that the cable comes off the circuit

board, take hold of the cable when it's clear, and pull toward the tape so that the tape lifts off. Figure 19-7 shows the battery coming free.

11. Using a small pair of wire-cutters, cut each of the battery's wires close to where it is soldered to the iPod.

Figure 19-4

A guitar pick can come in handy on the iPod's second side, as it reaches a bit deeper than a spudger.

Figure 19-5

The iPod nano (right) with its back plate (left) off. You can't miss the battery—it's the big rectangular thing with the three-wire cable running to it.

Figure 19-6

Use the spudger to unstick the battery. The glue strips are usually positioned nearer the middle of the iPod than the edge.

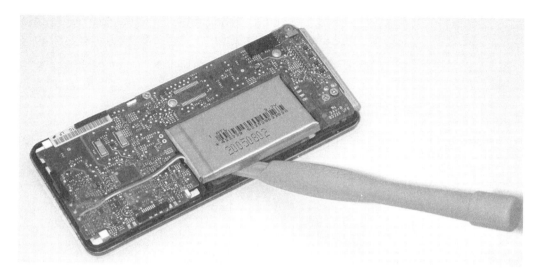

Figure 19-7

The battery cable is held down by two pieces of tape.

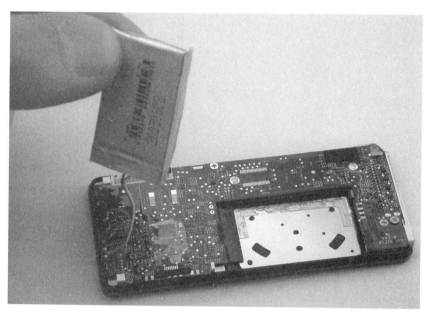

12. Prepare the replacement battery. Strip off any extra insulation on the ends of the wires, and remove any unnecessary labels.

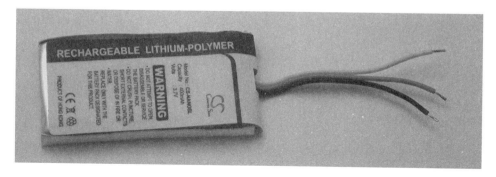

13.   Heat up your soldering iron. Don't forget to lubricate the tip.

14.   Very carefully solder each battery wire in turn to the correct connector: white on the left, red in the middle, and black on the right (looking from the back of the iPod with the dock connector at the bottom).

15.   Place the battery in its compartment. The glue strips that secured the original battery should hold it in place. (If these glue strips came out with the original battery, scrape them off and reinstate them in the battery compartment.)

16.   Lay the battery cable as flat as possible, making sure its three wires aren't twisted, and then tape it down with the two pieces of tape that you removed.

17.   Working from the top end of the iPod, put the back on again. Start by getting the hold switch and the top clip into place, and then the rest should follow easily. You're on the home stretch, but take it easy. Each clip takes a little force to click into place, but if you find yourself applying strength, the front and the back of the iPod probably aren't aligned. Take your time.

Now that the iPod is back together, charge the battery before trying to use it. The full charge takes between three and four hours. Be patient.

tip *If your iPod nano exhibits odd behavior when you restart it after charging the battery, restore its firmware using the latest version of iTunes. See Project 17 for instructions on restoring the iPod's firmware.*

Replace the Battery in an iPod with Video

What You'll Need:

- iPods Covered: iPod with video (original model)
- Hardware Required: iPod with video battery, soldering iron, spudger
- Cost: $25–50 U.S.

I f you've bought an iPod with video, you probably want to be able to use it to play videos back on the screen. The videos look great—but they chew through the battery faster than a hyperactive teenager through a stack of pancakes. As a result, you'll quickly notice any deterioration in battery life. While you can probably tolerate battery life dropping from eight or so hours of music playback to two hours without your commute becoming frustrating, having your video-watching time cut down to half an hour is always going to hurt.

Like the other iPods' batteries, the iPod with video's battery is rated at 500 charge cycles. That means you should be able to recharge it fully 500 times before the battery starts to decline noticeably. Some batteries will do better than this—and others will do worse.

Step 1: Make Sure the iPod Is Out of Warranty

Before you even think of opening your iPod with video, make sure that its one-year warranty has expired. If the battery loses 50 percent or more of its charge time, you should be able to get Apple to fix it under warranty.

If you've bought an AppleCare Protection Plan for iPod ($59), your iPod has two years' coverage from the original date of purchase. In this case, you should let Apple do the work, even though it'll mean you being without your iPod for days or weeks.

note *Replacing the iPod with video's battery requires a spudger and a trusty hand. If you choose not to replace the battery yourself, you can have Apple replace it for you for $59 plus shipping. Other battery retailers may charge less, so you might benefit from shopping around.*

Step 2: Get the Replacement Battery and the Tools

Before assaulting your iPod's case, get a suitable replacement battery and all the tools you need:

- **iPod with video battery**   You can find replacement batteries for the iPod with video at various sites (see the sidebar). To find the widest range of batteries and prices, put the search phrase **iPod video replacement battery** into your favorite search engine and see what it produces. You'll need to choose the battery that's right for your iPod with video model and generation—for example, a 30 GB first-generation iPod with video rather than an 80 GB second-generation iPod with video.

- **Spudger**   To get inside the iPod's case, you should use a *spudger*, a prying tool made of plastic or similar material soft enough to avoid marking the iPod but strong enough to get it open. Many replacement battery kits include a spudger (or a pair of spudgers); if the kit you order doesn't include one, the store that sells you the battery will almost certainly be happy to sell you a spudger separately. You can also use a credit card that you don't mind damaging, a heavy guitar pick, or a similar object with a thin, strong, and nonscratching edge.

- **Small flat-blade screwdriver**   You'll also need a screwdriver with a small, flat blade, such as you might use for electrical work.

- **Another pair of hands**   Disconnecting the battery cable and reconnecting it are tricky maneuvers that benefit from another pair of hands—so have someone standing by to help if possible.

> **note**   *If you don't have a spudger, you can open the iPod using a small flat-blade screwdriver—but you're likely to mark or bend the iPod while opening it.*

Where to Get a Replacement Battery for Your iPod

You can find replacement batteries for iPods at many sites online, including the following.

- PDASmart (www.pdasmart.com) sells replacement batteries (including a higher-capacity battery for the 30 GB model) and also offers a battery-replacement service for a little more.

- Laptops for Less (www.ipodbattery.com) has replacement batteries for many models of iPods.

- We Love Macs (www.welovemacs.com) sells replacement batteries for the iPod with video models.

- Batteries.com (www.batteries.com) sells a wide variety of replacement batteries, including batteries for some iPod models.

Step 3: Back Up Any Valuable Data from the iPod

Replacing the iPod's battery shouldn't affect what's stored on the iPod's hard disk—but it's better to be safe than sorry. If you have a mishap when opening the iPod and replacing the battery, you may need to restore the iPod (thus erasing all files on its disk) to get it functioning again.

So before you open the iPod, then, back up any valuable data from the iPod to your computer. You don't need to back up songs that are in your music library, because iTunes will put them back on the iPod at the next synchronization. But if you're using the iPod's disk mode to transport valuable files, copy them to your computer.

Step 4: Open the iPod with video and Replace the Battery

To open the iPod with video and replace its battery, follow these steps:

1. Lay the iPod on its back on a flat surface with iPod's left side facing toward you. Use a soft surface such as a mouse pad, cloth, or pad of paper rather than a hard surface that might scratch the iPod.

2. At a point on the right side, level with the middle of the Click wheel, work the spudger's blade into the crack between the iPod's front plate (the white or black part) and the back plate (the chrome plate). Don't force the spudger's blade in: instead, slide it back and forth along the seam repeatedly, applying only gentle pressure, until the front plate and the back plate spring apart slightly (see Figure 20-1).

Figure 20-1

Start by working the spudger into the crack between the front plate and the back plate.

3. Once you've opened up a crack, work the spudger along the crack to widen it. Work back and forth all the way along the seam from top to bottom, gradually widening the crack until the clips holding the front and back of the iPod together pop open, as shown here.

4. Work your way around the other side of the iPod with the spudger. Now that you've got the first side loose, the clips on the second side should pop open with minimal force.

5. With the back of the case loose, put the iPod face down on your flat surface and lift the back off the case off carefully an inch or two so that you can see inside. This is the first point at which you'll probably want the second pair of hands.

 Most of the iPod's innards are in the front part of the case, but the battery is stuck to the back of the case and connected to the rest of the innards by delicate cables. If you open the iPod too far or too roughly, you may damage these cables.

6. Use the flat-head screwdriver to pry up the brown plastic catch that holds the end of the long, straight cable in place, and then pull the cable out gently. You can now open the back of the iPod all the way and lay it down next to the front of the iPod. Figure 20-2 shows the iPod open so that you can see the catch and the cable.

7. Pry the battery loose, remove it, and then replace it with the new battery.

Figure 20-2

The battery cable runs from the battery stuck on the back of the iPod's case to the electronics on the front.

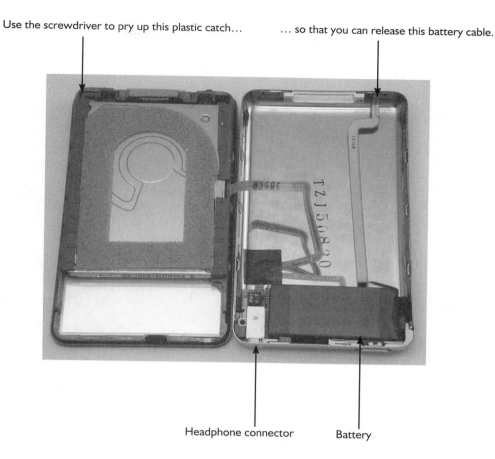

Use the screwdriver to pry up this plastic catch…

… so that you can release this battery cable.

Headphone connector

Battery

8. Close the iPod's back partway so that you can bring the battery cable across to its socket. This is the other point at which you'll probably want the second pair of hands.

9. Slide the battery cable into the socket, and then gently push the brown plastic catch back down until it holds the battery cable securely.

10. Align the back of the iPod with the front, and then gently clip first one side into place and then the other. You shouldn't need to use much pressure. If the back seems to get stuck, make sure it's correctly aligned.

Now that the iPod is back together, charge the battery before trying to use it. The full charge takes between three and four hours. Wait until the iPod indicates it's fully charged before you try using it, because not giving the battery a full charge first time may reduce battery life in the long run.

Share Your Songs with Your Household via iTunes or a Server

What You'll Need:

- iPods Covered: Any iPod
- Hardware Required: An old PC or Mac
- Windows Software Required: An extra copy of Windows or Linux
- Mac Software Required: An extra copy of Mac OS X or Linux
- Cost: $100 U.S. or less

If you live alone and have only one computer, you never need worry about sharing your songs with others: just put all your songs on your computer and play them from there. But it's more likely you live with other people, have multiple computers, or both—in which case, you'll probably want to share your songs with the other people or other computers. This project shows you three different ways of doing so: sharing songs by using iTunes' sharing features, sharing songs by putting them in a folder that all users of a particular computer can access, and sharing songs by putting them on a shared drive or music server.

Step 1: Decide Which Type of Sharing You'll Use

Your first step is to decide which type of sharing you'll use. Table 21-1 summarizes the types of sharing. The following three sections give you the details on each type of sharing and explain how to implement it.

Sharing Type	How It Works	What It's Good For	Limitations
iTunes sharing	Turn on iTunes' sharing features to stream songs from one computer to another.	Effortless sharing of your entire music library or some songs. Listening to songs other people are sharing.	Only five computers per day can access your shared songs. Songs are available only when the sharing computer is running.
Shared music folder	Set up each user of a shared computer to use the same music folder.	Sharing songs among all users of the same computer.	Each user may need to add new songs to their music library manually.
Music server	Create a dedicated computer to hold all your home's song files.	Sharing many songs with all members of the household.	Takes more effort to set up. The server must run all the time that songs are required.

Table 21-1   Pros and Cons of the Three Ways of Sharing Songs

Step 2: Share Songs with iTunes' Limited Sharing Feature

The swift and painless way to share songs with other people in your household is to use iTunes' built-in sharing features. As long as all the computers are running a recent enough version of Windows (Windows 2000, Windows XP, or a later version) or Mac OS X (10.2.4 or a later version), you just need to configure sharing, and then you're ready to start.

Understand How Sharing Works

To get the most out of iTunes' sharing—and avoid being disappointed—you should understand the basics of how it works. Here's what you need to know:

- You can share either your entire music library or selected playlists with other users on your network. Sharing playlists makes the list of songs faster to load and more manageable.

- You can share MP3 files, AAC files, AIFF files, WAV files, Apple Lossless Encoding files, and links to radio stations. You can't share Audible files or QuickTime sound files.

- iTunes' music sharing is limited to computers on the same TCP/IP subnet as your computer is on. (A *subnet* is a logical division of a network.) If your computer connects to a medium-sized network, and you're unable to find a computer that you know is connected to the same network somewhere, it may be on a different subnet.

- You can share your music with up to five other computers per day, and your computer can be one of up to five computers accessing the shared music on another computer on any given day. Apple has changed the sharing limitations in the past and may change them again.

- Shared music remains on the computer that's sharing it, and when a participating computer goes to play a song, the song is streamed across the network. This means that the song isn't copied from the computer that's sharing it to the computer that's playing it in a way that leaves a usable file on the playing computer.

- When a computer goes offline or is shut down, any music it has been sharing stops being available to other users. Participating computers can play the shared music but can't do anything else with it; they can't burn the shared music to CD or DVD, download it to an iPod, or copy it to their own libraries.

Set Up Sharing and Looking for Shared Music

To set up iTunes to share some or all of your songs with other people on your network, or to look for songs other people are sharing, follow these steps:

1. Display the iTunes dialog box or the Preferences dialog box:

    - In Windows, choose Edit | Preferences or press CTRL-COMMA or CTRL-Y to display the iTunes dialog box.

    - On the Mac, choose iTunes | Preferences or press either ⌘-COMMA or ⌘-Y to display the Preferences dialog box.

2. Click the Sharing tab to display it. Figure 21-1 shows the Sharing tab of the iTunes dialog box with settings chosen.

3. If you want to share music, follow these steps:

    - Select the Share My Music check box. (This check box is cleared by default.) By default, iTunes then selects the Share Entire Library option button. If you want to share only some playlists, select the Share Selected Playlists option button and then select the check boxes in the list box for the playlists.

    - The Shared Name text box controls the name that other users trying to access your music will see. The default name is *username*'s music, where *username* is your username—for example, Anna Connor's Music. You might choose to enter a more descriptive name, such as **Tech Metal Zone** or **Kitchen Computer**.

    - By default, your music is available to any other user on the network. To restrict access to people with whom you share a password, select the Require Password check box and enter a strong (unguessable) password in the text box.

Figure 21-1

Choose whether to look for shared music and whether to share part or all of your music library.

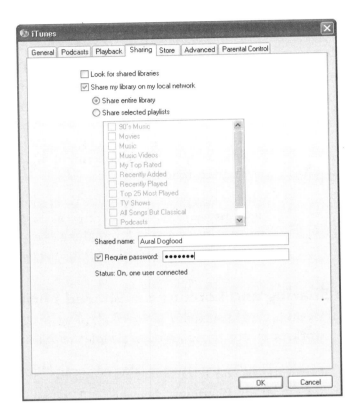

tip *If there are many computers on your network, use a sharing password to help avoid running up against the five-users-per-day limit. If your network has only a few computers, you may not need a password to avoid reaching this limit.*

4. If you want to listen to music other people are sharing, select the Look For Shared Music check box.

5. Click the OK button to apply your choices and close the dialog box.

note *When you set iTunes to share your music, iTunes displays a message reminding you that "Sharing music is for personal use only"—in other words, remember not to violate copyright law. Select the Do Not Show This Message Again check box if you want to prevent this message from appearing again.*

Disconnect Other Users from Your Shared Music

To disconnect other users from your shared music library, follow these steps:

1. Display the iTunes dialog box or the Preferences dialog box:

- In Windows, choose Edit | Preferences or press CTRL-COMMA or CTRL-Y to display the iTunes dialog box.

- On the Mac, choose iTunes | Preferences or press either ⌘-COMMA or ⌘-Y to display the Preferences dialog box.

2. Click the Sharing tab to display it.

3. Clear the Share My Music check box.

4. Click the OK button. If any other user is connected to your shared music library, iTunes displays this message box to warn you:

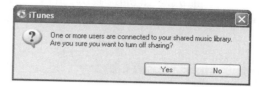

5. Click the Yes button or the No button, as appropriate. If you click the Yes button, anyone playing music from it will be cut off abruptly without notice.

Browse and Play Shared Songs

Once you've selected the Look For Shared Music check box on the Sharing tab of the iTunes dialog box or the Preferences dialog box, iTunes automatically detects shared music when you launch it while your computer is connected to a network. If iTunes finds shared music libraries or playlists, it displays them in the Source pane. Figure 21-2 shows an example of browsing the music shared by another computer.

Figure 21-2

Quickly browse the music that's being shared in the iTunes Source pane.

If a shared music source has a password, iTunes displays the Music Library Password dialog box. Type the password and click the OK button to access the library. Select the Remember Password check box before clicking the OK button if you want iTunes to save the password to speed up future access to the music library.

tip *Double-click the entry for a shared music library in the Source pane to open a separate window that shows its contents.*

Disconnect a Shared Music Library

To disconnect shared music you've connected to, click the Eject icon next to the music library in the Source pane. You can also click the music library in the Source pane and then press CTRL-E (Windows) or ⌘-E (Mac) or choose Controls | Disconnect "*Library*" from the shortcut menu (where *Library* is the name of the shared music library and appears between double quotation marks—for example, Disconnect "John's Music"). Alternatively, right-click the music library in the Source pane (or CTRL-click on the Mac) and choose Disconnect from the shortcut menu.

Step 3: Share Your Songs More Effectively with Other Local Users

As you saw in Step 2, sharing via iTunes could hardly be simpler, but it's a bit limited; it works only with users of other computers, not users of your own computer, and the songs are available only when the computer sharing them is powered on and attached to the network. No surprises there, but if you enjoy sharing your songs, you'll probably want to have them available all the time.

This section shows you how to share songs among all the users of the same PC or Mac. The next section explains how to create a music server that makes music available to all users on the network.

Share Your Music Library with Other Users of Your PC

Like Mac OS X, Windows XP normally prevents other users from accessing your personal files, assigning each user a user account and keeping them out of other users' accounts. The result of this is that your iTunes music library, which is stored in your My Music\iTunes\iTunes Music folder by default, is securely protected from other users of your computer. This protection is great if you want to keep your music to yourself, but not so great if you want to share it with your friends, family, or coworkers.

note *Windows Media Player, the audio and video player that Microsoft includes with Windows at this writing, gets around this restriction by making the music and video files that any user adds to their music library available to all users. This openness is great if you want to share all your files but less appealing if you want to keep some of them private.*

The easiest way to give other users access to your music library is to move it to the Shared Music folder, which Windows XP automatically shares with other users of your computer but not with other computers on the network. The Shared Music folder is located in the \Documents and Settings\All Users\Documents\My Music folder. Alternatively, you can put the music library in another shared folder. This example uses the Shared Music folder; if you're using another folder, substitute it where appropriate.

Moving your music library to the Shared Music folder involves two steps: moving the files, and telling iTunes where you've moved them to.

To move your music library files to the Shared Music folder, follow these steps:

1. Close iTunes if it's running (for example, press ALT-F4).

2. Choose Start | My Music to open a Windows Explorer window showing My Music.

3. Double-click the iTunes folder to open it. You'll see an iTunes Music Library .xml file, an iTunes Music Library.itl file, and an iTunes Music folder. The first two files must stay in your My Music folder. If you remove them, iTunes won't be able to find your music, and it will create these files again from scratch.

4. Right-click the iTunes Music folder and choose Cut from the shortcut menu to cut it to the Clipboard.

5. In the Other Places task pane, click the Shared Music link to display the Shared Music folder. (If the Shared Music folder doesn't appear in the Other Places task pane, click the My Computer link, click the Shared Documents link, and then double-click the Shared Music folder.)

6. Right-click in open space and choose Paste from the shortcut menu to paste the iTunes Music folder into the Shared Music folder.

7. Close the Windows Explorer window.

Next, you need to tell iTunes where the song files are. Follow these steps:

1. Start iTunes (for example, double-click the iTunes icon on your desktop).

2. Press CTRL-COMMA or choose Edit | Preferences to display the iTunes dialog box.

3. Click the Advanced tab.

4. Click the Change button to display the Browse For Folder dialog box.

5. Navigate to the Shared Music folder (for example, click the My Computer item, click the Shared Documents item, click the Shared Music item, click the iTunes Music item, and then click the iTunes Music item) and then click the OK button.

6. Click the OK button to close the iTunes dialog box.

After you've done this, iTunes knows where the song files are, and you can play them back as usual. When you rip further song files from CD or import files, iTunes stores them in the Shared Music folder.

You're all set. The other users of your PC can do either of two things:

- Move their music library to the Shared Music folder, using the techniques described here, so that all music is stored centrally. Instead of moving the iTunes Music folder itself, move the folders it contains. Users can then add songs they import to the shared music library, and all users can access them.

- Keep their music library separate, but add the contents of the shared music library folder to it. To do so, follow these steps:

  1. Choose File | Add Folder To Library to display the Browse For Folder dialog box.

  2. Navigate to the Shared Music folder.

  3. Select the iTunes Music folder.

  4. Click the Open button. iTunes adds all the latest songs to your music library.

In either case, there's a small complication songs that other users have added to the shared music library don't appear automatically in your music library. To add all the latest tracks, use the Add To Library dialog box, as described in the previous list.

Share Your Music Library with Other Users of Your Mac

Mac OS X's security system prevents other users from accessing your Home folder or its contents—which by default include your music library. So if you want to share your music library with other users of your Mac, you need to change permissions to allow others to access your Home folder (or parts of it) or move your music library to a folder they can access.

The easiest way to give other users access to your music is to put your music library in the Users/Shared folder and put an alias to it in its default location. To do so, follow these steps:

1. Use the Finder to move the iTunes Music folder from your ~/Music/iTunes folder to the /Users/Shared folder.

2. Press ⌘-COMMA (or ⌘-Y) or choose iTunes | Preferences to display the Preferences dialog box.

3. Click the Advanced button to display the Advanced sheet.

4. Click the Change button and use the resulting Change Music Folder Location dialog box to navigate to and select the /Users/Shared/iTunes Music folder.

5. Click the Choose button to close the Change Music Folder Location dialog box, and then enter the new path in the iTunes Music Folder Location text box on the Advanced sheet.

6. Select the Keep iTunes Music Folder Organized check box.

7. Click the OK button to close the Advanced sheet. iTunes displays the Changing The Location Of The iTunes Music Folder dialog box.

8. Click the OK button. iTunes displays the Updating Song Locations dialog box as it updates the locations in its database. iTunes then displays the dialog box asking whether you want to let it organize your music preferences.

9. Click the Yes button to move the music files in your library to the new, shared music library.

10. If you want other users to be able to put song files in the shared music library (for example, if they import them from CD), you need to give them Write permission for it. To do so, follow these steps:

   A. Open a Finder window to the /Users/Shared folder.

   B. CTRL-click or right-click the iTunes Music folder, and then choose Get Info from the shortcut menu to display the iTunes Music Info window (shown here with the Ownership & Permissions area expanded).

   C. In the Ownership & Permissions area, click the Details arrow to expand its display, if necessary.

   D. In the Others drop-down list, select the Read & Write item instead of the Read Only item.

E. Click the Apply To Enclosed Items button. Mac OS X displays this dialog box:

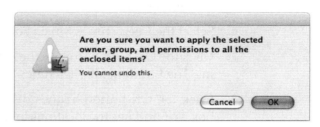

F. Click the OK button.

G. Click the Close button (the X button) to close the Info window.

After you move your music library to the /Users/Shared folder, the other users of your Mac can do one of two things:

- Move their music library to the /Users/Shared folder, using the technique just described, so that all music is stored centrally. Users can then add songs they import to the shared music library, and all users can access them.

- Keep their music library separate, but add the contents of the shared music library folder to it:

  1. Press ⌘-Q or choose File | Add To Library to display the Add To Library dialog box.

  2. Navigate to the /Users/Shared/iTunes Music folder.

  3. Click the Open button. iTunes adds all the latest songs to your music library.

In either case, there's a small complication: songs that other users have added to the shared music library don't appear automatically in your music library. To add all the latest tracks, use the Add To Library dialog box, as described in the previous list.

Step 4: Build a Music Server for Your Household

If you find that trying to play songs stored in music libraries that keep disappearing off the network is too tedious, another option is to build a music server for your household. You can either build a server from scratch on a new computer or change the role of one of your existing computers—even a pensioned-off computer that's too old to run Mac OS X or Windows at a decent speed.

note *Another possibility is to use disk space on one of your existing computers to hold a shared folder for songs. You don't need to specifically turn the computer into a server to do this—but the computer must be running (and connected to the network) all the time you want any songs to be available.*

Whether you buy (or build) a new computer or repurpose an existing computer will color your choices for your server. Here are notes on the key components for the server:

- **Operating system**   The server can run Windows or Mac OS X if you have a copy that you can spare. If not, consider using a less expensive (or even free) operating system, such as one of the many distributions of Linux.

- **Processor**   The server can run on a modest processor—even an antiquated one by today's standards, such as a 500 MHz or faster processor for a Windows or Linux server or a slower G3 processor for a Mac server.

- **RAM**   The server needs only enough RAM to run the operating system unless you'll need to run applications on it. For example, 256 MB RAM is adequate for a server running Windows XP or Mac OS X.

- **Disk space**   The server must have enough disk space to store all the songs and videos you want to have available. A desktop computer is likely to be a better bet than a notebook computer, because you can add internal drives to it. Alternatively, you might use one or more external USB or FireWire drives to provide plenty of space.

- **Network connection**   The server must be connected to your network, either via network cable or via wireless. A wireless connection is adequate for serving a few computers, but in most cases, a wired connection (Fast Ethernet or Gigabit Ethernet) is a much better choice.

- **Monitor**   If the server will simply be running somewhere convenient (rather than being used for other computing tasks, such as running applications), all you need is an old monitor capable of displaying the bootup and login screens for the operating system. After that, you can turn the monitor off until you need to restart or configure the server.

- **Keyboard and mouse**   Like the monitor, the keyboard and mouse can be basic devices, because you'll need to use them only for booting and configuring the server.

- **Optical drive**   After you install the operating system, the server needs an optical drive only if you'll use it for ripping. If you'll rip on the clients, the server can get by without one.

- **Sound card**   The server needs a sound card only if you'll use it for playing music.

- **Reliability**   Modest the server may be, but it must be reliable—otherwise the music won't be available when you want to play it. Make sure also that the server has plenty of cooling, and configure its power settings so that it doesn't go to sleep.

● **Location** If you choose to leave your server running all the time, locate it somewhere safe from being switched off accidentally. Because the running server will probably make some noise, you may be tempted to hide it away in a closet. If you do, make sure there's enough ventilation so that it doesn't overheat.

After setting up the server and sharing a folder that will contain the songs, configure iTunes on the client computers to use that folder for the music library. Use the techniques described in Step 3 to tell iTunes where to find the song files.

Boot Your Mac from Your iPod

What You'll Need:

- iPods Covered: First-, second-, third-, or fourth-generation regular iPod; or iPod with video
- Cost: Free

One of the attractions of early iPods for Mac users was that you could *boot* (start up) your Mac from the iPod instead of from the Mac's hard disk. To do so, you must install Mac OS X on the iPod's hard disk, and then tell the Mac to use the iPod as its startup disk instead of using the hard disk as usual.

Booting your Mac from an iPod can be useful in several situations, such as (but not limited to) the following:

- If you've got an old iPod, you can prepare it as an emergency boot device for that evil day when your Mac's hard disk goes south. Having an extra hard disk is particularly comforting when you're on the road.

- Even better, you can use your iPod to create daily backups of your hard disk—and bootable backups at that. If the hard disk suffers corruption, or if it fails, you can use your iPod to recover.

- If you need to maintain tight security, you can make your iPod the only bootable disk for your Mac. By taking the iPod with you wherever you go, you can prevent other people from booting your Mac.

Step 1: Understand the Limitations of Booting from the iPod

Booting your Mac from your iPod is a cool trick and can save your bacon when things go wrong. But you should understand the limitations before you install Mac OS X on your iPod:

- This trick is Mac-only: It doesn't work for the PC and never has.

- It works only for the regular iPods—the full-size iPods that have hard disks. The iPod mini (which had a tiny hard disk) and iPod nano (which uses flash memory) have never had this capability—which is probably just as well, given their limited capacity.

- You can boot a Power-based Mac from a FireWire iPod or an Intel-based Mac from either a FireWire iPod or a USB iPod with video. At this writing, you can't boot a Power-based Mac from a USB iPod with video.

note *A Power-based Mac is one with a Power processor, such as a G3, G4, or G5 processor. An Intel-based Mac is one with an Intel processor in it. Apple switched from Power processors to Intel processors in 2005–2006.*

- Apple acknowledges that you can use your iPod as a bootable disk but doesn't support booting as a feature.

- To start up a Power-based Mac from a FireWire iPod, the Mac must have a built-in FireWire port. (Almost all Power-based Macs do, so you're unlikely to have a problem here.)

- Even though FireWire and USB are fast connections, booting from your iPod will take much longer than booting from your hard disk, and your Mac will run more slowly than usual. Be prepared for this before you make grand plans for your iPod.

Step 2: Determine What Kind of Mac and iPod You Have

Now that you understand the limitations of booting your Mac from your iPod, make sure you know whether your Mac is Power-based or Intel-based and what kind of iPod you have.

To tell whether your Mac is Power-based or Intel-based:

- If the Mac has "Power" in the name (for example, Power Mac or Power-Book), it's Power-based. If you bought your Mac before January 2006, it's Power-based.

- If the Mac is called MacBook or Mac Pro, it's Intel-based.

- If it's not clear from the first two bullet points, choose Apple | About This Mac and look at the Processor readout in the About This Mac dialog box. Figure 22-1 shows an example of a Mac with a PowerPC G4 processor. Click the Close button (the red button on the title bar) to close the dialog box.

You probably know by now which kind of iPod you have. If not, have a look at the packaging, the Apple website (www.apple.com/ipod/), or any iPod-enthusiast site.

Figure 22-1

If in doubt about the type of processor in your Mac, check the Processor readout in the About This Mac dialog box.

Step 3: Put Mac OS X on Your iPod

The next step is to put Mac OS X on your iPod. How you do this depends on whether the iPod uses FireWire or USB.

If the iPod uses FireWire, you can put Mac OS X on it in either of two ways:

- **Install Mac OS X directly on the iPod** This method gives you a clean installation of Mac OS X, which you should update (via Software Update) to make sure that it contains all the latest patches. To install Mac OS X directly on your iPod, you need to have an install DVD (rather than install CDs—the install process usually fails when switching from the first CD to the second CD). See the next section for instructions.

- **Clone an existing installation of Mac OS X** This method lets you copy your existing installation of Mac OS X—fully up-to-date and with all your applications and settings—onto your iPod. The easiest way to clone your existing installation is to use a utility such as the freeware Carbon Copy Cloner. See the section after next for instructions.

If your iPod uses USB, you need to use a different technique. See "Put Mac OS X on a USB iPod," later in this project, for details.

Install Mac OS X Directly on a FireWire iPod

To install Mac OS X directly on a FireWire iPod, you run the installation routine from your Mac OS X installation DVD exactly as you would to install the operating system on your Mac, but you specify your iPod, rather than your Mac's hard disk, as the destination disk for the install.

To install Mac OS X on your iPod, follow these steps:

1. Make sure your iPod has plenty of free space. You need between 2GB and 4.8GB for Tiger, depending on which files you choose to install. Leopard will probably need more.

2. Connect your iPod to your Mac via FireWire.

3. Enable disk mode on your iPod if it isn't already enabled (see the section "Enable Disk Mode" in Project 13 for instructions).

4. If you're not certain that your iPod is formatted with the Mac OS X Extended file system rather than the FAT32 file system, right-click the iPod's icon on the Desktop and choose Get Info from the shortcut menu. In the Info window, check the Format readout. If the iPod is formatted with FAT32, you must use the iPod Updater to restore the iPod to Mac OS X Extended before you can boot from it. (Use the technique described in the section "Restore the iPod" in Project 17.) Restoring the iPod loses all the songs and other data it contains, so back up the iPod before taking this drastic step.

5. Insert the Mac OS DVD in your Mac's optical drive. If Mac OS X doesn't automatically open a window showing the DVD's contents, double-click the DVD's icon on your desktop or in a Finder window.

6. Double-click the Install Mac OS X application icon to display the Install Mac OS X window (see Figure 22-2).

Figure 22-2

The Install Mac OS X window.

Launching the Mac OS X installation may feel like you're going to wipe your Mac's hard drive, but you get to specify your iPod as the destination drive after your Mac restarts.

7. Click the Restart button. Mac OS X displays the Authenticate dialog box (shown here).

8. Type your username and password and then click the OK button. (You must have administrator-level privileges to install the operating system, even on your iPod rather than on your Mac.) Your Mac restarts and displays the installation screen on which you select the language to use.

9. Choose the language—for example, select the Use English As The Main Language item—and then click the arrow button. The Install Mac OS X window appears.

10. Follow through the installation procedure until you reach the Select Destination screen.

11. Click your iPod's icon to set it as the destination for the installation, and then click the Continue button.

caution *The Mac OS X installation routine offers you the option of erasing your hard drive and formatting it using either Mac OS Extended (HFS Plus) or Unix File System. Don't use this option. Erasing the disk will do more harm than good.*

12. When installing Mac OS X, it's a good idea to customize the installation to reduce the amount of space it takes up. On the Installation Type screen, click the Customize button instead of accepting the default Easy Install option. On the resulting Custom Install screen, clear the check boxes for the items you don't want to install. Keep these points in mind:

● You must install the Essential System Software item, so the Installer doesn't let you clear its check boxes.

● Consider installing only some printer drivers rather than all of them (1.6 GB altogether), not installing the Additional Fonts (129MB; for Chinese, Korean, Arabic, and other exotic languages), the Language Translations (1.1 GB), or X11 (89 MB).

13. Click the Install button to start the installation, and then let it run. At the end of the installation, your Mac automatically boots from your iPod, and you see the Welcome screen for Mac OS X. You'll then need to go through the Mac OS X setup routine of selecting your country, choosing a keyboard layout, registering Mac OS X, and setting up a user account.

Clone Your Existing Mac OS X Installation onto Your iPod

The second way to make your iPod bootable is to clone your existing Mac OS X installation onto it. This method gives you an iPod with an up-to-date and fully patched installation—and all your files and settings.

This section shows you how to close Mac OS X using Carbon Copy Cloner, which you can download from Mike Bombich's website (www.bombich.com/software/ccc .html). Carbon Copy Cloner is donationware: if you like it, you can make a donation to the author.

tip   *Another powerful cloning utility for the Mac is SuperDuper!, which you can buy for $27.95 from Shirt Pocket Software (www.shirt-pocket.com/SuperDuper/SuperDuperDescription.html). Shirt Pocket offers a trial edition that you'll probably want to test before buying the full version.*

To clone your installation of Mac OS X, follow these steps:

1. Prepare your installation of Mac OS X for cloning:

   ● Run Software Update and apply any new patches or updates.

   ● Install any applications that you want to have on your iPod when you boot from it. For example, you might want to install troubleshooting tools.

   ● If you've been meaning to clear out old files, now is a good time to do so.

   ● Empty the Trash.

2. Connect your iPod to your Mac via FireWire.

3. Enable disk mode on your iPod if it isn't already enabled (see the section "Enable Disk Mode" in Project 13 for instructions).

4. Make sure your iPod has enough free space for the installation of Mac OS X that you want to clone.

5. Run Carbon Copy Cloner. It displays the Cloning Console (shown in Figure 22-3 with the source disk and target disk selected).

6. In the Source Disk drop-down list, choose the disk that contains the installation of Mac OS X that you want to clone. Carbon Copy Cloner displays a list of the disk's contents in the Items To Be Copied list box.

7. By default, Carbon Copy Cloner clones everything on your disk. To remove an item, select it in the Items To Be Copied list box and then click the Delete button (the button bearing a red circle with a line through it above the Items To Be Copied list box).

Figure 22-3

Select the source disk and target disk in the Cloning Console.

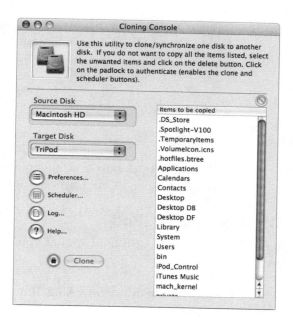

8. In the Target Disk drop-down list, select your iPod.

9. Click the lock button in the lower-left corner of the Carbon Copy Cloner window to display the Enter Your Administrative Password pane.

10. Type your password, and then click the OK button. Carbon Copy Cloner closes the pane and activates the Clone button.

11. Click the Clone button to start the cloning operation. Carbon Copy Cloner displays a progress readout (in the bottom-left corner of the Cloning Console) as it works (see Figure 22-4).

Figure 22-4

Carbon Copy Cloner shows its progress as it clones your disk to the iPod.

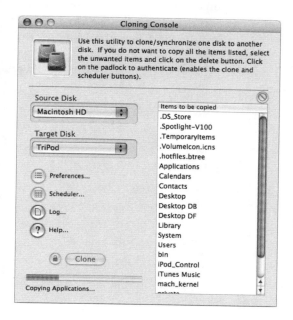

12. Carbon Copy Cloner displays a message box to tell you when it has finished cloning your Mac OS X installation:

The clone operation has completed.

Donate   OK

13. Click the OK button to close the message box. Then press ⌘-Q or choose Carbon Copy Cloner | Quit Carbon Copy Cloner to quit Carbon Copy Cloner.

Put Mac OS X on a USB iPod

To put Mac OS X on a USB iPod so that you can boot an Intel-based Mac from it, follow these steps:

1. Connect the iPod to your Mac. If it's set to synchronize automatically, allow it to do so.

2. Check that your iPod is formatted with the Mac OS Extended file system. Right-click the iPod's icon on the Desktop, and then choose Get Info from the shortcut menu. In the Info window, check the Format readout. If the iPod is formatted with FAT32, you must use the iPod Updater to restore the iPod to Mac OS X Extended before you can boot from it. (Use the technique described in the section "Restore the iPod" in Project 17.) Restoring the iPod loses all the songs and other data it contains, so back up the iPod before taking this drastic step.

3. Enable disk mode on your iPod if it isn't already enabled (see the section "Enable Disk Mode" in Project 13 for instructions).

4. Open a Terminal window (as shown here). For example, click the Finder button on the Dock, choose Go | Utilities to open a window showing the Utilities folder, and then double-click the Terminal item.

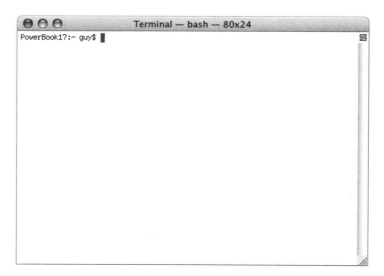

Terminal — bash — 80x24

PowerBook17:~ guy$

5. Make sure you know what your Mac's hard disk and the iPod are called. Issue the **ls /Volumes** command and press ENTER to list the volumes mounted on your Mac. You'll see something like the following, which indicates that Mac OS X knows the Mac's hard disk as "Macintosh HD" and the iPod by the name "VideoPod":

```
PowerBook17:~ guy$ ls /Volumes
Macintosh HD    VideoPod
```

6. Use the following **sudo** command (sudo is "do as super-user") and press ENTER to tell Apple Software Restore (**asr**) to copy the Mac's hard disk to the iPod. Substitute the name of your hard disk for "Macintosh HD" and the name of your iPod for VideoPod in the following command. If either name includes a space, put it within double quotation marks (as with "Macintosh HD" here).

```
sudo asr -source /Volumes/"Macintosh HD" -target /Volumes/VideoPod
```

7. When you press ENTER, Terminal prompts you for your password. Type it, and then press ENTER. You'll see messages as Terminal validates the target, the source, and sizes, and then copies your Mac's hard disk to the iPod.

8. When Terminal has finished copying the files, it displays a message about the target not being "blessed"—not being recognized as a bootable drive:

```
asr: did not copy blessed information to target, which may have
missing or out-of-date blessed folder information.
```

9. To bless the folder, use the following **sudo** command, substituting the name of your iPod for VideoPod and pressing ENTER at the end of the command.

```
sudo bless -folder /Volumes/VideoPod/System/Library/CoreServices
```

10. Press ⌘-Q or choose Terminal | Quit Terminal to close the Terminal window.

Step 4: Set the Mac to Boot from the iPod— and Then Boot!

The next step is to set the Mac to boot from the iPod. To do this, you tell the Mac to use the iPod as its startup disk.

note *If you've installed Mac OS X from scratch on the iPod, you don't need to take this step, as your Mac will already have booted from the iPod at the end of the installation.*

To designate your iPod as the startup disk, follow these steps:

1. Choose Apple | System Preferences to display the System Preferences window.

2. Click the Startup Disk icon in the System area to display the Startup Disk sheet (shown here).

3. Select the item that represents your iPod.

4. To restart immediately and check that your bootable iPod works, click the Restart button. Mac OS X displays this confirmation dialog box:

5. Click the Restart button. Your Mac restarts and boots the operating system from your iPod.

If you don't want to restart your Mac immediately, press ⌘-Q or choose System Preferences | Quit System Preferences to quit System Preferences. Then restart your Mac as normal whenever you want to.

Step 5: Set Up Your Mac to Boot from Its Hard Disk Again

To make your Mac boot from its hard disk again instead of from the iPod, follow these steps:

1. Choose Apple | System Preferences to open System Preferences.

2. Click the Startup Disk item to display the Startup Disk sheet.

3. Select the entry for your hard disk, and then click the Restart button. Mac OS X displays a confirmation dialog box.

4. Click the Restart button in the confirmation dialog box. Mac OS X restarts from your hard disk.

If you installed Mac OS X directly on your iPod, keep it updated by booting to it regularly and using System Update to check for and apply updates as they become available. If you cloned your Mac's hard disk, keep the hard disk up-to-date, and perform the cloning operation whenever you need to update the iPod's copy.

Display All Available Startup Disks

If your Mac fails to boot from your iPod, you may have a nasty moment—or your Mac may give up on looking for your iPod and decide to boot from its hard disk anyway. If it *doesn't* boot at all, and you find yourself looking at a blank screen, take the following steps:

1. Press ⌘-CONTROL-POWER to force a restart.

2. When your Mac plays the system sound, hold down OPTION to display a graphical screen of the available startup disks.

3. Click the disk from which you want to start the computer.

4. Click the arrow button on the screen to start your Mac using that startup disk.

Install iPodLinux on Your iPod and Record Full-Quality Audio

What You'll Need:

- iPods Covered: First-, second, third-, and fourth-generation regular iPod, iPod with video
- Windows Software Required: iPodLinux
- Mac Software Required: iPodLinux
- Cost: Free

The iPod's operating system is well designed and easy to use—but if you're looking to push your iPod to its limits, you need a different operating system. This project discusses one operating system, iPodLinux. The next project discusses another, RockBox.

iPodLinux is an extremely ambitious project and has much to recommend it. Apart from playing music, you can run an impressive array of applications on your iPod, including text editors and drawing and painting programs. iPodLinux includes a battery of straightforward games, and you can even install demanding games such as ports of DOOM, the classic first-person shooter.

For the audio enthusiast, one of the most appealing features of iPodLinux is that it enables you to record high-quality stereo audio on iPods that normally can record only mono audio at inadequate bitrates with their own firmware. At this writing, recording works only with third- and fourth-generation iPods (both the iPod photo and the fourth-generation iPod with the monochrome screen)—but given that the iPod with video and second-generation iPod nano can already record in CD quality (given a suitable microphone, as discussed in Project 3), and that the first-generation iPod nano, iPod mini, and first- and second-generation iPods can't record at all because of hardware limitations, that's still a great boon.

Step 1: Back Up Your iPod

Installing iPodLinux is "nondestructive," so you shouldn't lose any data—but it's always possible that something might go wrong.

So before you install iPodLinux, back up any files on your iPod whose loss you'd miss. If your iPod contains only song and video files, contacts, calendars, and notes synchronized from your computer, you needn't back any up. But if you've been using your iPod to store or transfer files, make sure you have copies of them.

Step 2: Turn On Disk Mode

Also before you install iPodLinux, you need to turn disk mode on for your iPod, so that it appears to Windows or Mac OS X as a disk. To turn on disk mode, follow these steps:

1. Connect your iPod to your computer and allow iTunes to synchronize with the iPod if it is set to do so.

2. Click the iPod's entry in the Source pane. iTunes displays the iPod's information.

3. On the Summary tab, select the Enable Disk Use check box. iTunes displays a warning dialog box, telling you that using disk mode requires you to manually unmount the iPod before each disconnect, even when you're automatically updating music.

4. Select the Do Not Warn Me Again check box, and then click the OK button.

5. Click the Apply button to apply the change.

6. Choose File | Exit (Windows) or iTunes | Quit iTunes (Mac) to close iTunes.

Leave your iPod connected to your computer for the time being.

Step 3: Install iPodLinux

You're now ready to install iPodLinux on your iPod. The following sections discuss the procedure for Windows (first) and Mac OS X (second).

Install iPodLinux on an iPod from Windows

To install iPodLinux on an iPod from Windows, follow these steps:

1. Open your browser, go to the iPodLinux website (www.ipodlinux.org), and download the iPodLinux Installer file for Windows.

2. In the Download Complete dialog box, click the Open button to open a Windows Explorer window showing the contents of the zip file.

3. In the Folder Tasks pane, click the Extract All Files link, and then follow through the Extraction Wizard to extract the contents of the zip file and open a Windows Explorer window showing its contents (a folder called ipodlinux-installer and a version number).

4. Open the folder, and then double-click the installer.exe program to run the installer. Windows may display an Open File – Security Warning dialog box telling you that the publisher cannot be verified. If so, click the Run button. The first screen of the iPodLinux Installer appears.

5. Click the Next button. The iPodLinux Installer detects the iPod, and then shows the details of what it has found (see Figure 23-1).

Figure 23-1

Make sure the iPodLinux Installer has correctly identified your iPod.

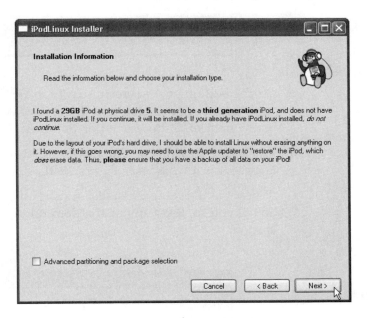

note   *If you're experienced with Linux, you'll probably want to select the Advanced Partitioning And Package Selection check box.*

6. Verify that the iPodLinux Installer has found your iPod. (Unless you've connected the wrong iPod, there shouldn't be any confusion.)

7. Click the Next button to continue with a standard installation. The iPodLinux Installer displays the second Installation Information screen (see Figure 23-2).

8. Select the Standard Loader With iPodLinux Default option button if you want your iPod to boot iPodLinux unless you actively choose to boot the iPod's own operating system. To keep booting the iPod's operating system unless you choose to boot Linux, select the Standard Loader With Apple Firmware Default option button.

Figure 23-2

Choose whether to make iPodLinux or the iPod's own operating system the default.

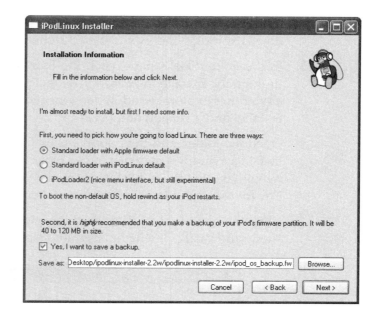

9. At the bottom of the screen, select the Yes, I Want To Save A Backup check box, and specify the location in the Save As text box. You can type a folder path or click the Browse button and then use the resulting dialog box.

10. Click the Next button. The iPodLinux Installer keeps you up-to-date on its progress as it works (see Figure 23-3).

11. When the iPodLinux Installer finishes the installation, it displays a screen to tell you so. Read any instructions on the screen, and then click the Finish button.

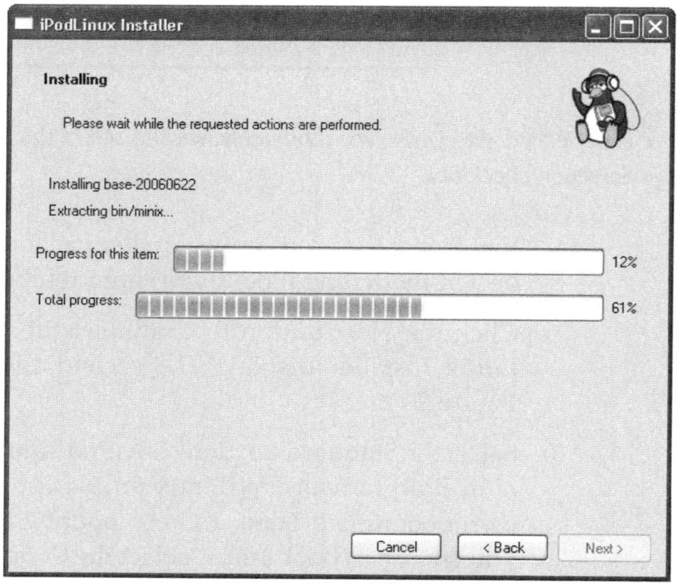

Figure 23-3

You can watch each operation the iPodLinux Installer is performing—or else go for a cup of coffee while the installation runs.

Install iPodLinux on an iPod from the Mac

To install iPodLinux on an iPod from the Mac, follow these steps:

1. Open your browser, go to the iPodLinux website (www.ipodlinux.org), and download the iPod-Linux Installer disk image file for the Mac.

2. If Mac OS X doesn't automatically mount the disk image and open a Finder window showing its contents, double-click the disk image file to mount the disk image, and then double-click the disk image itself to open a window.

3. Double-click the iPod-Linux Installer item to start the installer. A disclaimer dialog box appears.

4. Click the I Agree button to agree that you won't blame the iPod-Linux Installer's author for any harm that "may occur to you, your iPod, or anything else as a result of using this software." You then see the whole of the iPod-Linux Installer window (see Figure 23-4).

Figure 23-4

The iPod-Linux Installer lets you choose whether to make Linux the default OS on your iPod.

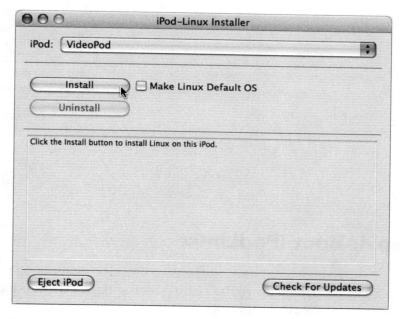

5. In the iPod drop-down list, select the iPod on which you want to install iPodLinux.

6. If you want to make iPodLinux the default operating system on the iPod, so that the iPod boots iPodLinux unless you prevent it from doing so, select the Make Linux Default OS check box. You can easily override the default operating system and boot the other, so don't feel you need to select this check box.

7. Click the Install button to start the installation. The iPod-Linux Installer displays progress messages as it works, as shown here.

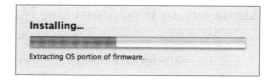

8. When the iPod-Linux Installer finishes the installation, it displays a screen such as the one shown in Figure 23-5. Click the Eject iPod button to eject your iPod, and then press ⌘-Q or choose iPod-Linux Installer | Quit iPod-Linux Installer to close the installer.

Figure 23-5

When the iPod-Linux Installer finishes, read the instructions, and then click the Eject iPod button to eject your iPod.

> **iPod–Linux Installer**
>
> **iPod:** VideoPod
>
> (Re–Install) ☐ Make Linux Default OS
> (Uninstall)
>
> Linux was installed successfully. To use, unplug your iPod and hold the menu and select buttons down until it resets. If you want to use Linux, hold the rewind button down as the iPod reboots. If you want to use the Apple supplied OS, do not hold any buttons when you reboot the iPod.
>
> If you want to switch between either OS at a later point, repeat the steps mentioned above. These instructions are available in the Read Me file that should have come with the installer.
>
> (Eject iPod)   (Check For Updates)

Step 4: Boot iPodLinux

To boot iPodLinux, restart your iPod. For example, on the iPod with video or the iPod nano, hold down the Menu button and the Select button for about five seconds, until you see the Apple logo appear.

If you chose to make iPodLinux your iPod's default operating system, your iPod boots iPodLinux automatically. (If you want to boot the iPod's own firmware, hold down the Previous/Rewind button for a few seconds as the iPod restarts.)

If you chose not to make iPodLinux your iPod's default operating system, hold down the Previous/Rewind button as the iPod restarts. When you see the image of Tux (the Linux penguin), you can release the button.

You'll see various text-based screens as Linux loads. iPodLinux's interface, which is called podzilla, then appears, as shown here.

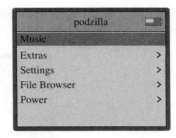

Step 5: Listen to Music on Your iPodLinux iPod

podzilla can read the iPod's database of songs you've transferred via iTunes, so you can start listening to music right away. Select the Music item on podzilla's main menu, and you're in business.

If you wiped your iPod clean before installing iPodLinux, you can add songs in two ways:

- Use iTunes to install songs. You can then play the songs through both iPod-Linux and the iPod's own firmware.

- Simply put song files into folders in the Linux file system, and then use podzilla's File Browser to locate songs. You won't be able to play these songs using the iPod's own firmware.

If you want to play games on the iPod, or investigate programs such as iPod Paint, open the Extras menu (shown here) and explore its contents.

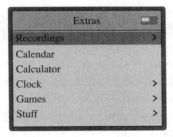

Step 6: Record Audio on Your Third- or Fourth-Generation iPod

To record audio on a third or fourth-generation iPod, follow these steps:

1. Connect a microphone to the iPod. Most microphones for these generations of iPods connect via the headphone connector and the remote-control connector at the top of the iPod.

2. From the podzilla menu, choose Extras | Recordings to display the Recordings screen (shown here).

3. Scroll down to the Sample Rate item, and then press the Select button to select the recording quality you want: 8 kHz, 32 kHz, 44.1 kHz (CD quality), 88.2 kHz, or 96 kHz. Usually 44.1 kHz is the best choice unless you need super-high quality.

4. On a third-generation iPod, select the Mic Record item or the Line In Record item. On a fourth-generation iPod, select the Mic Record item (fourth-generation iPods can record only via Mic).

5. Press the Select button to display the Record screen.

6. Press the Select button to start the recording, and then press the Select button again to stop the recording.

To listen to a recording, go to the Recordings screen, scroll to the Playback item, and then press the Select button. Select the file, and then press the Select button.

Step 7: Boot Your iPod's Own Firmware

To boot your iPod's own firmware, restart your iPod. For example, on the iPod with video or the iPod nano, hold down the Menu button and the Select button for about five seconds, until you see the Apple logo appear.

If you chose not to make iPodLinux your iPod's default operating system, your iPod boots its own firmware automatically. If you chose to make iPodLinux your iPod's default operating system, press the Previous/Rewind button as the iPod restarts.

Step 8: Uninstall iPodLinux

If you decide to get rid of iPodLinux, you can do so easily enough. Connect your iPod to your computer, run the installer (as discussed in step 2), and then choose the Uninstall iPodLinux option.

Install Rockbox on Your iPod for Even Better Audio Playback

What you'll need:

- iPods Covered: iPod with video, iPod nano, fourth-generation iPod with color screen, fourth-generation iPod with monochrome screen, third-generation iPod, iPod mini
- Windows Software Required: Rockbox
- Mac Software Required: Rockbox
- Cost: Free

Apple has designed the iPod to appeal to as wide an audience as possible, and most people find that the iPod delivers more than adequate audio quality—especially when you're listening to songs encoded using Apple Lossless Encoding or AAC at a high bitrate. But if you're a true audiophile, you may find the iPod's audio quality somewhat disappointing. You may also want to listen to music encoded using the Free Lossless Audio Codec (FLAC) or the Ogg Vorbis codec, neither of which the iPod supports.

tip *Audiophiles tend to rate the audio quality of the iPod photo above that of the iPod with video and iPod nano. If you've got an iPod photo, don't be in too much of a hurry to trade it in for one of the newer and sleeker models.*

To get higher audio quality on your iPod, you can replace your iPod's firmware (the iPod's operating system) with Rockbox, an open-source jukebox program designed for various music players. At this writing, Rockbox runs on the iPod with video, iPod nano, fourth-generation iPod (both the iPod photo and the iPod with the monochrome screen), third-generation iPod, and the iPod mini. Rockbox is freeware (you can donate if you like it) that plays audio in more than ten formats (including MP3, AAC, FLAC, and Ogg Vorbis), offers highly configurable sound settings, and even provides a suite of games.

Step 1: Back Up Your iPod

Before you install Rockbox, back up any files on your iPod whose loss you'd miss. If your iPod contains only song and video files, contacts, calendars, and notes synchronized from your computer, you needn't back any up. But if you've been using your iPod to store or transfer files, make sure you have copies of them.

When installing Rockbox on an iPod you're using with Windows, you shouldn't lose any files—but it's always possible that something might go wrong. When installing Rockbox on an iPod you're using with a Mac, however, you'll most likely have to reformat the iPod using the FAT32 file system. Reformatting deletes all the existing files, so you'll lose them even if everything goes to plan.

Step 2: Turn Off Auto-Launching of iTunes

Next, turn off auto-launching of iTunes for the iPod on which you will install Rockbox. Follow these steps:

1. Connect your iPod to your computer, and allow iTunes to synchronize with the iPod if it is set to do so.

2. Click the iPod's entry in the Source pane. iTunes displays the iPod's information.

3. On the Summary tab, clear the Open iTunes When This iPod Is Connected check box.

4. Click the Apply button to apply the change.

5. Choose File | Exit (Windows) or iTunes | Quit iTunes to close iTunes.

Leave your iPod connected to your computer.

Step 3: Download Rockbox and OS-specific Files

Your next step is to get the files you need. Follow these steps:

1. Open your browser, and then go to the Rockbox web site (www.rockbox.org).

2. Click the Downloads link, find the latest version of Rockbox for your iPod, and then download it.

3. Download the latest version of the iPod manual as well.

4. Download the OS-specific Rockbox files, as discussed in the next two subsections.

Rockbox consists of a bootloader and firmware files:

- **Bootloader**   The bootloader is a small file that you install to your iPod's flash memory. When your iPod boots, the bootloader instructs it to load the Rockbox firmware image.

- **Firmware files**   The firmware files consist of a file called rockbox.ipod and a folder called .rockbox. You install these files on your iPod's hard drive or (in the case of an iPod nano) its main flash memory storage.

Get the ipodpatcher and ipod_fw Files for Windows

For Windows, apart from the main Rockbox software, you'll also need to download the ipodpatcher.exe file and the ipod_fw.exe file from www.rockbox.org/twiki/bin/view/Main/IpodInstallation/.

Choose Start | My Documents, create a new folder named Rockbox in the My Documents folder, and then put these two files in it. If you decide to use a different folder, you'll need to change the paths in the commands you issue in the next step.

Get the diskdump and ipod_fw Files for the Mac

For the Mac, apart from the main Rockbox software, you'll also need to download the diskdump file and the ipod_fw file from www.rockbox.org/twiki/bin/view/Main/IpodInstallationFromMacOSX.

Click the desktop to activate the Finder, choose Go | Home to open a Finder window to your Home folder (represented by ~ in Unix notation), and then create a folder named Rockbox. Put the files you downloaded in this folder. If you decide to use a different folder, you'll need to change the paths in the commands you issue in the next step.

Step 4: Install the Bootloader and Rockbox Operating System

Now that you've got the Rockbox software, it's time to install the bootloader and the operating system. The process is different for Windows and the Mac, so follow the first section (Windows) or second section (Mac) below, as appropriate.

Install the Bootloader on Windows

To install the Rockbox bootloader on Windows, follow these steps:

1. Choose Start | All Programs | Accessories | Command Prompt to open a command prompt window.

2. Issue the following command to change directory to the Rockbox directory inside your My Documents folder:

```
cd %userprofile%\My Documents\Rockbox
```

3. Run the ipodpatcher.exe program using ascending numbers to find out which drive represents the iPod: ipodpatcher 0, ipodpatcher 1, ipodpatcher 2, and so on. Start with this command:

```
ipodpatcher 0
```

4. For each drive that isn't an iPod, you'll get the message "Error reading from disk: The device is not ready." When the ipodpatcher command finds the iPod, it displays details of its partition table. Here's an example:

```
C:\Documents and Settings\Jon\My Documents\Rockbox>ipodpatcher 5
ipodpatcher v0.3 - (C) Dave Chapman 2006
This is free software; see the source for copying conditions.  There is NO
warranty; not even for MERCHANTABILITY or FITNESS FOR A PARTICULAR PURPOSE.

[INFO] Reading partition table from \\.\PhysicalDrive5
Part      Start Sector     End Sector     Size (MB)   Type
   0                63         160649         78.4   Empty (0x00)
   1            160650       58605119      28537.3   W95 FAT32 (0x0b)
```

5. Note the drive number, because you'll use it in the following commands in place of the placeholder *drive*.

6. Issue the following command to copy the iPod's firmware partition to a file on your computer:

```
ipodpatcher -r drive bootpartition.bin
```

7. You'll see output like the following as ipodpatcher.exe reads the partition table and writes the information to the output file:

```
ipodpatcher v0.3 - (C) Dave Chapman 2006
This is free software; see the source for copying conditions.  There is NO
warranty; not even for MERCHANTABILITY or FITNESS FOR A PARTICULAR PURPOSE.

[INFO] Reading partition table from \\.\PhysicalDrive5
Part      Start Sector     End Sector     Size (MB)   Type
   0                63         160649         78.4   Empty (0x00)
   1            160650       58605119      28537.3   W95 FAT32 (0x0b)
[INFO] Seeking to sector 63
[INFO] Writing 160587 sectors to output file
[INFO] Done.
```

8. Issue the following command to extract the iPod's firmware from the partition, noting that the character before "bootpartition.bin" is a zero rather than a capital O:

```
ipod_fw -o apple_os.bin -e 0 bootpartition.bin
```

note   *Keep a copy of bootpartition.bin so that you can restore your iPod's original firmware later if you want.*

9. For the iPod with video, you must perform an extra step to extract the Broadcom firmware. Issue the following command:

```
ipod_fw -o apple_sw_5g_rcsc.bin -e 1 bootpartition.bin
```

10. Merge the Rockbox bootloader into the Apple firmware, creating a file called rockboot.bin. The command varies depending on the iPod model.

   ● For the iPod with video, issue this command:

```
ipod_fw -g video -o rockboot.bin -i apple_os.bin bootloader-video.bin
```

   ● For the iPod nano, issue this command:

```
ipod_fw -g nano -o rockboot.bin -i apple_os.bin bootloader-nano.bin
```

   ● For the iPod photo, issue this command:

```
ipod_fw -g color -o rockboot.bin -i apple_os.bin bootloader-color.bin
```

   ● For the grayscale fourth-generation iPod, issue this command:

```
ipod_fw -g 4g -o rockboot.bin -i apple_os.bin bootloader-4g.bin
```

   ● For the first-generation iPod mini, issue this command:

```
ipod_fw -g mini -o rockboot.bin -i apple_os.bin bootloader-mini1g.bin
```

   ● For the second-generation iPod mini, issue this command:

```
ipod_fw -g mini -o rockboot.bin -i apple_os.bin bootloader-mini2g.bin
```

11. Use ipodpatcher.exe to copy the rockboot.bin file you just created to the iPod. Issue the following command, replacing *drive* with the drive number that represents the iPod:

```
ipodpatcher -w drive rockboot.bin
```

12. You'll see output like the following as ipodpatcher writes rockboot.bin to your iPod.

```
ipodpatcher v0.3 - (C) Dave Chapman 2006
This is free software; see the source for copying conditions.  There is NO
warranty; not even for MERCHANTABILITY or FITNESS FOR A PARTICULAR PURPOSE.

[INFO] Reading partition table from \\.\PhysicalDrive5
Part    Start Sector    End Sector    Size (MB)   Type
  0              63         160649       78.4      Empty (0x00)
  1          160650       58605119    28537.3      W95 FAT32 (0x0b)
[INFO] Input file is 11792384 bytes
[INFO] Writing input file to device
[INFO] Wrote 11792384 bytes plus 0 bytes padding.
```

13. Next, unzip the Rockbox distribution file to your iPod. Follow these steps:

   ● Choose Start | My Documents to open a Windows Explorer window to your My Documents folder.

   ● Double-click the Rockbox folder to open it.

   ● Double-click the Rockbox zip file to open it.

   ● In the Folder Tasks pane, click the Extract All Files link to launch the Extraction Wizard, and then click the Next button.

- On the Select A Destination screen of the wizard, click the Browse button, use the Select A Destination dialog box to select the drive that represents your iPod, and then click the OK button.

- Click the Next button to extract the files to the iPod.

- Click the Finish button. When Windows Explorer displays the contents of the destination folder, you should see a folder named .rockbox (with a period at the beginning) and a file named rockbox.ipod.

14. Unplug the iPod. The iPod restarts automatically and boots Rockbox.

Install the Bootloader and Rockbox on the Mac

On the Mac, there's a hurdle you have to surmount before you can start installing the bootloader: if the iPod is formatted using the Mac OS Extended file system, you must reformat it using the FAT32 file system.

 Reformatting your iPod deletes all the files it contains. Back up any files you want to keep before you reformat the iPod.

Check Whether Your iPod Is Using the Mac OS Extended File System

To check whether your iPod is using the Mac OS Extended file system, go to the iPod's Settings menu, select the About item, and then scroll down to the bottom. If there's a Format line that says "Windows," the iPod is using FAT32. If there's no Format line, the iPod is using Mac OS Extended.

Reformat Your iPod with the FAT32 File System

The easy way to reformat your iPod with FAT32 is to use a Windows computer that has the iPod Software installed. If you have access to such a Windows computer, follow these steps:

1. Connect your iPod to the computer. Windows displays an iTunes dialog box (shown here) saying that it has detected a Macintosh-formatted iPod.

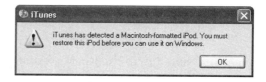

2. Click the OK button. iTunes selects the iPod in the Source pane and displays the Summary tab of information for it.

3. Click the Restore button to start the restoration.

4. iTunes checks the iPod Updater site for the latest version of the iPod Updater software, and then displays a confirmation dialog box.

5. Click the Restore button, and then follow through the restore process. Wait until your iPod appears in the Source pane in iTunes.

6. Disconnect the iPod, and then connect it to your Mac.

If you don't have access to a Windows computer with the iPod Software installed, you must reformat the iPod the hard way. Follow these steps:

1. Click the desktop to activate the Finder, and then choose Go | Utilities to display the contents of your Utilities folder.

2. Double-click the Terminal icon to launch an instance of Terminal.

3. Issue the mount command to list all the volumes on your Mac so that you can see what Mac OS X thinks your iPod is called:

```
mount
```

4. In the resulting list, identify the device name that refers to your iPod. Here's an example in which the iPod appears as /dev/disk1s2:

```
/dev/disk1s2 on /Volumes/nanoPod (local, nodev, nosuid, journaled)
```

5. Issue the diskutil unmount command with the device name you found in the previous step to unmount the device:

```
diskutil unmount /dev/disk1s2
```

6. When Mac OS X has unmounted the device, Terminal displays a message to tell you so—for example, "Volume /dev/disk1s2 unmounted."

7. Issue the following command to reformat the partition using the FAT32 file system, replacing the numbers in rdisk1s2 with the numbers of the device that represents your iPod:

```
newfs_msdos -F32 -v iPod /dev/rdisk1s2
```

Install the Bootloader and the Rockbox Software

Once your iPod is formatted with the FAT32 file system, you can install the bootloader and the Rockbox software. Follow these steps:

1. Click the desktop to activate the Finder, and then choose Go | Utilities to display the contents of your Utilities folder.

2. Double-click the Terminal icon to launch an instance of Terminal.

3. In Terminal, issue the following command to switch to the Rockbox folder inside your Home folder:

```
cd ~/Rockbox
```

4. Issue the following command to apply the "executable" attribute to the diskdump and ipod_fw files, so that you can execute them:

```
chmod +x diskdump ipod_fw
```

5. Issue the mount command to list all the volumes on your Mac so that you can see what Mac OS X thinks your iPod is called:

```
mount
```

6. In the resulting list, identify the device name that refers to your iPod. Here's an example in which the iPod appears as /dev/disk1s3:

```
/dev/disk1s3 on /Volumes/nanoPod (local, nodev, nosuid, journaled)
```

7. Issue the diskutil unmount command with the device name you found in the previous step to unmount the device:

```
diskutil unmount /dev/disk1s3
```

8. When Mac OS X has unmounted the device, Terminal displays a message to tell you so—for example, "Volume /dev/disk1s3 unmounted."

9. Next, issue the following diskdump command to copy the partition containing the iPod's current firmware to a file in your Rockbox folder:

```
~/Rockbox guy$ ./diskdump -r /dev/disk1 bootpartition.bin
```

10. The diskdump command takes a few minutes to run. You'll see output like the following as it reads the partition table and writes the file to your Mac.

```
diskdump v0.1 - (C) Dave Chapman 2005
This is free software; see the source for copying conditions.  There is NO
warranty; not even for MERCHANTABILITY or FITNESS FOR A PARTICULAR PURPOSE.

[INFO] Reading partition table...
Part    Type    Start Sector    End Sector    Size (MB)
   0    0x00             63         160649           78
   1    0x0b         160656        7984304         3820
[INFO] Seeking to sector 63
[WARN] Seek error - reading 63 sectors instead
[INFO] Writing 160587 sectors to output file
[INFO] Done.
```

11. Once diskdump has finished copying the partition, extract the iPod's firmware from it. Issue the following command, noting that the character before "bootpartition.bin" is a zero rather than a capital O:

```
./ipod_fw -o apple_os.bin -e 0 bootpartition.bin
```

note   *Keep a copy of bootpartition.bin so that you can restore your iPod's original firmware later if you want.*

12. For the iPod with video, you must perform an extra step to extract the Broadcom firmware. Issue the following command:

```
./ipod_fw -o apple_sw_5g_rcsc.bin -e 1 bootpartition.bin
```

13. Merge the Rockbox bootloader into the Apple firmware, creating a file called rockboot.bin. The command varies depending on the iPod model.

● For the iPod with video, issue this command:

```
./ipod_fw -g video -o rockboot.bin -i apple_os.bin bootloader-video.bin
```

● For the iPod nano, issue this command:

```
./ipod_fw -g nano -o rockboot.bin -i apple_os.bin bootloader-nano.bin
```

● For the iPod photo, issue this command:

```
./ipod_fw -g color -o rockboot.bin -i apple_os.bin bootloader-color.bin
```

● For the grayscale fourth-generation iPod, issue this command:

```
./ipod_fw -g 4g -o rockboot.bin -i apple_os.bin bootloader-4g.bin
```

● For the first-generation iPod mini, issue this command:

```
./ipod_fw -g mini -o rockboot.bin -i apple_os.bin bootloader-mini1g.bin
```

● For the second-generation iPod mini, issue this command:

```
./ipod_fw -g mini -o rockboot.bin -i apple_os.bin bootloader-mini2g.bin
```

14. Copy the rockboot.bin file you just created to the iPod. Issue this command, using the iPod's volume name as the destination but omitting the s and the number from the end of the name. For example, instead of /dev/disk1s3, use /dev/disk1.

```
./diskdump -w /dev/disk1 rockboot.bin
```

15. The diskdump command takes a minute or so to run. You'll see output like the following as it writes rockboot.bin to your iPod:

```
diskdump v0.1 - (C) Dave Chapman 2005
This is free software; see the source for copying conditions.  There is NO
warranty; not even for MERCHANTABILITY or FITNESS FOR A PARTICULAR PURPOSE.

[INFO] Reading partition table...
Part    Type    Start Sector    End Sector    Size (MB)
   0    0x00             63         160649           78
   1    0x0b         160656        7984304         3820
[INFO] Seeking to sector 63
[WARN] Seek error - reading 63 sectors instead
[INFO] Writing input file to device
[INFO] Wrote 5630528 bytes.
```

16. Use the unzip command to unzip the Rockbox distribution file and place its contents on the iPod's drive. This time, use the iPod's volume name from step 6, putting it in place of "nanoPod" in the following example. You'll need to substitute the name of the Rockbox distribution file for "rockbox-ipod-nano-20060729.zip."

```
unzip rockbox-ipodnano-20060729.zip -d /Volumes/nanoPod
```

17. Choose Terminal | Quit Terminal or press ⌘-Q to close Terminal.

18. Unplug your iPod. When the iPod restarts automatically, it boots into Rockbox.

Step 5: Load Songs on Your Rockbox iPod

To load songs on your iPod running Rockbox, don't use iTunes. Instead, simply copy folders containing your songs from your computer to the iPod using Windows Explorer (on Windows) or the Finder (on the Mac).

To be able to browse easily by artist, organize your songs into artist folders with album subfolders. For example, you might have a Bruce Springsteen folder that contains subfolders such as We Shall Overcome, Born in the U.S.A., and Born to Run.

Step 6: Enjoy Music and Other Diversions with Your Rockbox iPod

The Rockbox interface is easy to navigate using the iPod's controls. The following list shows the basics that you need to know in order to get started. For details, download the Rockbox manual for your iPod model from the Rockbox website.

● From the File Browser (shown here), you can select an item that appears on the first level of the iPod's folder structure. If you sort your songs into artist folders, each artist appears here, together with your Contacts, Calendars, Notes, and Photos folders.

- To play a song on your iPod using Rockbox, navigate to the song, and then press the Play button.

- From the main menu (shown here), you can access recent bookmarks, settings, playlist options, and more. If you've chosen to use Rockbox so that you can get higher-quality audio out of your iPod, select the Sound Settings item to access Rockbox's many sound settings, which allow you to tweak the sound to how you want it.

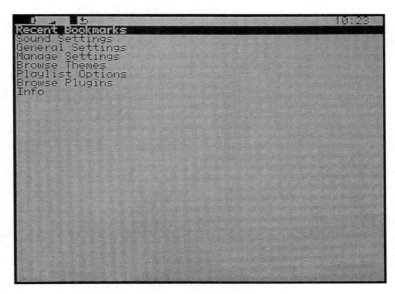

- To turn off your iPod, hold down the Play button for a few seconds.

Step 7: Make Rockbox Boot Your iPod's OS

Even with Rockbox installed, you can still run your iPod's own operating system and play back music using the iPod's regular codecs. To do so, follow these steps:

1. Hold down the Select button and the Menu button for about five seconds to make your iPod restart.

2. When the iPod begins restarting, release the Select button, but keep holding down the Menu button.

3. When you see the Rockbox message, "Loading original firmware," release the menu button. The iPod's operating system then starts.

To return to Rockbox, hold down the Select button and the Menu button for about five seconds, and then release both buttons when the iPod restarts.

Step 8: Restore Your iPod's Firmware

If you decide you don't want to keep Rockbox on your iPod, you can restore the iPod's operating system in two ways:

- By restoring the original bootpartition.bin file.

- By using the Restore feature in iTunes to wipe your iPod clean and put a fresh version of the iPod firmware on it.

Restore the Original bootpartition.bin File

To restore your iPod's firmware without deleting the iPod's contents, restore the original bootpartition.bin file that you extracted from the iPod.

This solution works better for Windows-based iPods than for Mac-based iPods. Because you converted your Mac-based iPod to the FAT32 file system in order to install Rockbox, your iPod keeps the FAT32 file system. This means that the iPod works fine with a Mac, but you cannot use the iPod Updater to update the iPod's firmware when Apple releases new versions. (To update the firmware, you must restore the iPod first.)

Restore the Original bootpartition.bin File on Windows

To restore the original bootpartition.bin file on Windows, follow these steps:

1. Choose Start | All Programs | Accessories | Command Prompt to open a Command Prompt window.

2. Issue the following command to change directory to the Rockbox directory inside your My Documents folder:

```
cd %userprofile%\My Documents\Rockbox
```

3. Run the ipodpatcher.exe program using ascending numbers to find out which drive represents the iPod: ipodpatcher 0, ipodpatcher 1, ipodpatcher 2, and so on. When ipodpatcher.exe finds the iPod, it displays details of its partition table.

4. Issue the following command, replacing *drive* with the drive number at which ipodpatcher.exe found the iPod:

```
ipodpatcher -w drive bootpartition.bin
```

5. Disconnect your iPod from the computer and allow it to restart.

Restore the Original bootpartition.bin File on the Mac

To restore the original bootpartition.bin file on the Mac, follow these steps:

1. Click the desktop to activate the Finder, and then choose Go | Utilities to display the contents of your Utilities folder.

2. Double-click the Terminal icon to launch an instance of Terminal.

3. Issue the mount command to list all the volumes on your Mac so that you can see what Mac OS X thinks your iPod is called.

4. Issue the following diskdump command, replacing "disk3" with the number of the disk indicated by the mount command. Omit the last part of the device name—for example, use "disk3" instead of "disk3s1."

```
./diskdump -w /dev/disk3 bootpartition.bin
```

5. Disconnect your iPod from the Mac and allow it to restart.

Restore Your iPod Using the iTunes

If you're prepared to lose all the iPod's contents, you can restore its firmware by using the Restore feature in iTunes. See the section "Restore the iPod" in Project 17 for instructions on restoring your iPod.

Index